The
Card Games
Bible

The
Card Games
Bible

Over 150 Games and Tricks

hamlyn

An Hachette UK Company
www.hachette.co.uk

First published in Great Britain in 2014 by
Hamlyn, a division of Octopus Publishing Group Ltd
Carmelite House
50 Victoria Embankment
London, EC4Y 0DZ
www.octopusbooks.co.uk
www.octopusbooksusa.com

Distributed in the US by
Hachette Book Group
1290 Avenue of the Americas
4th and 5th Floors
New York, NY 10104

Distributed in Canada by
Canadian Manda Group
664 Annette Street
Toronto, Ontario, Canada M6S 2C8

ISBN 978-0-600-62994-8

A CIP catalogue record for this book is
available from the British Library

Printed and bound in China

10 9 8 7

This material was previously published in
*Card Games for One, The Complete Book
of Card Games, How to Play Poker, Card
Games for Kids, 101 Clever Card Tricks.*

Editorial Director: Trevor Davies
Production Controller: Sarah-Jayne Johnson

Produced for Octopus Publishing Group Ltd
by Tracy Killick Art Direction and Design
and EditorsOnline.org
Senior Editor: Sarah Tomley
Editor: Alice Bowden
Art Director: Tracy Killick
Proofreader: Louise Abbott

Contents

Introduction

A deck of cards is a wonderful thing to have to hand: it's about the same size as a smartphone, but cheaper, lighter and infinitely more sociable. With a pack of cards, you'll never be bored again.

Playing cards were invented in China in the 9th century, and by the 11th century they had spread throughout the Asian continent. They first arrived in Europe in the late 14th century, probably via Egypt. Like all exotic imports, these early hand-painted sets of cards were initially the preserve of royalty and the rich, but the invention of wood-block printing in the 15th century made it possible to produce playing cards much more cheaply, widening their appeal. Women and men from all walks of life were soon playing card games at home and in taverns. New games – and different decks of cards – were rapidly invented in every region as the popularity of playing cards spread across Europe and went on to cross the Atlantic.

The red and black suitmarks – spades, hearts, diamonds and clubs – that are familiar to players today and feature in a modern standard international deck of 52 playing cards, originated in France around 1490. Some of the card games we play now are almost as old as their marks: they can be traced back to drinking and gambling games from the 16th century.

A game for every occasion

In some card games, winning is a matter of pure luck; other games require skill to win, while in many games, success depends on a combination of the two. In *The Card Games Bible*, there is a card game for every mood and occasion, from Klondike (page 24), the most popular of the one-player games of patience or solitaire, to games for up to ten players that will liven up any party, such as Red Dog (page 202).

This book also includes games that are particularly suitable for younger players (see the chapter on Card Games for Kids, pages 152–83) as well as more adult-friendly casino classics including Baccarat (page 208) and Vingt et Un (page 224). And if you're not in the mood for a game, you can always practice some card tricks (see pages 280–313).

Winner takes all

As soon as two or more players are involved, keeping score becomes a matter of great importance: the peg board traditionally used in games of Cribbage (page 52) makes this particularly easy, but a pen and a piece of paper will do just as well. Most card games are fast, so you can play as many or as few rounds as you like, with plenty of chances to chat between deals.

Games like Canasta (page 111), Hearts (page 131) and Rummy (page 148) are entertaining, addictive and easy to learn, while other games are rather more involved, pitting two pairs of players against each other in a battle of strategy, skill and memory. Introduced in the United States in the 1920s, Contract Bridge (page 85) quickly took the English-speaking world by storm, and is now played by millions of players around the globe, with official leagues and international tournaments.

Playing for prizes always makes games more fun, even if the only things at stake are piles of matches or sweets.

Card games based on betting or bluffing have been played for centuries, one of the most popular of these being Poker. The game of Poker (page 229) as we know it today was developed in the United States in the early 1800s. In recent years, internet gaming and televised championships have brought Poker to a whole new audience and it has since become a commonplace recreational activity in popular culture to be played in or outside the home.

A 'dip in' book for everyone

So whatever mood you're in, be it passing the time of day alone, spending an evening with your partner, or having a full-on riotous night of fun with friends and family, a pack of cards and a copy of this book is all you need.

Accordion

Accordion is one of the simplest of one-pack patience or solitaire games. The aim is to get all the cards into one pile, by building.

How to play

There is no starting layout and the cards are shuffled and dealt from the hand one at a time. The first card is dealt to the top left of the board and succeeding cards to the right of the one before, so a row is built up from left to right. The object is to finish with all the cards in one pack.

If, after dealing a card, it matches its left-hand neighbour either in suit or rank it can be packed on it. Similarly, if it matches the card three places to its left (i.e. with two other cards intervening) it can also be packed upon that. If a card can be packed in either position, the player chooses which option to take. When a card topping a pile is moved, the whole pile moves with it. All moves should be carried out as soon as they become possible.

If a long string of cards is built up, it is easier to start a second or third row, in which case the lines are to be considered continuous. Often the length of the line expands and contracts, like an accordion, after which the game is named. Success is almost entirely a matter of chance, and is rarely achieved. To finish with no more than three piles is a good result.

In the illustration below, if the next card dealt is the ♣6, it can be packed on the ♠6, the pile topped by the ♣Q packed on it, the ♥3 packed on the ♥8 and the ♣Q pile packed on the ♣10, thus reducing the piles to two. If the next card dealt were the ♣3 or ♥Q, they would be reduced to one. Notice that the ♥3 must be packed on the ♥8 before the ♣Q is packed on the ♣10 – otherwise it will not go.

Card dealt

Agnes

How to play

Deal 28 cards face up in one row of seven cards, one of six, and so on, down to one card. For convenience the cards may overlap. The 29th card is dealt face up to the centre as a foundation card. As they become available, either from the layout or the hand, the other three cards of the same rank will be placed in line with it.

The object of the game is to build ascending, round-the-corner suit sequences onto the foundation cards.

The bottom card of a column in the layout is termed exposed. It may be built on a foundation or packed on another exposed card in the layout. Within the layout, cards are packed in descending sequences of the same colour (not necessarily of the same suit), but it should be borne in mind that a sequence may be moved from one column to another only as a whole and only if all the cards of the sequence are of the same suit. If a vacancy occurs through all the cards of a column being moved, it may be filled with any available card, or same-suit sequence of cards, if wished.

After all possible moves have been made, cards are dealt face up to the bottom of all the columns, and the game continues until the stock is exhausted. After the third deal has been made from the stock, there will be two cards left in the hand and these may be played to either a foundation or the layout.

In the illustration, play the ♥10 to the foundation row. Pack the ♥5 on the ♥6 and the ♥4 on the ♥5. Pack the ♠2 on the ♣3, and the ♠6 on the ♣7. Move the ♦Q into the vacancy, and pack the ♥6, ♥5 and ♥4 together on the ♥7. Pack the ♣5 on the ♠6 and move the ♥7, ♥6, ♥5 and ♥4 together into the vacancy. Then deal seven more cards and continue.

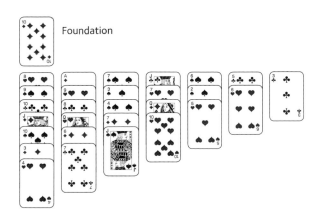

Foundation

Block Eleven

Block Eleven, or Calling Out, will occupy a couple of minutes if you are so unlucky as to have a couple of minutes with nothing better to occupy them.

How to play

Remove the first 12 numeral cards (i.e. Ace to 10) from the pack and lay them face up on the table in three rows of four, or four rows of three: it doesn't matter which. Shuffle the rest of the cards until a picture card lies at the bottom of the pack – if you do not, the game cannot be won.

Where, added together, two cards in the layout total 11, a card is dealt on each from the stock. Once a picture card has been dealt on one of the piles, no more cards can be added to it. The game is won when all 40 cards of the stock have been dealt and the 12 picture cards cover the layout. It is an inane game that requires no skill, but does have a pretty ending.

In the illustration of a game in progress (see right), four piles have so far been blocked by picture cards. Play continues by placing cards from the stock on one of the 8s and the ♦3, and on the ♠9 and ♦2.

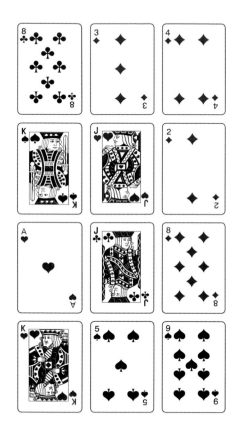

Calculation

Calculation, or Broken Intervals, is well named, because it is necessary to calculate at the turn of every card and it offers great scope for skilful play.

How to play

Any Ace, any 2, any 3 and any 4 are placed in a row on the table to form four foundations. The object of the game is to build, regardless of suits, the remaining 48 cards on them, in the following order:

On the Ace – 2, 3, 4, 5, 6, 7, 8, 9, 10, Jack, Queen, King
On the 2 – 4, 6, 8, 10, Queen, Ace, 3, 5, 7, 9, Jack, King
On the 3 – 6, 9, Queen, 2, 5, 8, Jack, Ace, 4, 7, 10, King
On the 4 – 8, Queen, 3, 7, Jack, 2, 6, 10, Ace, 5, 9, King

The cards are dealt from the pack one at a time and every card must either be built on a foundation or played to any of the four waste heaps below the foundation (see right). At any time the top card of a waste heap may be built on a foundation, but it may not be played to another waste heap. The pack is dealt only once, but play from a waste heap may continue after it is exhausted.

The cards in the pack are now dealt one at a time. Suppose a 10 is dealt: as it cannot be built on a foundation it is best played to a vacant waste heap. Next a 6

is dealt; it is built on the 3 foundation. Next comes an 8, and is built on the 4 foundation. The next card is a King. It must be played to a waste heap, but because the Kings are the last cards to be built on the foundations it would be wrong to play it to, for example, the waste heap containing the 10. It should be played to another waste heap, and experienced players would now reserve this for Kings. Play continues in this way until all 48 cards have been dealt.

If the play is carefully thought out, by building cards on the waste heaps in descending sequences of two to four or, hopefully, more, excellent progress will be made towards the end of the game.

Foundations

Waste heaps

The Carpet

See how quickly you can unweave the carpet of cards!

How to play

Remove the four Aces from the pack and play them to the centre as foundations. Below them, deal 20 cards face up in four rows of five cards each (see illustration).

The object of the game is to build ascending suit sequences to the Kings on the Aces.

All of the cards in the layout (the carpet) may be built on the foundations, and the resulting vacancies are filled from the waste heap or from the stock if there is no waste heap. Cards cannot be packed on the layout. The stock is turned one card at a time and any card that cannot be built on a foundation is played to the waste heap, the top card of which is always available to be played.

In the illustration below, the ♣2 is built on the ♣A, the ♣3 on the ♣2 and the ♣4 on the ♣3. The ♦2 is built on the ♦A and the ♦3 on the ♦2. The five vacancies are filled from the stock and play continues.

The game ends when the stock has been dealt once.

Clock

This is a simple five-minute game that relies entirely on chance.

How to play

First, 13 piles of four cards are dealt face down one at a time: 12 in a circle to represent the numbers on a clock face and the 13th in the centre. The top card of the centre pile is turned over and placed behind the pile representing its number on the clock face (Jacks count as 11 and Queens 12). The top card of that pile is then exposed and placed in its appropriate position, and a card from that pile exposed. When a King is exposed it is played to the centre and another card exposed from there. The object is to end with all cards exposed.

Once the fourth King is exposed, the game ends, as there is not another card in the centre to turn over. For the game to succeed, therefore, the last card exposed must be a King, so the chance of success is one in 13.

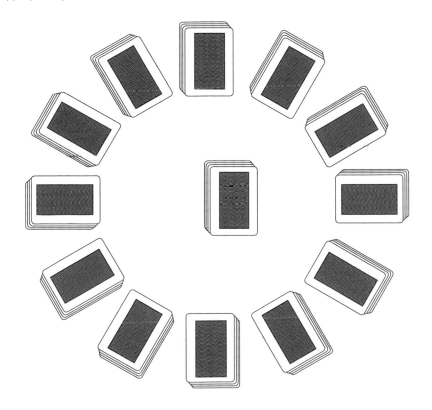

Crossword

How to play

The 12 court cards are removed from the pack and temporarily set aside. The top card of the pack is played to the table, and the rest of the pack is turned one card at a time. Each card in turn is played to the table in a position adjoining a card already played, at top or bottom, to either side, or diagonally.

The object of the game is to complete a square of seven cards in each direction in which the pips of the cards in each row and column add up to an even number. The court cards are only used when needed to serve as stops, much the same as the black squares in a crossword

puzzle; at least nine, if not all of them, will have to be used. Bear in mind that the pips of the cards between two court cards, or between a court card and the outer edge of the square, must also add up to an even number (see illustration).

When there is only one square to fill, the player may look at the four cards in the hand and choose one needed to complete the game.

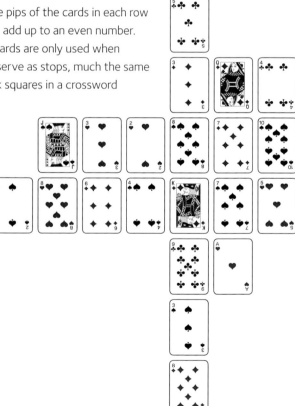

Eagle Wings

Eagle Wings, or 13 Down, is one of those games that depend for success entirely on the order in which the cards are dealt.

How to play

Deal 13 cards to the table face down in a pile (the heel). On each side of the heel four cards are dealt face up in a row (the wings). Above the heel a card is dealt face up as the first foundation (see illustration). As they become available, the other three cards of the same rank will be placed in the row with it.

The object of the game is to build same-suit, ascending, round-the-corner sequences on the foundation cards. The eight cards in the wings are available to be played to the foundations, and the vacancies are filled with cards from the heel turned face up. The stock is dealt one card at a time, and any card that cannot be played to a foundation is played to a waste heap. When only one card remains in the heel, it is turned face up and may be played direct to a foundation, without first filling a vacancy in the wings. When the heel is exhausted any vacancy in the wings may be filled with a card from either the stock or the waste heap.

The stock may be dealt three times in total, but must not be shuffled between deals.

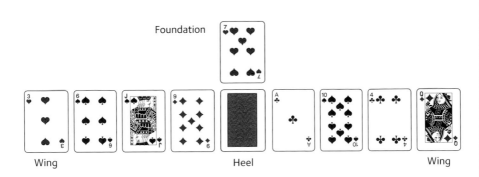

Foundation

Wing · · · Heel · · · Wing

Eight Off

A fascinating game for an idle quarter of an hour, with an estimated chance of winning one in two games.

How to play

Deal the pack face up in six rows of eight cards each (see illustration). Play the Aces, as they occur, to a foundation row. The object of the game is to build suit sequences up to the Kings on the Aces.

The bottom card of any column is exposed so once it has been played the card above it becomes available. The player may take up to eight exposed cards into the hand. These cards are collectively known as the reserve and are retained until they are required for building on a foundation or for packing onto an exposed card in a column.

Exposed cards at the foot of columns may be built on a foundation, or packed on another exposed card in descending suit sequence. Only one card may be moved at a time. A vacancy caused by all the cards of a column being played may only be filled by a King.

In the layout illustrated, the ♦Q is packed on the ♦K, the ♠8 on the ♠9 and the ♣5 taken into the reserve. The ♦7 is packed on the ♦8 and the ♣2 built on the ♣A. The ♥5 is taken into the reserve, the ♦J packed on the ♦Q and the ♣3 built on the ♣2. The ♦7 and ♦8 are taken into the reserve, the ♠7 packed on the ♠8 and the ♠2 built on the ♠A.

Tactics

Aim to release low cards and build them on the foundations. Retain as many openings as possible in the reserve, as these are more valuable than creating vacancies in the layout.

Foundations

  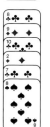    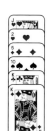 

Florentine

Florentine is a quick and easy game, where all the cards are moved to the foundation, just like in most solitaire games. It can be won about half of the time.

How to play

Deal five cards face up to the table in the form of a cross, then deal the sixth card above it as the first of the four foundations (see illustration). As the other three cards of the same rank as the foundation card are dealt, they are added to the foundation row.

The object of the game is to build ascending, round-the-corner suit sequences on the foundation cards.

The card in the centre of the cross may not be packed on, but the remaining cards in the cross are available for building on the foundations or for packing on each other in descending sequence regardless of suit and colour. When one of these cards is built on a foundation, or packed on another card of the cross, the vacancy is filled either with the top card of the waste heap or with the centre card of the cross and the vacancy in the centre of the cross filled with the top card of the waste heap. Cards are dealt from the stock one at a time and those that cannot be built or packed are played to a waste heap. One redeal is allowed by turning the waste heap, but it may not be shuffled.

In the game in progress shown in the illustration (left), the foundation cards are to be built up to their respective 7s. The ♦6 is packed on the ♠7 and the vacancy filled with the ♠10, or with the ♣2 and the ♠10 played to the centre of the cross. And so on.

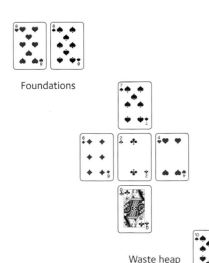

Foundations

Waste heap

Flower Garden

The Flower Garden, sometimes called the Bouquet and sometimes the Garden, is a fascinating one-pack patience with the added merit that some degree of skill is needed.

How to play

Create six fans of six cards each. These are known as the beds. The remaining 16 cards are kept in the hand and become the bouquet. The object of the game is to release the four Aces, play them to a row above the beds, and build on them ascending suit sequences to the Kings.

While only the right-hand card in a bed is exposed, all of the cards in the bouquet are exposed and may either be built on the Ace foundations or packed on the outer card of a bed in descending sequence irrespective of suit and colour. A sequence may be moved from one bed to another provided the sequence is retained. When a bed has been cleared, the space may be filled either with a card from the bouquet, or by an exposed card or sequence from another bed.

In the layout illustrated, the ♣A is played to the foundation row, the ♣2 built on it, followed by the ♣3 from the bouquet. The ♦Q is packed on the ♦K, and the ♦J on the ♦Q, followed by the ♦10 from the bouquet then the ♥9, ♠8 and the ♠7. Now the ♠6 is packed on the ♠7 and the ♦A played to the foundation row. The ♦5 is packed on the ♠6, the ♣6 on the ♦7 and the ♠2 on the ♠3.

Tactics

The hand shown below will be hard to win because of the high cards in the bouquet and on top of the beds. Avoid packing a card from the bouquet on a bed if an alternative play is possible, as reducing the number of cards in the bouquet reduces the number of cards that may be played at any one time. The main aim of the player should be to release the Aces, 2s and 3s, because a game may well be lost if even one low card is immobilized.

The beds (six fans)

Bouquet

Fortune

How to play

Remove the four Aces from the pack and lay them at the top of the table as foundation cards. Below them, deal 12 cards face up. For convenience, these may be arranged on the table in three rows of four cards each (see illustration).

The object of the game is to build ascending suit sequences up to the Kings on the Aces.

The cards in the layout are available to be built on the foundations, or packed onto each other in descending suit sequences. Only one card may be moved at a time.

The stock is dealt one card at a time and any card that cannot be built on a foundation or packed on the layout is played to a waste heap, the top card of which is always available for play.

Any vacancy in the layout is filled with the top card of the waste heap, or the top card from the stock if there is no waste heap. Only one deal is allowed.

With the layout in the illustration, the ♦2 is built on the ♦A. The ♠5 is packed on the ♠6 and the ♠4 on the ♠5. The ♣8 is packed on the ♣9, and the ♦9 on the ♦10, followed by cards from the waste heap or stock as necessary.

Foundations

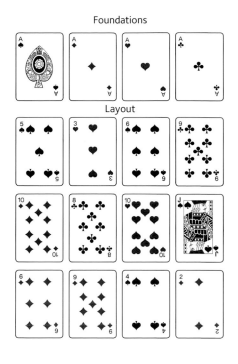

Layout

Grandfather's Clock

This patience game has a similar layout to Clock (see page 15), but is quite different and less mechanical.

How to play

Remove from the pack the ♥2, ♥6 and ♥10, the ♠3, ♠7 and ♠J, the ♦4, ♦8 and ♦Q and the ♣5, ♣9 and ♣K.

Arrange these cards on the table face up in a circle comparable to the hours on the face of a clock, placing the ♣9 at noon, and the others in sequence round the dial.

These serve as foundation cards to be built on in ascending, round-the-corner suit sequences until each reaches the number appropriate to its position on the dial, with the Jack at 11 o'clock and the Queen at noon. (The 10, Jack, Queen and King foundations will each need four cards built on them, the others only three cards.)

The remaining 40 cards are dealt face up below them, in five rows of eight cards, which for convenience may overlap (see illustration, opposite).

The cards at the bottom of the columns are available to be built on a foundation or be packed on other exposed cards, in descending, round-the-corner sequences regardless of suit. Only one card may be moved at a time, and if all the cards of one column have been moved the vacancy may be filled by any available card.

With the layout illustrated, the ♠Q may be built on the ♠J, the ♣A on the ♣K, the ♠4 on the ♠3, the ♥7 on the ♥6, the ♦9 on the ♦8, the ♦10 on the ♦9 and the ♠K on the ♠Q. The ♥Q may be packed on the ♥K, the ♦K built on the ♦Q, the ♠2 may be packed on the ♣3 and the ♦J then built on the ♦10 and so on, as the cards become exposed.

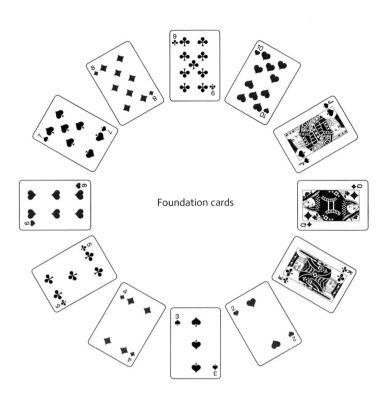

Foundation cards

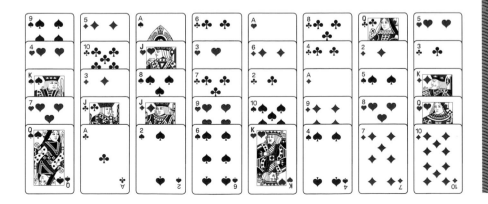

Klondike

Demon (see page 160) and Klondike are probably the two best-known and most popular one-pack patience games. In the UK the name of Canfield is sometimes attached to Klondike. This, however, is a misnomer, because Canfield is the name that in America is given to the patience that in the UK is called Demon.

How to play

Deal 28 cards face down in seven columns, by dealing a row of seven, then six, five, four, and so on, down to one (see illustration). Turn the bottom card of each column face up.

As they become available, the Aces are played as foundations to a row above the layout; the object of the game is to build ascending suit sequences up to the Kings on the Aces.

An exposed card at the bottom of a column is available to be built on a foundation, or packed in a descending sequence of alternating colours. A sequence may be moved from one column to another only as a whole and when it can be placed in sequence, e.g. ♦10, ♠9, ♥8, must be placed onto a black Jack. When an exposed card is played, the card above it is turned face up; when a whole column is moved, the

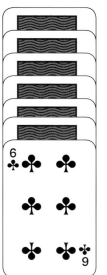
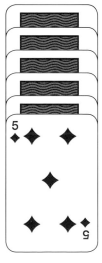

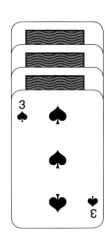

space may be filled only by a King, either with or without a sequence attached.

The stock is dealt one card at a time to a waste heap, of which the top card is available for building on a foundation or packing on a column in the layout. Only one deal is allowed.

The Aces must be played to the foundation row as soon as they become available, but all other cards may be left in position if the player prefers to wait in hope of finding a better move later.

In the layout shown, the ♦ 5 is packed on the ♣6, and the card under the ♦ 5 is turned face up. The ♣J is packed on the ♥Q, and the ♦K moved to fill the space vacated by the ♣J. The card under the ♦K is now turned face up. Once all of the moves within the layout have been made, play from the stock can begin.

JOKER KLONDIKE

Klondike has been the subject of several variations. One of the best is Joker Klondike. It is played in the same way as the parent game, but with the Joker added to the pack. Whenever the Joker becomes available for play it must be built on a foundation as the next card in sequence. Other cards, if they are in correct sequence, can be built on it, but when the natural card that it replaces becomes available it is substituted for the Joker, which is then built on another foundation.

A player may choose on which foundation to build the Joker. If it becomes available for play before a foundation has been started it must remain in its position until an Ace turns up and a foundation is started.

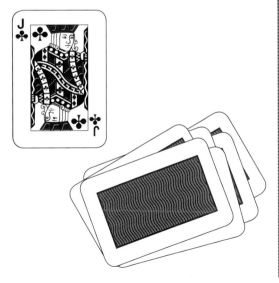

La Belle Lucie

La Belle Lucie, or The Fan, is one of the classic one-pack patience games and it has a very pleasing layout. A word of advice: since all cards are visible after the deal, the basic strategy is to think before making each move.

How to play

The entire pack is spread on the table in 17 fans of three cards and one of a single card, as illustrated.

As the Aces become available they should be placed above the layout as foundations and built on in ascending suit sequences to the Kings. Only the fully exposed card of each fan and the single card are available for play. These cards may be built on a foundation, or packed on the end card of another fan in descending suit sequence. Note that a space made by playing all the cards from a complete fan is not filled.

When all possible moves have been made, all of the cards not yet played to the foundations are picked up, shuffled and redealt in fans of three. If one or two cards are left over they make separate fans. Two redeals are allowed.

In the layout illustrated opposite, the ♥A and ♣A are played to the foundation row. The ♥2 is built on the ♥A, and the ♣7 is packed on the ♣8. This releases the ♣2 that is built on the ♣A. The ♦J is packed on the ♦Q, the ♥J on the ♥Q, and the ♠A and the ♠2 go to the foundation row. After a few further moves it will become necessary to shuffle the cards and redeal.

Labyrinth

Labyrinth is quite a simple game and nothing like as fiendishly difficult as its name suggests.

How to play

The four Aces are played to the centre as foundation cards and built on in ascending suit sequence to the Kings. Below them eight cards are dealt face up to the table in a row. Any cards available are built on the foundations and the vacancies filled from the stock.

When all available cards have been built on the foundations and the vacancies filled, a second row of eight cards is dealt below the first. Cards from it are built on the foundations, but the vacancies are not filled: this only happens in the first row.

Dealing out rows, building on the foundations and filling gaps in the top row is continued in this way until the stock is exhausted. Only the cards in both the top and bottom rows are available to be built on the foundations while these rows are complete. But when a card is played from the top row the card below it becomes available, and when one is played from the bottom row the card above it becomes exposed and available. As only vacancies in the first row are filled, during the game there may be a number of unfilled vacancies in the layout (see illustration). It may suggest a labyrinth.

The game succeeds if all four foundations are built up to the Kings. Only one deal is allowed, and if the game has not been won when the stock has been exhausted, the player has one last resort: the option of playing any one card from the layout to a foundation, then continuing with normal play.

In the illustration, the ♠3 is built on the ♠2, the ♥4 on the ♥3 exposing the ♠4, which is built on the ♠3. The ♥5 is built on the ♥4, the ♥6 on the ♥5, the ♥7 on the ♥6, and the ♥8 on the ♥7. Once all the available moves have been made, the holes in the top row are filled, another row of cards is dealt at the bottom and play continues as before.

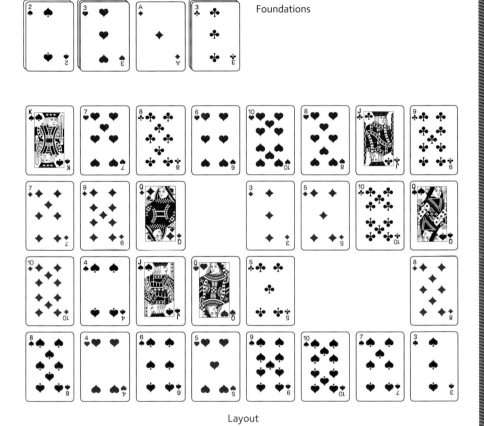

Foundations

Layout

Little Spider

Little Spider is a solitaire game using all 52 cards. Because of its form of game play and dealing, it should not be confused with two other solitaire games: Spider and its one-deck cousin, Spiderette.

How to play

The red Aces and black Kings (or the black Aces and red Kings) are placed in a row on the table to serve as foundations. Then eight cards are dealt, face up, in two rows of four cards, one above the foundation cards, the other below them, as illustrated.

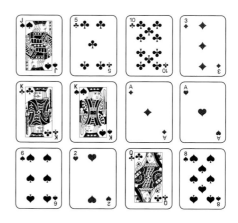

The object of the game is to build on the Aces ascending suit sequences to the Kings, and descending suit sequences on the Kings to the Aces.

During the deal (i.e. after each round of eight cards), cards from the upper row may be built on any of the four foundation cards, but a card from the lower row may be built only on the foundation card directly above it.

After all six batches of eight cards have been dealt, the top cards of all eight piles are playable and may be built on any foundation cards or packed on any other pile in the layout. The piles are packed in ascending or descending continuous sequences (an Ace ranks below a 2 and above a King) regardless of suit. A space made by removing an entire pile is not filled.

In the layout illustrated, which shows the game after all the cards have been

dealt (as happens rarely, no cards were played to the foundations during the deal), the ♣Q may be built on the ♣K and the ♥2 on the ♥A. The ♣10 may be packed on the ♠J, and the ♣5 on the ♠6. The cards exposed by these moves may then be played, if possible.

Martha

Martha is a solitaire card game with an unusual layout: half the cards in the tableau are faced down.

How to play

Remove the Aces from the pack and lay them in a row at the top as foundation cards. Deal the rest of the pack in 12 columns of four cards, the first and third cards of each column face down, the second and fourth face up. The rows may overlap for convenience (see illustration).

The object of the game is to build on the Aces ascending suit sequences up to the Kings.

The bottom cards of the columns are available to be built on the foundations, or packed on other exposed cards in the layout in descending sequences of alternating colours. Provided the order and alternating colours are retained a

sequence may be moved either wholly or in part from one column to another. Vacancies in the layout, however, may be filled only by a single card. The face-down cards in the layout are turned face up when the cards below them have been played.

In the layout shown below, the ♥2 is built on the ♥A and the face-down card turned. The ♣2 is built on the ♣A and the face-down card turned. The ♠9 is packed on the ♥10, the ♥8 on the ♠9, the ♣7 on the ♥8 and the face-down cards turned after each move. Not knowing where almost half of the cards are makes this game a good challenge.

Foundations

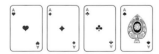

Layout

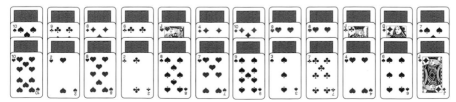

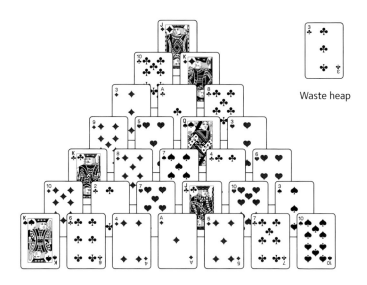

Pyramid

Pyramid, or Pile of Twenty-eight, is an interesting form of patience, and not an easy one, having one chance of succeeding in about 50 games.

How to play

First, 28 cards are dealt face up to the table in seven rows, beginning with one card and adding one per row so the seventh row contains seven cards. The cards should be arranged in the form of a pyramid, so that every card (except those in the bottom row) will be overlapped by two cards in the row below it. The removal of two adjacent cards in a row exposes one card in the row above.

The object of the game is to discard the whole pack. Kings are discarded singly, but all other cards are discarded in a pair whose pips add to 13 (Queens counting as 12 and Jacks as 11). Only exposed cards may be discarded.

The cards that form the stock are turned one by one to a waste heap, the top card of which is exposed and can be paired with an exposed card or the next dealt from stock.

In the layout illustrated, the ♠K is discarded; the ♣7 and ♣6 are paired and discarded; the ♠10 and ♣3 (from the waste heap) are paired and discarded; the ♦10 and ♠3 are paired and discarded. As no further discards can be made, the next card of the stock is dealt to the waste heap. And so on.

Waste heap

Royal Parade

Royal Parade is a popular two-pack patience with the alternative names of Financier, Hussars and Three Up.

How to play

Two packs of cards are used and Aces are discarded from the layout. 24 cards are dealt in three rows of eight cards each. The aim first is to arrange the layout so that the top row consists of eight 2s, the middle row of eight 3s, and the bottom row of eight 4s, then to build on these in suit sequences at intervals of three cards:

2	3	4
5	6	7
8	9	10
J	Q	K

In the layout illustrated below, the ♦A in the top row, and the ♣A in the bottom row, are discarded; the ♠4, in the middle row, is moved to the space in the bottom row left vacant by the discard of the ♣A, and the ♠7, in the top row, built on it. Either the ♥3 or ♣3, both in the top row, may be moved to fill the space in the middle row left vacant by the ♠4, and clearly the ♥3 should be chosen because the ♥6 in the bottom row may be built on it.

When all moves have been made, eight cards are dealt to waste heaps below the layout. Aces are discarded as dealt; other cards are used to build on the foundations or, if they are 2s, 3s or 4s, to fill spaces in the layout. Play continues in this way until the pack is exhausted. Only the top cards of the waste heaps may be moved to the layout.

Scorpion

Scorpion is a simple solitaire game that is quick to play but difficult to win!

How to play

Seven cards, four face down and three face up, are dealt in a row. Two more rows are dealt in the same way, and then four rows of face-up cards. For convenience the cards may overlap slightly (see illustration). The remaining three cards are temporarily set aside.

Leaving the four Kings within the layout, the object of the game is to build descending suit sequences down to the Aces on them.

The cards at the bottom of the columns are exposed, and they may be packed with the next lower cards in suit sequence. To do this a card may be taken from anywhere in the layout, but if a card is not taken from the bottom of a column, all the cards below it in the column must be taken with it.

In the layout shown, the ♦3 may be packed on the ♦4, but the ♣2 must go with it. In the same way, the ♠5 may be packed on the ♠6, but the ♠7, ♥6, ♣A and ♦10 must be moved with it. Nothing, of course, is packed on an Ace.

When a face-down card is cleared, it is turned face up, and when a whole column is cleared the space is filled by a King, together with any cards below it in the column from which it is taken.

When no further moves can be made, the three cards, temporarily set aside, are now dealt face up, one to the foot of each of the three columns at the extreme left of the layout.

The game is by no means an easy one and calls for some care and forethought if it is to succeed. As a start, the layout should be inspected closely.

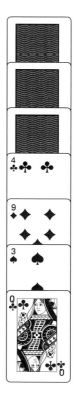

If there is a reverse sequence, such as ♦Q, ♦J, ♦K, in one column the game can never be won; nor can it if there is a 'criss-cross', such as the ♠9 on the ♦6 in one column and the ♦5 on the ♠10 in another. In such cases as these it is a waste of time to continue.

If the layout offers promise of success, the first aim should be an attempt to uncover the face-down cards. In the layout illustrated, for example, it will be seen that the ♣4, together with the ♦9, ♠3 and ♣Q, will free a face-down card if the combination is packed on the ♣5.

The first move, therefore, is to pack the ♠5, together with the ♠7, ♥6, ♣A and ♦10, on the ♠6.

Tactics

Careful thought should always be given to a situation before a move is made. Carelessness may well end in the player blocking the game.

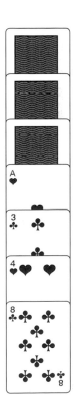

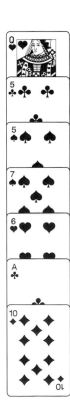

Simple Simon

Simple Simon, despite its name, is actually a very skilful game to play. It has some similarities to Klondike (see page 24) but differs in not having a stock pile and in having all cards laid out face up from the beginning.

How to play

Deal the whole pack face up to the table in eight rows (cards may overlap for convenience). The first row should consist of ten cards, the second row of nine, etc. down to a row of three cards (see illustration).

The object of the game is to build, within the layout, descending suit sequences from the exposed Kings to the Aces. The bottom card of each column (other than a King) may be packed in a descending sequence regardless of suit and colour. Only one card may be moved

at a time, except that a sequence may be moved as a whole if it consists of cards all of one suit.

A vacancy left by the removal of all the cards from a column may be filled by any exposed card or by a sequence if all the cards are of one suit.

This is an excellent game, but the name given to it is a mystery because it is far from easy or simple.

In the layout illustrated, the ♣Q may be built on the ♣K, the ♠10 may be packed on the ♠J, the ♥9 on the ♠10, and the ♠9 on the ♦10.

Now, the ♦6 may be packed on the ♥7, the ♥5 on the ♦6, and the vacancy filled with the ♠K. The ♠Q may be built on the ♠K, and the vacancy filled with the ♣K and ♣Q in sequence.

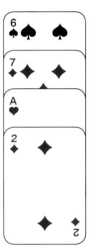

Sir Tommy

No one knows, and probably no one ever will know, which is the original patience from which all of the others were derived. This one, which is sometimes known as Try Again or Old Patience, may be it. Certainly, the game could hardly be simpler.

How to play

The cards are dealt face up one by one, and played at the discretion of the player to four waste heaps. As they occur, the Aces are played to a foundation row and built on in ascending sequences to the Kings, regardless of suits and colour.

In the game in progress as illustrated, two Aces have so far been played to the foundation row and then built on.

Suppose the next card from the stock is the ♥A; it is played to the foundation row and the ♣2 built on it.

Tactics

The top cards of the waste heaps are available to be played to the foundations but, as there is only the one deal, and a card may not be transferred from one waste heap to another, the best that can be done is to reserve one waste heap on which to play the Kings and hope that they will show up early in the game.

Foundations

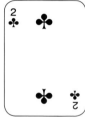

Waste heaps

Six by Six

Six by Six is a simple building-up patience that may not be as well known as it deserves to be.

How to play

The object of the game is to release the Aces, play them to the centre as foundation cards, then to build on them in ascending suit sequences to the Kings. To start, 36 cards are dealt face up to the table in six rows (cards may overlap).

The bottom card of each column is exposed. It may be built on a foundation, or packed on an exposed card in the layout in descending sequence regardless of suit and colour. Provided the order is retained, a sequence may be moved, either wholly or in part, from the foot of one column to that of another. When all the cards of a column have been played, the vacancy may be filled by any exposed card or by a sequence. The stock is dealt one card at a time, and any card that cannot be built on a foundation or packed on the layout, is played to the foot of the left-hand column. Only one deal is allowed.

In the layout illustrated, the ♦A becomes a foundation card and the ♦2 is built on it. The ♣A joins the foundation row. The ♣5 is packed on the ♥6. The ♥J is packed on the ♣Q, the ♥10 on the ♥J, the ♣9 on the ♥10, the ♠8 on the ♣9, the ♥7 on the ♠8 and the ♦6 on the ♥7. The ♥A joins the foundation row and the ♥2 is built on it. Once no more moves can be made within the layout, cards can start being dealt from the stock.

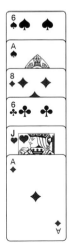

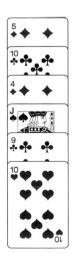

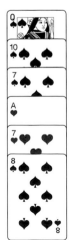

Three Blind Mice

This is a simple patience that more or less operates itself. It does not turn out very often (about one time in ten) and has a way of getting stuck very near the end, which you may find amusing or aggravating depending on your temperament.

How to play

Five rows of ten cards are dealt out, with the cards overlapping. The cards in the seven columns to the left should be placed face up, but the three cards in the top three rows of the three right-hand columns should be face down. The two odd cards are kept on one side to be played whenever it becomes possible to do so, as shown in the illustration below. The object is to build the four suits in descending sequence (Queen on King,

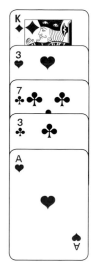

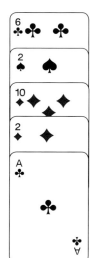
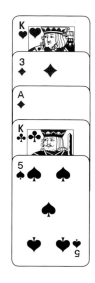

8 on 9, and so on) from King down to Ace. For this game, only the exposed cards can be built onto, but the card doing the building can be anywhere except farther up the same column, so long as it is face up. Any other cards below the one being taken to build are carried with it.

When one of the 'blind' cards is exposed it is turned over and can join in the play.

Kings may be played into the vacancies that arise when one of the ten columns becomes empty.

The illustration shows the start of a game. The ♠Q may be played onto the ♠K, but the ♦5 has to wait until the ♦6 is exposed. The building might start with the ♣7 being played on the ♣8, keeping the ♣3 and ♥A with it. This exposes the ♥3, so the ♥2 (and ♦7) can be built on the ♥3. Now one of the blind cards is exposed and should be turned over.

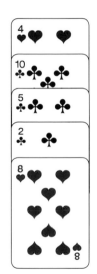
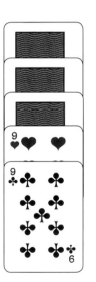
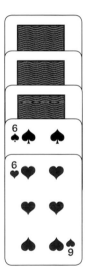
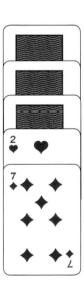

♣

Vacancies

Vacancies is more usually known as Gaps, and sometimes as Spaces. It is an excellent game with the merit that it is one of the few patience games in which the lucky order of the cards is less important than the player's skill. At every move the player is faced with four vacancies to fill, and much depends on the order in which they are filled.

How to play

The whole pack is dealt face up to the table in four rows of 13 cards, and the Aces are discarded, leaving four vacancies (see illustration). The object of the game is to arrange the cards so that every row consists of one suit in sequential order, with the 2 on the extreme left and the King on the extreme right. The player decides which row he will allocate to each suit, and, having decided, must stand by this order throughout the game.

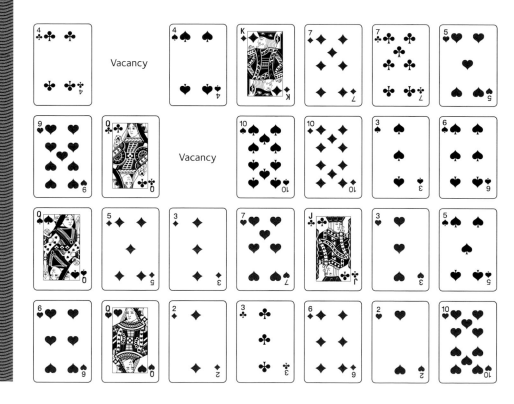

A vacancy may be filled only by the card that is next higher in rank and of the same suit as the card on the left of the vacancy. Obviously, filling a vacancy leaves another vacancy to be filled and this is done in the same way until the run of the game is brought to a halt by the position of the four Kings.

Three deals are permitted. When no further moves can be made after the first deal, all the cards that are not in their final positions are picked up, shuffled, and the layout remade by dealing them to the table, leaving a vacancy in each row to the immediate right of the cards that are in sequence. If a row has no cards in sequence then the vacancy is left on the extreme left of the row.

In the deal as illustrated below, the ♠6 is played to the right of the ♠5, and the ♠4 to the right of the ♠3. The ♣5 is played to the right of the ♣4, and the ♣6 to the right of the ♣5.

The ♠Q is played to the right of the ♠J and the player is now in a position to begin the third row by playing the 2 of the suit chosen for that row into the vacancy left by the ♠Q.

All Fours

All Fours was mentioned in Charles Cotton's *Compleat Gamester* in 1674 as being 'much played in Kent'. It became popular in the United States, where it acquired other names such as Seven-up, High-low Jack or Old Sledge.

Number of players

All Fours is a game for two players, but it can be adapted for four players as described in Seven-up (see opposite).

Cards

The full pack of 52 cards is used, the cards ranking from Ace (high) to 2 (low).

Six cards are dealt in two lots of three to both players, and the 13th card is turned up to determine the trump suit.

The deal passes in rotation.

How to play

The game is won by whoever first scores seven points. Points are scored for:

High. The player who is dealt the highest trump in play scores one point.

Low. The player who is dealt the lowest trump in play scores one point.

Jack. The player who wins the Jack of trumps (if it is in play) scores one point.

Game. Each player counts the honours among the tricks he has won, and, counting the Ace as four, the King as three, the Queen as two, the Jack as one and the 10 as ten, the player with the highest total scores one point. If

both players score the same total then the non-dealer scores the point.

The points are not counted until the end of the deal, but they should be understood from the start because they illustrate the object of the game.

The non-dealer now declares whether he will stand or beg. If he says 'I stand' he accepts the turned-up card as the trump suit and play begins. If he says 'I beg' he rejects the turned-up card as the trump suit, and the dealer must either accept or refuse the proposal to make another suit trumps. To refuse he says 'Take one'. The non-dealer then scores one point and play begins. To accept he says 'I run the cards'. He deals three more cards to his opponent and three to himself, and turns up the next card to determine the trump suit. If this is the same suit as the original trump suit, he runs the cards again, and continues to run them until a different trump suit is turned up. In the rare, but not impossible, event of the pack being exhausted without a different trump suit being turned up, there is a redeal by the same player. If the turned-up card is a Jack, the dealer scores one point, and if, when the cards are run, the turned-up card is again a Jack, the dealer again scores one point.

Play begins when the trump suit has been determined, and if the cards have been run, the players first discard from their hands enough cards to reduce the number held to six. The non-dealer leads the first trick. His opponent must follow suit or trump, as in Whist (see page 58). Unlike most other games, however, a player may trump even though he is able to follow suit, but he must not discard if he holds either a card of the suit led or a trump. If he does he has revoked and his opponent scores one point.

The winner of a trick leads to the next, and so on until all six tricks have been played. The players then turn up their tricks and score for High, Low, Jack and Game.

These four scoring features are fundamental to the game and are counted whenever it is possible to do so. If, for example, there is only one trump in play it counts two points, because it is both High and Low.

SEVEN-UP

This is a variation of the parent game that takes its name from the method of scoring.

Both players (or both sides if four are playing) begin with seven counters each. Every time that a point is scored the player (or side) that wins it puts a counter aside, and the player (or side) who first gets rid of his counters wins the game. If both go out in the same deal, the winner is he who first counts out when the points are scored for High, Low, Jack and Game.

ALL FIVES

This variation of the parent game is played for 61 points up. For convenience the score is best kept on a cribbage board.

The mechanics of the game are the same as those of the parent game, and points are pegged when the following trumps are won in a trick: Ace four points, King three points, Queen two points, Jack one point, 10 ten points and 5 five points.

After the hand has been played, the honours are counted as in the parent game, to determine the point for Game, with the addition that the player who has won the 5 of trumps scores five points for it.

California Jack

California Jack is a game arising from All Fours (see page 46), but it uses the full pack and is more complex and skilful. It is thought by most to be better than the original game.

Number of players

California Jack can only be played satisfactorily by two players.

Cards

California Jack is played with all 52 cards, the Ace ranking high, the 2 low.

The non-dealer cuts the pack and exposes the bottom card to decide the trump suit. The dealer deals six cards, one at a time, to each player, and places the remainder of the pack face upwards on the table, making sure to square it up so that only the top card can be seen.

How to play

The non-dealer leads the first trick. The winner of a trick takes the top card of the stock, the loser the next card. A player must follow suit or play a trump if he can, otherwise he loses one point.

When the stock is exhausted and the last six cards have been played, the tricks won by each player are examined, and one point is scored for winning High (Ace of trumps), Low (2 of trumps), Jack (Jack of trumps) and Game (majority of points, counting each Ace won as four points, each King as three points, each Queen as two points, each Jack as one

point and each 10 as ten points). The game is won by the player who first scores ten points.

The player should aim to keep both winning and losing cards in his hand because if the exposed card of the stock is valuable he will wish to win it, but if it is not, he will wish to lose the trick on the chance of the next card of the stock being a more valuable one. The 10s, of course, are the cards to go for.

SHASTA SAM

This is a variation of the game in which the stock is placed face downwards on the table instead of face upwards. It is a less skilful game as, of course, the winner of a trick does not know what card he will draw.

A good California Jack hand. There are two good cards for trick-winning and three for losing.

Casino

Casino is a game of Italian origin, sometimes spelt as Cassino, but this is believed to be an early printing error which was perpetuated. The game possibly takes its name from the casino – where gambling takes place.

Number of players

Although Casino is essentially a game for two, it may be played by three or four. The only difference is that if three players take part they all play against each other, whereas if four players take part, two play in partnership against the other two.

Cards

The full pack of 52 cards is used.

The numeral cards count at their pip values. The Ace counts as 1, and the court cards are used only for pairing: they have no pip value.

The dealer deals two cards face downwards to his opponent, then two face upwards to the table, and then two face downwards to himself. This is repeated, so that both players end with four cards each, and there are four exposed cards (the layout) on the table. The remaining 40 cards (the stock) are placed face downwards on the table.

The object of the game is to take in cards which score as follows:

♦10 (great casino)	2
♠2 (little casino)	1
Majority of cards (27 or more)	3
Majority of spades (7 or more)	1
Aces	1
All cards in layout (the sweep)	1

How to play

Each player in turn, beginning with the non-dealer, plays a card until both players have exhausted their four cards. When this occurs, the same dealer deals four more cards to his opponent and four to himself but none to the layout. Play continues in this way until the stock has been exhausted. In all, therefore, there are six deals to complete the game, and before making the final deal the dealer must announce it. If he does not, his opponent has a right to cancel the deal.

When a player plays a card from his hand he has the choice of several plays.

He may *Pair*. If, for example, there are one or more 5s in the layout, he may play a 5 from his hand and take it up as a trick with all the other 5s in the layout. A court card, however, may be paired with only one card of the same rank at a time.

He may *Combine*. It is an extension of pairing that allows a player to pick up cards from the layout of the total pip value of a card in his hand. Thus a player playing a 9 may take up a 7 and a 2, or a

Layout

Hand

6 and a 3 from the layout, or all four cards if they are in the layout.

He may *Build*. He may play a card onto a card in the layout to make up a total that he is in a position to take with another card in his hand. If, for example, a player holds a 9 and a 2, and there is a 7 in the layout, he may build the 2 on the 7, so that the next time he plays (provided his opponent has not forestalled him) he may play the 9 and take all three cards as a trick. The build may be continued by either player up to a maximum of five cards, but a build can be taken only as a unit. The player who has built must take up the combination

when next it is his turn to play, unless he prefers to win something else, or he decides to make another build.

He may Call. It is an extension of building that allows a player to earmark one or more combinations for subsequent capture. Suppose, for example, a player holds in his hand two 8s and that there is a 5 and a 3 in the layout (see illustration above). He could, of course, combine one of his 8s with the 5 and 3 in the layout, but this would only give him three cards in the trick. The better play, therefore, is for him to play one of his 8s to the layout and announce 'Eight'. Then, when next it is his turn to play, provided his opponent has not forestalled him, he may play his other 8 and pick up all four cards in the trick.

When a player cannot pair, combine, build or call, he must play one of his cards to the layout. This is known as trailing. It is advisable to play a low card, but not an Ace, little casino or a spade.

When the last eight cards have been played any left in the layout are the property of the winner of the final trick, but this does not count as a sweep.

This ends the game, except for the formality of the players examining their tricks and counting their scores.

There is no penalty for making a build incorrectly, or for capturing cards to which a player is not entitled, because his opponent has the opportunity to see the error and demand that it is corrected. If, however, a player makes a build when he has no card in his hand to capture it or trails when he has a build in the layout, he automatically forfeits the game. If a card is accidentally face-up in the pack, or if the dealer when dealing exposes a card (other than when dealing cards to the layout), the exposed card is added to the layout and the dealer plays the hand with fewer than four cards.

Casino is sometimes considered a game for children. It is, however, very far from being so. Among card players it is widely spoken of as one of the best of all two-handed games and it is often played for high stakes. To be successful a player needs an elephantine memory, and the capacity to deduce from the card played by an opponent what cards he is most likely to be holding in his hand.

ROYAL CASINO

This is an improvement on the parent game because the court cards play a more important part. The Aces count 1 or 14 (at the option of the player), the Kings 13, the Queens 12 and the Jacks 11, and they may be used for combining and building. Thus an 8 and a 4 may be taken with a Queen, a 6, a 4 and a 3 with a King, and so on. Twenty-one points constitute the game.

DRAW CASINO

In this version of the game, after the first round of a deal, the 40 undealt cards are placed face downwards on the table to form a stock. Then each player, after playing, draws a card from the stock to bring the number of cards in his hand up to four. When the stock is exhausted the hands are played out and the count made in the same way as in the parent game.

SPADE CASINO

This version may be played either as royal casino or as the parent game, with the addition that the ♠A, ♠J and ♠2 count two points each, and all the other spades one point each.

Game is 61 points, and it is convenient and customary to keep the score on a cribbage board.

Comet

Comet was probably devised around 1759, when Halley's Comet reappeared and caused great excitement.

Number of players

Comet is a game for two players.

Cards

Two 52-card packs, with the same design on their backs, are used alternately. The packs must be prepared by rejecting all the Aces, putting all the red cards into one pack and all the black cards into another, and interchanging a red and a black 9.

Taking one of the packs, 18 cards are dealt to each player, one at a time, and the remaining 12 cards are put aside; they play no part in the game.

How to play

The non-dealer begins the game by playing one of his cards, face upwards, to the centre of the table. The players then, alternately, build up on it by rank only. Suits are disregarded. Any number of cards, provided they are of the proper rank, may be played in one turn. The four 8s, for example, may be built on a 7, the four Jacks on a 10, and so on. When a player is unable to build it is classed as a stop, and his opponent begins a new sequence by playing any card he chooses. Obviously a King is always considered as a stop.

The 9 of the opposite colour, when it appears, is called the comet. It may represent any card that the holder chooses, but can only be played in turn. It is a stop card, which means that the player who plays it begins a new sequence.

The player who is first to get rid of all the cards in his hand is the winner. He scores the total of pips left in his opponent's hand, the court cards counting as 10 each. If both players are stopped and both are left with cards in their hands, both hands are counted. The lower hand wins and scores the value of his opponent's hand less the value of his own.

If a player wins the hand while the comet is in the hand of his opponent he scores double. If a player wins by playing the comet, he doubles his score, and if he wins the hand by playing the comet as a 9 he quadruples his score.

Cribbage

Cribbage is believed to have been developed out of the older card game of Noddy by Sir John Suckling in the reign of Charles I. In the manner of scoring it is unique, and the play calls for no effort of memory. Good judgment and concentration are the chief qualities that lead to success.

Number of players

Originally cribbage was a two-handed game as described first, but variations for three and four players are now played and are described later.

The two-handed game is the most popular, and of it there are three variations: five-, six- and seven-card.

Cards

The full pack of 52 cards is used, and they rank from King (high) to Ace (low). The King, Queen and Jack count as ten each, and the other cards their pip values.

Five-card Cribbage for two players, which is the original game, is generally considered the most scientific of the variations.

The players cut for the deal; the lower deals first. Five cards are dealt to each player, and the non-dealer pegs three holes (Three for Last) as compensation against the advantage of the first deal of a game.

How to play

Points won are marked with a peg on what is known as a cribbage or noddy

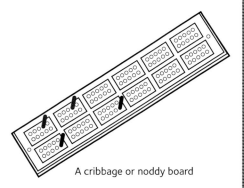

A cribbage or noddy board

board (see illustration above). It is oblong in shape, has a double row of holes, 30 in each row, and is divided, for convenience in scoring, into groups of five holes. The board is placed between the two players; both start from the same end of the board and peg their scores first along the outer row of holes and then along the inner row – once round the board in the five-card game, twice round in the six-card game and three times round in the seven-card game. In each case the game ends when one player reaches the hole from which he started. So in five-card cribbage the game is 61 holes, in six-card 121 holes, and in seven-card 181 holes.

The players look at their cards, and then each place two of them face

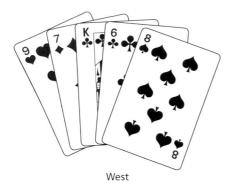

West

East

downwards on the right of the dealer. These four cards are known as the crib or box. The non-dealer then cuts the pack, and the dealer turns up the top card of the cut and places it on top of the pack. The card is known as the start, and if it is a Jack the dealer pegs two holes (Two for his Heels).

Scores are made partly in play and partly by the scoring values of the cards in hand. The latter, however, are not pegged until the play ends.

During the play of the hand, scores are made as follows:

If a player plays a card of the same rank as the previous one played, he pegs two for a pair, but court cards pair only rank with rank – that is to say King pair with King, Queen with Queen and Jack with Jack.

If a player plays a third card of the same rank as a pair he pegs six for pair-royal.

If a player plays a fourth card of the same rank as a pair-royal he pegs 12 for a double pair-royal.

A sequence (or run) is pegged at one for each card with a minimum of three cards and a maximum of seven. The cards need not be of the same suit, nor need they be played in sequential order, but, as the Ace is low, A, K, Q is not a sequence, and a sequence is destroyed by a pair or an intervening card. If the dealer plays a 7 and the non-dealer a 5, the dealer may now play a 6 and peg three, and the non-dealer may continue either with a 4 or an 8 and peg four.

If a player plays a card which, with those already played, adds up to 15 he pegs two, and, again, if they total 31 he pegs two.

Out of this an important point arises. If, when the player whose turn it is to play cannot do so without exceeding 31, he says 'Go'. His opponent then plays a card or cards up to the limit. If the cards that he plays bring the total up to exactly 31 he pegs two; if not he pegs one (One for Last).

This ends the play, and the players, beginning with the non-dealer, count their scores by combining their own cards with the start. The dealer then exposes the crib (it is his exclusive property) and any values that he finds in it (making full use of the start) he pegs to his score. Should either player hold the Jack of the same suit as the start he pegs one (One for his Nob). If a player holds in his hand three cards all of the same suit he pegs three for a flush, and four if the start is of the same suit. In the crib, however, nothing is scored for a flush unless, with the start, it is a flush of five; if it is the dealer then he pegs five.

Two other features of the scoring call for special mention. First, a player must count his hand aloud, and if he overlooks any score, either in play or otherwise, his opponent may call 'Muggins', point out the omission, and peg the score for himself. Secondly, if a player reaches the game hole before his opponent has gone halfway round the board, a lurch is scored, that is to say that the winner scores two games instead of only one.

Points are scored during the play by a player adding the value of the card played by the opponent to a card played from his own hand. Thus if a 10 or court

Start

Crib

West

East

55

card is led, and a player plays a 5, he scores 15 and pegs two holes (*fifteen-two* as it is called for short). If a 6 is led, and he plays another 6, he scores for a pair and pegs two. Again, if a 4 is led and he plays a 6 and the opponent plays a 5: he pegs three for a sequence and two for 15. And so on.

Example play

The general principles may be illustrated in the elementary deal.

East is the dealer.

West (see illustration on page 54) holds a sequence of four. As a result the ♣K will go to the crib, and for his other card he must choose between the ♣6 and the ♥9. There is not much in it, but as the ♣6 is of the same suit as the King, there is a slight advantage in discarding the ♥9, because the ♣6 (along with the King) might help to give East a flush.

East has an easy choice of discards. Indeed, it is obvious that he will discard the ♣A and ♦3.

West cuts the cards, and East turns up the ♠K.

The position is now as shown in the illustration on page 55.

West leads the ♦7 and says 'Seven'. It is his best lead because if East plays an 8 and pegs two for 15, West can play the ♣6 and peg three for sequence. He will not, of course, play the ♠8, because if East holds another 8 he will play it and not only peg for a pair-royal but for 31 as well.

In the event, East cannot play an 8 and score for 15. His best play, therefore, is the ♣10, announcing 'Seventeen'. This makes it impossible for a 15 to be scored against him.

West has no better play than the ♠8, announcing 'Twenty-five', because the closer the total to 31 the better the chance that East will be unable to play.

East plays the ♠5, announcing 'Thirty'.

West says 'Go' and as East has not got an Ace he pegs One for Last.

The hands are now counted.

West is not helped by the start. All he can score is two for 15 and three for sequence. This, with his Three for Last (as non-dealer), gives him eight.

East pegs six for 15 (two 10s and the ♠K in the start, each combined with the ♠5) and two for the pair of 10s. In the crib he finds an Ace, a King, a 9 and a 3. With the start this gives him two for the pair of Kings. He therefore pegs 10 holes, making 11 in all as he has already pegged One for Last.

Six- and seven-card cribbage

The six- and seven-card variations of cribbage differ very little from the five-card game. There is, in fact, no difference in the play nor in the crib, and very little in the mechanics of the game. The only differences of importance, apart from the number of cards, are that the non-dealer does not receive Three for Last, that the cards are played out to the end (the player failing to score for go leading again, thus giving his opponent the chance of making a pair or 15).

In the six-card variation the play is twice round the board (121 holes) and in the seven-card three times round (181 holes).

The general principles explained for the parent game are the same as for the six-card variation. It is to be noted, however, that in the six-card variation the number of cards in hand and in the crib are the same, from which it follows that it is not so important for the non-dealer to make the effort of trying to baulk the crib by his discard. The two objectives – preserving any values in hand and baulking the opponent's crib – are in this case on the same level, which means that either objective may be preferred, as the nature of the hand dictates.

Three-handed cribbage

With three players, five cards are dealt to each player, and an extra one to the crib, to which each player contributes one card only. There is no Three for Last. The start is cut in the same way as for two-handed cribbage. The player on the left of the dealer plays first and has first Show. He deals the succeeding hand. The score may be pegged on a triangular board open in the centre, or on the standard board with a pivoted arm that permits a third player to peg. The game is played once round the board.

Four-handed cribbage

With four players, two play as partners against the other two, the partners sitting facing each other. Each player is dealt five cards and discards one to the crib, which is the property of the dealer. The player on the left of the dealer plays first. The others follow in clockwise rotation. Consultation between partners is not allowed, nor may they prompt each other, but a player may help his partner in the count of the hand or crib. The cards are played out to the end, as in the six and seven-card variations. Game is usually played as twice round the board (121 holes).

German Whist

German Whist was invented for two players who like Whist and cannot find another pair. It is a simple game but to play it well requires a good memory.

Number of players
German Whist is essentially a game for only two players.

Cards
The full pack of 52 cards is used. Cards rank from Ace (high) to 2 (low).

Each player is dealt 13 cards. The remaining 26 cards are placed face down between the players and the top card is turned face up to denote the trump suit.

How to play
The non-dealer leads the first trick. Thereafter the player who wins a trick leads the next, and so on. A player must follow suit if he can, the higher-ranking card winning. If he cannot follow suit, he may either trump (to win) or discard (lose the trick by playing a card from another suit). The winner of a trick takes into his hand the exposed card from the top of the stock; the loser takes the next card from the stock (he does not show it to his opponent) and turns up the next card.

When the stock is exhausted, the players play out the remaining 13 cards, and at this stage of the game the player with a good memory will know exactly which cards his opponent holds.

The game is complete in one deal, and the player who wins the majority of tricks receives an agreed number of points per trick for all in excess of those won by his opponent. If both players win 13 tricks, there is, of course, no score.

Although German whist is a simple game it offers good memory training for those who aspire to succeed at more advanced games, and, at the same time, exercises the technique of card play.

If a player holds a strong trump suit he should lead his trumps early so that he can command the game later on. If the exposed card is a trump it is always good play to make an effort to win it.

On the other hand, it is not always good play to win a trick. Much depends on the value of the exposed card. For example, suppose the ♦9 is exposed. West leads the ♦7 and East holds ♦Q, ♦6, ♦3. East should play ♦3, and allow West to win the trick. It is not worth while wasting the ♦Q, which should be kept in hand for better things later in the game. However, if the ♦J is the exposed card, East should win the trick with the ♦Q, because in this case he would be exchanging the ♦Q for an equivalent card and adding a trick to his total.

Stock

West's hand

It is advisable to hold command of as many suits as possible, because it enables one to take a trick whenever the exposed card is worth winning, without losing control of the suit.

In the illustration above, West holds the hand. Spades are trumps, and the exposed card is ♣K. The ♣K is worth winning, but leading the ♣A is not the best play. West will win the trick, but the value of his hand will remain unchanged. West should prefer to lead the ♦K, because if it wins the trick his hand will be that much better, and if East is able to win the trick with the ♦A, West's ♦Q has been promoted to top diamond.

Gin Rummy

The invention of Gin Rummy has been credited to E. T. Baker, in a New York club in 1909. It is a variant of the parent game Rummy, which is frequently shortened to Rum, and acquired its name Gin by extension of the alcoholic drink theme. It became very popular due to the publicity it received when taken up by film stars in Hollywood in the 1940s.

Number of players

Gin Rummy is a game for two players only. There are forms of Rummy for more players – see Rummy on page 148.

Cards

The full pack of 52 cards is used, cards ranking from King (high) to Ace (low).

Dealer is determined by the players each drawing a card from the pack: higher has choice of dealing first or not. If cards of equal rank are drawn, the suit determines precedence in the order: spades (high), hearts, diamonds, clubs. After the first deal, the winner of each hand deals the next.

The dealer deals ten cards face down to each player, one at a time, beginning with his opponent. The remainder of the pack is placed face down between the players to form the stock. The top card of the stock is placed face up beside the stock and becomes the upcard, at the same time beginning a discard pile.

How to play

The object of the game is to form the hand into sets of three or more cards.

A set may be of two kinds: three or four cards of the same rank, or three or more cards in sequence in the same suit (Ace being in sequence with 2, 3, not King, Queen).

The non-dealer may take the first upcard into his hand or refuse it. If he refuses, the dealer has the option of taking it or refusing it. If the dealer also refuses it, the non-dealer draws the top card from the stock and takes it into his hand, discarding a card (the new upcard) face up on the discard pile. The discarded card may, in fact, be the card picked up, and the player may merely look at it and discard it immediately. Thereafter each player in turn draws a card, either the upcard or the top card of the stock, and discards, so that the number of cards in each player's hand remains at ten.

Cards which are not included in a set are 'unmatched' cards. After drawing (and only then), a player may 'knock', i.e. terminate the hand, whenever the pip value of the unmatched cards in his hand total ten or less. For this purpose, court cards (King, Queen, Jack) count as ten points each, the Ace counts as one, and the other cards as their face value. Knocking involves laying down the hand, arranged in sets, with unmatched cards separate, making the usual discard. The count of unmatched cards represent points against the player. If all ten cards are in sets, the player is said to 'go gin', and the count against him is zero.

If the player drawing the fiftieth card discards without knocking (i.e. there are only two cards left in the stock) the hand is abandoned and there is no score for that deal.

When a player knocks, there is one further stage before the calculation of the score, and that is the 'laying off'. The opponent of the knocker lays down his cards in sets, and, unless the knocker has gone gin, may lay off any of his unmatched cards on the sets of the knocker, thereby reducing the count against him.

The illustration below shows a completed deal in which the opponent of the knocker can lay two unmatched cards on the knocker's sets.

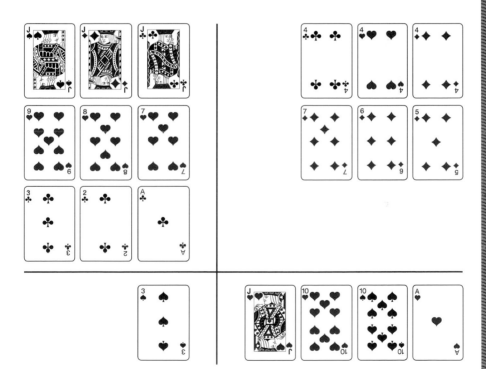

Knocker (left) goes out with a count of three. His opponent lays off with ♥J, ♥10 and is left with a count of 11

Scoring

If the knocker has the lower of the two counts in unmatched cards, he scores the difference in the counts (in the example on the previous page the knocker scores eight points). It is possible that the player who did not knock has the lower count. In this case he 'undercuts' the knocker and scores the difference in the count plus a bonus of 20 points. Should the count be equal, the opponent of the knocker still undercuts him, scoring the bonus 20 points, but nothing for difference in point count. The illustration below shows a completed deal, in which the knocker is undercut.

It must be remembered that cards cannot be laid off on a knocker who goes gin. Going gin therefore guards against being undercut.

A player who goes gin scores a bonus of 25 on top of the point count.

The first player to score 100 points wins the game, but scoring does not end there. The winner of the game adds a 100 points bonus to his score. Each player then adds 20 points to his score for each of his 'boxes' – each deal that he has won. The winner wins by the difference in the two scores. This difference is doubled if the lower did not score a point. This is called a 'shutout' or 'schneider'.

There is a more complex scoring system, which was used in the days of popularity in Hollywood and which is known as Hollywood scoring.

The scores are recorded on a sheet of ruled paper (see illustration, opposite, top). The first time a player wins a deal

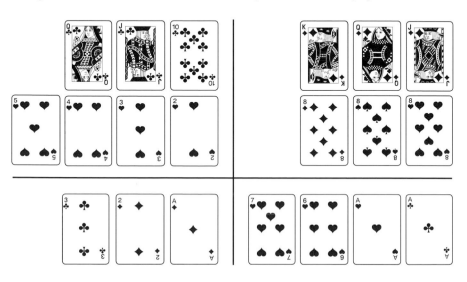

Knocker (left) is undercut when opponent lays off with ♥A, ♥6 and ♥7 on his sequence

	Me	Three	Me	Three	Me	Three
Box 1	25	17	2	3	12	
Box 2	27	20	14		18	
Box 3	39		20			
Box 4	45					
Box 5						
Box 6						
Box 7						

Hollywood scoring, with a game in progress

he enters the points in the first column only. The second time he enters the points in the second column and also adds them to the score in the first column. The third time he enters the points in the third column and adds them to the score in the first two columns. Thereafter, any points won should be added to the scores in all three columns on the sheet.

When the score of a player in a column reaches 100 points or more, the column is closed. The player winning it scores a bonus of 100 points, and each player scores 20 points for each box won, as in the orthodox scoring. The winner wins by the difference in the scores, and if the loser fails to score in a column, then the difference should be doubled. A player who is shut out in the first column must clearly make his first entry in the second column. A game ends when all three columns are won.

Strategy

Players must use judgment in deciding how long to hold high cards presenting a good chance of a set. For three or four draws it might pay to hold them, as high cards are likely to be discarded by the opponent. Many hands are won after only five or six draws, however, with six or seven cards in sets, and three or four unmatched. At this stage, therefore, a player should consider discarding these high cards in favour of lower ones.

Low cards ought to be retained, as they reduce the loss if your opponent wins, and they enable a player to knock as soon as he holds two or three sets.

A player in a position to knock will have to weigh the chances of being undercut. In the first four turns, a player might feel safe in knocking as soon as he can. From about the eighth turn, however, he might decide to knock only with a count of, say, five or lower. In deciding whether to knock he will consider the upcards which both players have taken and try to calculate how many sets his opponent has and what he might be able to lay off.

With an opportunity to knock with a low count it is usually a mistake to wait for gin. If your opponent goes gin first it is a costly error.

Jo-jotte

Although Jo-jotte was invented by Ely Culbertson in 1937 it is not altogether a modern game, but a variation of the old French game of Belotte, in itself very similar to Klaberjass (see page 68) and its several variations.

Number of players

Jo-jotte is a game for two players.

Cards

Jo-jotte is played with the short pack, namely a pack from which all cards below the rank of 7 have been removed.

The rank of the cards varies. If there is a trump suit, the cards of the suit rank in the order: Jack, 9, Ace, 10, King, Queen, 8, 7. In plain suits, or if the hand is played in no trumps, the order is: Ace, 10, King, Queen, Jack, 9, 8, 7.

Each player is dealt six cards (either singly, or in twos or threes) and the 13th card of the pack is placed face upwards on the table. This is known as the turned card.

Bidding

There are two rounds of bidding. The non-dealer bids first. He may either accept the suit of the turned card as trumps, or pass. If he passes, the dealer has the same option. If both players pass, the non-dealer may name any suit, other than that of the turned card, as trumps, or he may declare no-trumps or he may pass. If he passes for the second

time, the dealer has the same option. If both players pass twice the hand is abandoned and the deal passes, but if either player names a suit as trumps, his opponent may overbid it by declaring no-trumps, but not by naming another suit as trumps. Either player may double his opponent's declaration, and any double may be redoubled.

How to play

When the declaration has been determined (doubled, redoubled or passed) the dealer deals three more cards to his opponent and to himself, and he places the bottom card of the pack face upwards on top of the undealt cards of the pack. It has no significance in play but is solely informatory and, therefore, is known as the information card.

The player who has made the final declaration is known as the declarer: his opponent as the defender.

At this stage of the game the defender may announce that instead of defending against the declarer's contract he will himself become declarer at a nullo contract; a contract, that is, to lose every trick. The declarer may now

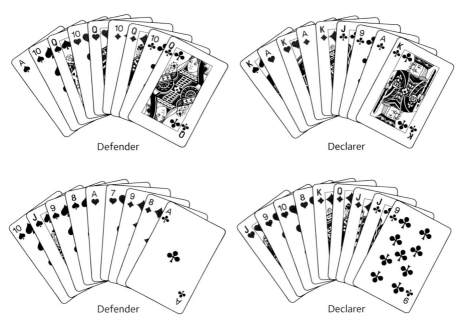

Defender

Declarer

Defender

Declarer

declare a slam, a contract to win every trick either in the suit originally named by him (he cannot change the suit) or in no-trumps.

The defender then announces his melds, if he holds any. A meld is four of a kind (except 9s, 8s and 7s at no trumps, and 8s and 7s in a suit declaration). A meld carries a score of 100 points and is scored (as at Bridge, see page 85) above the line. Only the player with the highest-ranking meld may score for it, and he may score for a second meld if he holds one.

Next, beginning with the defender, the players score for sequences, and for this purpose the cards take their normal rank of Ace (high), King, Queen, Jack,

10, 9, 8, 7. For a sequence of five cards the holder scores 50 points above the line, for a sequence of four 40 points, and for a sequence of three 20 points. If two sequences are of equal length, that headed by the highest card takes precedence. If both sequences are equal, a sequence in the trump suit wins over one in a plain suit; if both sequences are in plain suits neither is scored for. Only the player with the higher-ranking sequence may score for it, and he may score for any other sequences that he may hold.

In the top illustration above, clubs are trumps. Defender scores 200 points above the line for his melds of 10s and Queens, and the declarer cannot score for his meld of Kings because in the trump suit the 10 is higher than the King.

In the lower of the illustrations on page 65, hearts are trumps. Neither player has a meld. Defender declares his four-card sequence in spades but he cannot score for it because the declarer has an equal sequence in the trump suit (hearts). The declarer, therefore, scores 40 points above the line for his four-card sequence in hearts and a further 20 points for his three-card sequence in diamonds.

Finally, it is to be noted that if the declarer elects to play the hand in the same suit as the turned card, either player if he holds the 7 of the suit may exchange it for the turned card.

The player who leads to a trick may lead any card that he chooses. The second player is limited in his play; for he must obey the three rules that follow:

He must follow suit if he can.

If a trump has been led he must not only follow suit if he can, but win the trick by playing a higher trump if he holds one.

If a plain suit has been led and he is unable to follow suit, he must win the trick by trumping if he can.

Second player may discard a worthless card only when he is unable to obey one or other of these three rules.

Winning a trick has no value in itself. What counts is winning tricks with certain cards in them; these are scored as follows:

Jack of trumps	20
9 of trumps	15
Any Ace or 10	10
Any King or Queen	5
Last trick (except at nullo)	10

In the example that follows hearts are trumps. The turned card is ♠K: the information card ♦Q. The defender leads ♣A, and the play is as given below (underlining indicates the winning card):

Defender	Declarer
♣A	♣Q
♣10	♥10
♦8	♦A
♦J	♦7
♣8	♥8
♥9	♦9
♠10	♠9
♠Q	♥A
♥7	♥J

Declarer scores for taking:

Jack of trumps (♥)	20
♥A	10
♠A	10
♥10	10
♣10	10
♠Q	5
Last trick	10
	75 points

Defender scores for taking:

9 of trumps (♥)	15
♣A	10
♠10	10
♣Q	5
	40 points

Defender   Declarer

In addition to the above, if a player holds the King and Queen of the trump suit (if there is one) he may score 20 points provided he announces 'Jo' when he plays the King and later 'Jotte' when he plays the Queen. He cannot score for the combination if he plays the Queen before the King.

Game is won by the player who first scores 80 points below the line, which may be made in one hand or in a series of part-scores, and the player who wins the rubber (best out of three games) scores a bonus of 300 points.

The declarer of a nullo contract scores a bonus of 200 points if he loses every trick; if he takes a trick, however, his opponent scores 200 points for the first trick and 100 points for every subsequent trick.

The declarer of a slam scores a bonus of 500 points if he wins every trick; and if a player wins every trick but has not bid slam he still scores a bonus but of only 100 points.

Scoring below the line, towards game, is calculated as follows:

1. If the declarer's total score, including melds, sequences, trick scores and bonuses is greater than the defender's total score, he scores his trick score below the line, and the defender scores his trick score above the line.

2. If the defender's total score is greater than the declarer's, the two trick scores are added together and scored by the defender below the line.

3. If the contract is doubled or redoubled, the player with the higher total scores both his and his opponent's trick score, doubled or quadrupled, below the line.

4. If there is a tie in total points, the trick scores of both players are put in prison and awarded to the player who obtains the higher total in the following deal.

Klaberjass

Klaberjass is probably better known in the United States than in Britain, because it occurs in American author Damon Runyon's stories under the names of Clabber, Clobber, Clubby, Klab and Klob. It is possible that the game was taken to the New World by Central European immigrants as a variation of the Hungarian game of Kalabriás, which is a game for three or four players.

Number of players

Klaberjass is primarily a game for two players, but can be played by four, in two partnerships.

Cards

The game is played with a pack from which the 6s, 5s, 4s, 3s and 2s have been removed. In the trump suit the cards rank in the order Jack, 9, Ace, 10, King, Queen, 8, 7; and in the other three suits Ace, 10, King, Queen, Jack, 9, 8, 7.

Six cards are dealt to both players, in two lots of three cards each. The next card of the pack is turned face upwards on the table (it is known as the turn-up card) and the rest of the pack is placed face downwards so as partly to cover it.

Bidding

The non-dealer bids first. He may take-it (i.e. accept the turn-up card as the trump suit); pass (i.e. refuse to accept the turn-up card as the trump suit); or schmeiss (i.e. offer to play with the turn-up card as the trump suit or throw in the hand, as his opponent prefers). If the opponent says 'Yes' to a schmeiss there is a fresh deal; if he says 'No' the hand is played with the turn-up card as the trump suit.

If the non-dealer has passed, the dealer may either take-it, pass or schmeiss.

If both players pass there is a second round of bidding. Now the non-dealer may name any one of the other three suits as trumps, or he may schmeiss, or he may pass. If he passes, the dealer may name one of the other three suits as trumps, or throw in the hand.

When a player accepts or names a trump suit, the bidding ends, and the player who has accepted or named a suit as trumps is called the maker.

There are never more than two rounds of bidding, and, when the trump suit has been settled, the dealer deals three more cards, one at a time, to the two players. He then turns up the bottom card of the pack and places it on top of the pack. It takes no part in the play, and is put where it is only to be seen.

If either player has been dealt the 7 of the trump suit, he may exchange it for the turn-up card.

How to play

First the players inspect their hands for possible melds (card combinations that may score them points). Only sequences are melded, and for melding the cards rank in the order from Ace (high) to 7 (low). A three-card sequence counts 20 points, a four-card or longer one 50 points.

The non-dealer begins by announcing the value of his best sequence. If his best sequence is of three cards he says 'Twenty'; if of four or more cards he says 'Fifty'. If the dealer has a better sequence he says 'No good'; if he lacks a better sequence he says 'Good'; if he has an equal sequence he asks 'How high?' The non-dealer then announces the top card of his sequence. The dealer then says whether it is good, no good, or if he has a sequence headed by an equal card. In this last event neither player scores unless one of the sequences is in the trump suit, which wins over a sequence in a plain suit.

The non-dealer leads the first trick; thereafter the winner of a trick leads to the next. A player must follow suit if he can, and if not he must play a trump if he holds one. If a trump is led, the second player must win the trick if he can.

After the first trick has been played, the player with the highest meld shows it and scores for all sequences in his hand. His opponent cannot score for any sequences that he may hold.

A player who holds the King and Queen of the trump suit may score 20 points so long as he announces 'Bella' immediately after he has played the second of them to a trick. If a player holds the Jack of the trump suit, as well as the King and Queen, he may score for the sequence as well as for bella.

When all the cards have been played, each player examines his tricks and scores points for winning in his tricks:

Jasz (Jack of trumps)	20
Menel (9 of trumps)	14
Any Ace	11
Any 10	10
Any King	4
Any Queen	3
Any Jack (except Jasz)	2
Last trick	10

If the maker's total, including melds and cards won, is higher than the opponent's, each scores all the points he has won. If the totals of the two players are equal, the opponent scores the points he has won, the maker nothing. If the opponent's total is higher than the maker's, the two totals are added together and the opponent scores them.

The player who first reaches 500 points wins the game.

Pinocle

Pinocle is frequently spelt Pinochle, but the *Oxford English Dictionary* does not sanction the 'h'. It was derived from the old French game of Bezique, which likely came from the Italian card game Bazzica, and was highly popular in Europe in the mid-19th century as a two-handed game. It has become extremely popular in the United States, where it is played by three or more players. The original form is described here.

Number of players

Pinocle is for two players (although can be played by more).

Cards

From two packs of cards, take all the Aces, Kings, Queens, Jacks, 10s and 9s to make a pack of 48 cards. The ranking of the cards in Pinocle is as follows: Ace (high), 10s, King, Queen, Jack, 9.

Twelve cards are dealt to each player, either three or four cards at a time, and the next card is turned face upwards to indicate the trump suit. The rest of the pack is placed face downwards on the table to half cover the exposed card.

How to play

The object is to win tricks including cards which carry a scoring value when won in a trick, and to meld certain card combinations that carry a scoring value.

When taken in a trick each Ace scores 11 points, each 10 scores ten, each King four, each Queen three, and each Jack two. The player who wins the last trick scores 10 points.

The values of the melds are:

Class A

A, 10, K, Q, J of trumps	150
K, Q of trumps (royal marriage)	40
K, Q of a plain suit (common marriage)	20

Class B

Pinocle (♠Q and ♦J)	40
Dis (9 of the trump suit)	10

Class C

1 Ace of each suit	100
1 King of each suit	80
1 Queen of each suit	60
1 Jack of each suit	40

The non-dealer leads to the first trick. Thereafter the winner of a trick leads to the next. It is not necessary for a player to follow suit to a led card. The winner of a trick replenishes his hand by taking the top card of the stock; the loser of the trick takes the next.

After a player has won a trick and before drawing from the stock, he may meld any of the above combinations. To meld he places the cards face upwards on the table in front of him, where they remain until he decides to play them to a trick, or until the stock is exhausted. Melding is subject to the three rules that follow:

1. Only one meld may be made at a turn.

2. For each meld, at least one card must be taken from the hand and placed on the table.

3. A card already melded may be melded again so long as it is in a different class, or in a higher-scoring meld of the same class. That is to say, if hearts are trumps a player may meld ♥K, Q and score for the royal marriage, and later he may add ♥A, 10, J and score for the sequence. He cannot first declare ♥A, 10, K, Q, J and score for sequence and later declare the royal marriage.

If the dealer turns up a dis as the trump card he scores 10 points. Thereafter a player holding a dis may count it merely by showing it when winning a trick. He may count the dis and make another meld at the same time. After winning a trick, the holder of a dis may exchange it for the trump card.

The player who wins the twelfth trick may meld if he is able to. He then draws the last face-downwards card of the stock and must show it to his opponent. The loser of the trick takes the card exposed on the table.

The last 12 tricks are now played off. During this period of play a player must follow suit if he can to the card led; if he cannot he must trump the trick if he holds a trump. If a trump is led the second player must win the trick if he can.

Melds are scored when they are declared. The score for cards won in tricks are added after the hand has been played out; a total of seven, eight, or nine points is counted as ten.

Every deal may constitute a game, or the players may prefer that the winner will be he who first reaches an agreed figure.

At pinocle skill and experience count for much. An ability to remember which cards have been played contributes much towards success. When it comes to playing off the last 12 cards, the experienced player will never be in any doubt about which cards his opponent holds. Thus, when playing to the last trick before the stock is exhausted, a player should be able to weigh up the merits of winning the trick and melding, preventing his opponent from melding, or losing the trick and so obtaining the exposed trump card to add to his trump length in the final play off.

Russian Bank

Russian Bank is similar to some patience games, in that cards are built on foundations, but it is a competitive game. It is also called Crapette and Stop!

Number of players

Russian Bank is for two players.

Cards

Two full packs of 52 cards are used. The cards rank from King (high) to Ace (low).

Each player draws a card from one of the packs. The player with the lower card plays first. Each player has one complete pack and shuffles his opponent's pack, placing it face down before his opponent. Players sit opposite each other.

The first player deals 11 cards face down to a pile to his right, turning the 12th card face up and placing it on top of the pile. This is his depot. He deals the next four cards face up in a column to his left so that the column runs from his left hand to his opponent's right hand. This is his file. He places the rest of his cards face down to his left. This is his stock.

How to play

The object is to pack onto the cards in the files in descending sequences of alternate colours. Cards should be packed outwards from the centre. Any Aces are played to a foundation column to the right of the file. The Aces in the foundation column are built up to King,

as cards become available, in suit sequence. The cards initially available are the cards in the file and the card face up on the depot. One card in the file can be packed on another, and when a card in the file is packed upon, it is still available, and can be packed onto another card in the file provided all the cards packed on it are transferred with it.

When the first player has completed his layout as described, he first moves any Ace from the file to its foundation space. The space created in the file is filled by the top card of the depot, and the next card in the depot is turned face up. He then makes any further plays available, filling spaces created from the depot each time, until no further plays are possible. He then turns over the first card of his stock. If he can build it onto a foundation or pack it onto a file he does so, turning the next card. When he finally turns a card which cannot be played to a foundation or file, he plays it to a waste heap to his right, next to his depot. He then turns the next card from the stock face up to the waste heap ready for play on his next turn. His current turn ends.

The second player then deals a depot, a file and a stock in the same way,

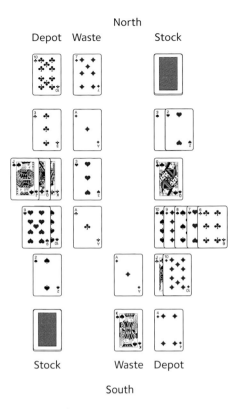

North

Depot Waste Stock

Stock Waste Depot

South

Russian Bank – a game in progress

stock. Each player from now on has these options on his turn. Cards available for play are those exposed at the top of a file, depot or waste heap. A turn ends when a player cannot play a card from stock except onto his waste heap.

When a player's stock is exhausted, he turns over his waste heap (without shuffling) to form a new stock. When his depot is exhausted, he fills spaces in his file from his stock.

Plays must always be made in the following order:

- A space in a file must be filled before any other play is made.
- A player must play from his depot before he plays from his file or from his waste heap.
- When a card is played from the depot, the next card must be turned face up before the next play is made.
- A player must play to a foundation if possible, before playing to a file.
- A player must play to a file if possible, before playing to a waste heap.

A player who sees his opponent violate any of these rules may cry 'Stop!' before his opponent has made a further play, and thus bring his turn to an end. He then points out the mistake, retracts the wrong play and makes the play his opponent failed to. He then takes over the turn himself.

The winner is the first player to get rid of all the cards in his stock and his waste heap.

so that his cards interlock with the first to form a complete tableau or layout. The second player makes his moves as the first, but he has the advantage of also being able to build to his opponent's foundations, and to pack onto his opponent's files. He can also play from his own depot and file onto his opponent's waste heap in either ascending or descending sequence, irrespective of suit or colour. However, he cannot pack onto his opponent's waste heap from his own waste heap or

Tablanette

Tablanette is a game that is easy to learn and worth learning because it is remarkably fascinating to play.

Number of players

Tablanette is for two players.

Cards

The full pack of 52 cards is used. Cards have their pip values, except that Ace can count as 11 or 1 at the discretion of the holder. King counts as 14 and Queen as 13. The Jack has no value, but plays a special part in the game, as will be seen.

Six cards are dealt face downwards to the two players, and four cards face upwards to the table between them. The rest of the pack is temporarily set aside. If any Jacks are dealt to the table they are removed, placed at the bottom of the pack, and the spaces filled with cards from the top of the pack.

Tablanette cards on table (above)

Hand 1

Hand 2

How to play

The non-dealer plays first. If he plays a card of the same rank as any of the four cards on the table, he takes the card; or, if there are any two or three cards on the table whose values if added together equal that of the card played, he takes these cards.

If the cards on the table are as shown above, a player with Hand 1 would play the ♥K and take the ♠K from the table. If the player held Hand 2 instead, he would play the ♥A and take the ♥2 and ♣9 from the table, because together they total 11, the value of an Ace.

The cards played and those taken from the table are kept in a pile face down by the player who took them.

If at any time a player is able to take all the cards on the table (there may be only one, or there may be more than four) he announces 'Tablanette' and scores the total value of all the cards taken plus the value of the card he has played. If, for example, the cards on the table are as illustrated above, and a player holds any of the other three Kings, he will be able to announce 'Tablanette', because his King will take the ♠K and the other three cards whose values total 14. The score for this will be 42 points (i.e. 14 x 3).

The special function of the Jack is that playing it allows the player to take all the cards on the table, but it does not allow him to score for a tablanette. A Jack is therefore an excellent card to hold, because playing it compels the opponent to play a lone card to the table and when there is only one card on the table the player whose turn it is to play is in a good position to score a tablanette.

The players play in rotation until they have exhausted their six cards. The dealer then deals another six cards to each, and so on until the pack is exhausted. When the last batch has been played, any cards left on the table are taken by the player who last took a card from the table.

The players examine their cards and score one point for the ♣2 and for every Ace, King, Queen, Jack and 10 (except the ♦10 which scores two points). If a player has taken 27 or more cards, he scores three points. The deal passes in rotation, and the game is won by the player who first scores a total of 251.

There is more skill in the game than may be first apparent. If, for example, there is only an 8 on the table and the player holds the cards shown below, his best play is the ♥4, because no one card has a value of 12 and the opponent, therefore, cannot score a tablanette.

It is important to keep in mind the cards that have been played. The opponent has scored a tablanette and the player holds the cards shown below.

This player has to play a card to the table, and the natural tendency is to play the ♥3, because this will give the opponent a minimum score if he can again announce 'Tablanette'. But if no 3s have been played, but a 10 has, then it is better to play one of the 10s, because the chances are against the opponent holding the remaining 10, and there is a possibility that he holds one of the remaining three 3s.

Trumps

The word 'trump' derives from 'triumph', documented as the name of a card game in 1529, which later became Whist.

Number of players

Trumps is for a minimum of two players.

Cards

The full pack of 52 cards is used. To determine who deals first, the players must cut the pack. The cards are placed in the centre of the table and each player in turn lifts off a small section from the deck. The card at the bottom of each section is shown to the other players and the player who has cut the highest card (Aces are high) deals first. Should two players draw cards of equal rank, a second cut is made. The job of dealer passes around the table in a clockwise fashion with each hand, or passes from one player to the other, if only two people are playing.

Before play begins, a trump suit must be chosen. The trump suit is defined by an extra cut of the deck prior to dealing. The suit of the chosen card is the trump suit for that round. For the rounds to follow, it is the winner of the round who chooses the trump suit.

The dealer now shuffles the cards and passes them to the player on their left, who cuts the deck and places the bottom half of the pack on the top half. The cards can now be dealt.

Cards are dealt one at a time and are placed face down in front of each player. The first card is dealt to the player on the left of the dealer, who works his or her way clockwise around the table. All the cards should be dealt, giving each player the same amount. If there are any cards left over, these should be placed in a pile in the centre of the table, with the top card turned face-up. It is this card that will start play. If the cards are equally distributed with no remaining cards, then it is the player to the left of the dealer who will start play by laying down a card of their choice face-up on the table.

Tricks

A trick is the name given to one complete round of Trumps; so, for example, if you have four players, the four cards on the table at the end of a round constitute a trick. The highest card played wins the trick and the victorious player gets to keep the cards, which will be counted up at the end to determine the round's winner.

How to play

The aim of the game is to win more tricks than your opponents. The starting card face-up in the centre of the table is the lead card and the other players must follow its suit if they can.

If the lead card is a six of diamonds, the next player must play a diamond if they have one. To stand a chance of winning the hand, he or she must play a diamond card of higher rank than the six their opponent played. If they have no diamonds, and they have no trump suit, they cannot follow and must instead discard a card of a different suit. You cannot win a trick with a discarded card, so its rank is irrelevant, and it is therefore advisable to put down the lowest ranking card that you hold. If, however, you do have a card from the trump suit, this will beat any other card except a trump of higher rank.

When all the cards are played, the winner is the one with the most tricks.

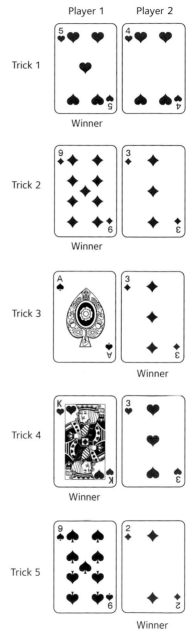

The trump suit is diamonds in each of the example hands shown above

500 Rum

The Game of 500 Rum is much more closely allied to the Rummy family than to Five Hundred (page 127).

Number of players

500 Rum is a game best for three.

Cards

The full standard pack of 52 cards is used. Cards rank in the order: King, Queen, Jack, 10, 9, 8, 7, 6, 5, 4, 3, 2, Ace. Cards also have values for scoring points as follows: King, Queen, Jack are each worth ten points, Aces are worth 15 points each if melded as Aces, but one point if used in a sequence of Ace, 2, 3. All other cards score according to their pip value.

Each player draws a card to decide dealer; lowest deals. The dealer shuffles the pack, which is cut by the player to his right, and deals seven cards, one at a time, to each player, beginning at his left. The remaining cards are placed face down to form the stock, and the top card is turned face up and placed beside the stock to begin the discard pile.

How to play

The object of the game is to form sets of three or four cards of the same rank, or sequences of three or more cards of the same suit. Sequences stop at Ace at one end and King at the other: Ace, King, Queen is not a sequence.

Beginning with the player left of the dealer, each player may take either a card or cards from the discard pile, or the top card of the stock. After drawing, the player may meld as many cards as he likes by placing sets and/or sequences on the table in front of him, and he then discards one card to the discard pile and the turn passes. Should a player draw from the discard pile, he must meld, and he must use the card taken from the discard pile in his meld.

This game differs from most kinds of Rummy in that all the cards in the discard pile are available, so the discard pile is not strictly a pile but a collection of cards spread out so that all their values can be seen (see opposite). When a player takes a card from the discard pile, he must also take all the cards above it. After melding with the card taken, he leaves on the table for one round any other cards taken from the discard pile which he has not melded, so that all other players may memorize them. On his next turn he takes them into his hand.

A player may on his turn add cards to any meld on the table, whether it is his meld or an opponent's. These cards are not actually attached to the melds, if they be opponents' melds, but kept on the table before the player, who will score for them later. It may happen that a card thus placed on the table would fit onto two existing melds, in which case the player must state which meld he is fitting his card or cards to. This is important because other players may subsequently add to the melds further.

Play continues until one player gets rid of all the cards in his hand or until the stock is exhausted. When the last card is drawn from stock, and the drawer has discarded, play may continue if the next player can draw from the discard pile and meld, and so on until one player passes.

At the end of the game, each player adds up the values of all the cards he has melded, and from the total he deducts the values of all the cards left in his hand, if any (an Ace in hand counts 15). Once a player has gone out, no further melds can be made by the other players, and any sets or sequences held, or cards which might be added to melds, are debited. A player may thus end with a minus score on the hand.

Throughout the game, a running total is kept of each player's score, and it is the first player to reach 500 who is deemed the winner.

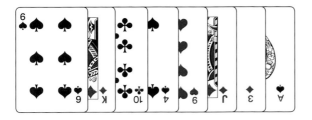

Discard pile

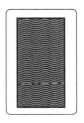

Stock

Hand

The player holding this hand will be advised to pick up ♦ 3. He can immediately meld
♦ 2, 3, 4; ♠ 4, 5, 6; ♦K, ♥K, ♠K. He must leave ♦J, ♥9 and ♣10 on the table
before him for one round, and should discard ♠Q

Auction Pitch

Auction Pitch, commonly known as Pitch and sometimes as Set Back, is a variation of All Fours (see page 46).

Number of players

Auction Pitch is at its best and most popular when played by four players, each playing for himself.

Cards

The full pack of 52 is used and cards rank from Ace (high) to 2 (low). Each player is dealt six cards in two lots of three each. No card, however, is turned up to determine the trump suit.

How to play

The player on the left of the dealer bids first, and each player, in his turn, may either make a bid or pass. A bid must be for at least two points, and for more than the preceding bid, except for the dealer, who is entitled to buy the hand for the same number of points as the preceding bid. The maximum number of points in a deal is four, and a player who expects to win them bids smudge. The dealer cannot take the declaration from him.

The successful bidder is known as the maker, and he leads the first trick. The card that he leads is the trump suit.

At each trick a player must follow suit to the card led, if he can, otherwise he may discard or trump. The winner of a trick leads the next.

Points are scored as follows:

High. The player who holds the highest trump scores one point.

Low. The player who holds the lowest trump scores one point.

Jack. The player who wins the trick that contains the Jack of the trump suit (if it is in play) scores one point.

Game. Counting the Ace as four, the King as three, the Queen as two, the Jack as one and the 10 as ten, the player with the highest total in the tricks he has won scores one point. If there is a tie no player scores the point.

Every player records what he scores, and if the maker fails to reach his bid he is set back by the full amount of it. He records the score and if it is a minus score he encircles it and is said to be in the hold.

The game is won by the player who first reaches seven points, and if the maker and one or more of the other players reach seven points in the same deal, the maker wins. As between the other players, the points are counted in the order High, Low, Jack, Game.

A player who smudges and wins all four points automatically wins the game regardless of his score, unless he was in the hole when he smudged. In this event he scores only four points.

Black Maria

Black Maria, sometimes known as Black Lady and sometimes as Slippery Anne, is very similar to Hearts (see page 131).

Number of players

Black Maria is a game best played by three players.

Cards

The full pack is used minus the ♣2, making a pack of 51 cards. Cards rank from Ace (high) to 2 (low).

Seventeen cards are dealt to each player. The deal passes in rotation clockwise. After a player has looked at his cards, he passes three of them to his right-hand opponent and receives three from his left-hand opponent. However, he must not look at the cards he receives before he has passed his chosen three on.

How to play

When the exchanges of cards have been made, the player on the left of the dealer leads the first trick. Thereafter, the player who wins a trick leads the next. A player must follow suit to the led card provided he can do so. Otherwise he may discard any card he chooses. There is no trump suit.

The object of the game is to avoid winning a trick which contains a penalty card. These cards, and the penalties that go with them, are:

All hearts	1
♠ A	7
♠ K	10
♠ Q (Black Maria)	13

The inexperienced player, if he is dealt a high spade, will assume that he cannot do better than pass it on to his right-hand opponent. It is, however, not always the best play. Provided a number of low spades are held in support of the high ones, it is very often better to retain the high cards with a view to controlling the suit during the play of the hand

Indeed, a player who has been dealt any spades or hearts lower than the Queen would be well advised to keep them in order to protect himself against any top cards in the suits that may be passed on to him. The main principle of discarding should be to try and set up either a void suit – in order to get rid of penalty cards by discarding them during the play – or at obtaining long suits, provided low cards in them are held.

A player who has been dealt the hand illustrated at the top of page 84 cannot do better than pass on the three diamonds. The spades must be kept to protect against receiving a high card in the suit, the hearts are adequately

protected, and there is nothing to fear in clubs.

An ability to count the cards is the first essential to success. Towards the end of a deal an experienced player will know pretty well which cards are still left to be played, and he will be able to make a shrewd guess as to who holds them. It is in the end-play, therefore, that opportunity comes for skilful play.

A three-card ending is illustrated below. After 14 tricks the players should know which remaining cards are in play: West is on lead and leads the ♠6, North plays the ♠2 and East is forced to win with the ♠K. Now, if East returns the ♦5, West must win with the ♦7 and North saddles him with the ♠Q (Black Maria). If, however, East returns the ♣3, North will have to win with the ♣6 on which West will have played the ♠A.

East's play will be directed by the score, and whether it is more advantageous to him to saddle West or North with all 20 points. The strategy is quite ethical so long as East puts his own interest first and is not moved by malice aforethought.

West

North

East

Bridge

Contract Bridge was developed out of Auction Bridge and introduced to card players in the early 1920s. It took firm root quickly to become the most popular game in the history of card-playing. Today it is played by millions, rich and poor, with a vast literature in many languages.

Number of players

Bridge is a game for four players, two playing in partnership against the other two, players sitting opposite each other.

Cards

The full pack of 52 cards is used. Although only one pack of cards is necessary, it is customary to use two, of different design or colour, and while one is being dealt the other is shuffled by the partner of the dealer, in readiness for the next dealer.

The cards rank in the order Ace (high) to 2 (low), and the Ace, King, Queen, Jack and 10 of a suit are known as the honour cards. The suits rank in the order spades, hearts, diamonds, clubs; the spade and heart suits are known as the major suits: the diamond and club suits as the minor suits.

To determine partners, a pack is spread on the table. The four players draw cards from it, and the two who draw the two highest cards play in partnership against the other two. If two players draw cards of equal rank, precedence is determined by the rank of the suits. The player who draws the highest card has the choice of seats and cards, and deals first. Thereafter the deal passes round the table clockwise. His partner sits opposite to him; the other two partners sit one on each side of him (i.e. opposite to each other). It is usual to denote the four players by the cardinal points of the compass.

Bidding

During the bidding, which the two partnerships compete against each other to establish which suit shall be made trumps or whether the hand shall be played without a trump suit.

The dealer bids first, and the bidding continues round the table clockwise. When a player bids he states the number of tricks in excess of six that he undertakes to win, and in the denomination that he undertakes to play. The lowest bid, therefore, is a bid of One (a contract to win seven tricks) and the highest is a bid of Seven (a contract to win all 13 tricks). As no-trumps takes precedence over the suits, the lowest possible bid is One Club, and the ascending scale is: One Club, One Diamond, One Heart, One Spade, One

No Trump, Two Clubs, Two Diamonds ... Seven Hearts, Seven Spades, Seven No Trumps. A contract of Six (to win 12 tricks) is called a small slam; a contract of Seven (to win all 13 tricks) is called a grand slam.

In turn each bid must name either a greater number of tricks than the previous one, or an equal number of tricks in a higher denomination. If a player has no wish to contract to win tricks he says 'No Bid', and if all four players do so, the hand is thrown in and the deal passes.

In his turn any player may double a bid made by an opponent. The effect of a double is to increase the score whether the contract succeeds or fails: and the partnership whose contract has been doubled may redouble thereby increasing the score, win or lose, still further. Doubling and redoubling, however, do not increase the size of a contract: e.g. a bid of Four Clubs is inferior to a bid of Four Diamonds and remains inferior to it even though it may have been doubled and redoubled.

The bidding period continues until the last and highest bid has been followed by three passes. The player who first mentioned the denomination in the final contract will then become the declarer.

Bridge is not a difficult game unless a player makes it so by ill-advised bidding. Its most important feature is that a player scores towards game only for the tricks that he has contracted to win, and, by a logical extension, he scores the big bonuses for slams only if the necessary amount of tricks has been contracted for. It follows that it is of paramount importance for the partners to estimate the trick-taking power of their combined hands, and not only must a player estimate as accurately as possible the position of the adverse high cards and distribution (as revealed by the bids of the other players) but convey by his bidding as much information as possible to his partner. In short, bidding may be defined as a conversation between the partners, and both must speak the same language.

Opening bids

Most modern players value their hands by means of the well-known Milton Work Point Count (devised by Milton Cooper Work). The method is as follows: 4 points for an Ace, 3 for a King, 2 for a Queen, and 1 for a Jack.

Suits The player who opens the bidding with a bid of One of a suit promises to make a further bid if his partner responds with One in a higher-ranking suit, or Two in a lower-ranking suit. For this reason a player should not open unless he can see a sound rebid in his hand over his partner's most likely response.

The strength to justify an opening bid varies, but in general it may be said that a hand totalling at least 13 points

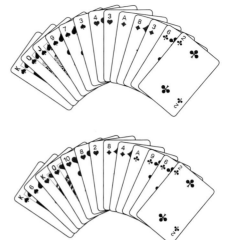

should be opened. It is clear, however, that the more points a player holds the less length does he need in the trump suit, and the fewer points in the hand the greater must be the length in the trump suit. With less than 13 points in the hand the practice is to open an 11- or 12-point hand with a reasonable five-card suit, and with only 10 points in the hand, sometimes less, a player needs a reasonable six-card suit, or two five-card suits.

Open One Heart. The hand totals only 11 points, but the heart suit is worth showing and if it is not shown at once it may be too late.

Open One Spade. The hand totals only 11 points, but is strong by reason of its distribution. With two suits of equal length it is proper to bid the higher-ranking before the lower-ranking one.

Open One Spade. The hand totals a mere 10 points, but the six-card spade suit (above, top) is too good to be held back.

A pre-emptive bid is defined as an opening bid at the level of Three or higher. It is a bid of great value because either it prevents the opponents from entering the auction or compels one of them to bid at a level that is dangerously high when he has no notion of what cards his partner may be holding. Postulating that the bid of Three is weak and that an opponent holds strength in the other three suits, the most practical way of countering the pre-emptive bid is to bid Three Diamonds over Three Clubs and Three No Trumps over Three Spades, Hearts or Diamonds. Either bid invites partner to bid his best suit.

When an opponent has bid a suit at the level of One, a player should enter the auction only if he can be reasonably sure that his bid, if passed out, will not

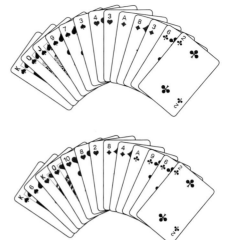

be defeated by more than two tricks if vulnerable and three if not vulnerable. This general rule, however, must be accepted with some reservation. It would, for example, not be wrong for a player who holds to bid One Heart over an opponent's One Diamond. The bid might prove costly, but not very often, and it is cowardly not to contest the part-score for fear of the worst happening. A player has a right to assume that even if his partner has a blank hand and only two or three low hearts, the hand will win three tricks in hearts and one in each of the black suits.

No trumps A bid of One No Trump is advised with a total of 16 to 18 points. The bid should never step outside the stipulated range, because your partner needs to rely on it for his response. With nine points he will jump to Three No Trumps; with seven or eight he will bid Two No Trumps and leave it to the opener to pass with a minimum, but bid Three with a maximum. A no trump range of 16 to 18 points is known as a strong no-trump. Some experienced players favour, particularly when not vulnerable, a range of 12 to 14 points. It is known as a weak no trump. Whether a strong or a weak no trump is played is a matter of personal choice, but it must be agreed between the partners before play begins, because if a weak no trump is played partner must increase his responses by four points.

In the same way, an opening bid of Two No Trumps is advised on 20 to 22 points. A partner should raise to Three if he holds five points, and to pass with less.

Opening bids of One No Trump and Two No Trumps postulate a balanced distribution of 4-3-3-3 or 4-4-3-2. A bid of Three No-Trumps is tactical. It shows a hand containing a solid minor suit, and altogether a hand that has a reasonable prospect of winning nine tricks if partner has one or two top cards in the right places.

This hand qualifies for an opening bid of Three No Trumps. There is every prospect of making the contract; if not it will not cost a lot and there is the consolation that it has probably stopped the opponents from bidding a game that would have been a greater loss.

Weak and strong bids An opening bid of Three of a suit is a weakness bid. It is made with a hand that has little, if any, defensive strength, offers small chance of success of game, and with one long suit that, if trumps, is unlikely to be defeated by more than two tricks if vulnerable and three if not vulnerable.

This type of hand (see above) qualifies for an opening bid of Three Spades if only because, even if doubled and a player's partner has no support, it cannot cost more than 500 points (two down). It is a reasonable loss if the opponents have a game in one of the other suits.

There is also a range of strong bids. The strongest of all is an opening bid of Two Clubs. It is strictly conventional and it may be made even if the player is void in the suit. The bid guarantees either five or more high cards and distributional strength, or 23 or more points and a balanced distribution. With one exception, the bid is forcing to game. A player's partner must respond no matter how weak his hand is, and with a weak hand he bids Two Diamonds. Any other response by him shows an Ace and a King or two King-Queen combinations, or the equivalent in high cards. The exception to the bid not being forcing to game occurs when the opener has bid Two Clubs with a balanced hand and, after the negative response of Two Diamonds, has rebid Two No Trumps.

West	East
West	*East*
♠ K, J, 3	♠ Q, 6, 2
♥ A, Q, 6	♥ 9, 7, 4
♦ A, K, 4	♦ 8, 5, 3, 2
♣ A, Q, ', 2	♣ 7, 4, 3
Bidding	*Bidding*
2 ♣	2 ♦
2 No Trumps	No Bid

West, with 24 points, is too strong to open with any other bid than Two Clubs, and over East's negative response he cannot do better than rebid Two No Trumps. East with only two points in his hand does well to pass, but another point in his hand would make a big difference and with three points or more he would bid Three No Trumps.

The opening bid of Two in any other suit is forcing for one round, and shows a hand containing not fewer than eight playing tricks and at least one powerful suit.

The hand illustrated above is best opened with Two Spades. If it is opened with One Spade there is no satisfactory way of coping with a response of Two Hearts.

A strong two-suited hand also qualifies for an opening bid of Two. The higher-ranking suit is bid first.

A one-suited hand may also be opened with a Two bid. This hand should be opened with a bid of Two Spades, and Three Spades should be bid over any response made by partner.

As well as an opening bid of Two Clubs there are several other bids that are forcing to game. The most frequent is a jump bid in a new suit.

West	East
♠ Q, 8, 4	♠ A, K, 6
♥ 9, 2	♥ A, Q, J, 10, 6, 4
♦ A, J, 3	♦ 8, 2
♣ A, K, 9, 3, 2	♣ J, 4

Bidding	*Bidding*
1 ♣	2 ♥

The situation is typical. East's bid of Two Hearts sets up a forcing situation. It is true that a bid of One Heart by East cannot be passed by West, but it is better for East to get the hand off his chest, and by bidding Two Hearts he makes certain that the bidding will not be dropped until a game level is reached.

It is much the same if the opener makes a jump in a new suit over his partner's response:

West	East
♠ K, J, 6	♠ A, Q, 9, 2
♥ A, K, J, 7, 4	♥ 10, 8, 3
♦ 6	♦ K, Q, 9
♣ K, Q, J, 7	♣ 10, 6, 3

Bidding	*Bidding*
1 ♥	1 ♠
3 ♣	

In this situation (or a similar one) West's bid of Three Clubs is a game force and East cannot pass it.

A forcing situation can be set up by reason of the logic behind the bidding.

West	East
♠ A, K, 9, 6, 3	♠ Q, 7, 4, 2
♥K, J, 9, 2	♥ Q, 10, 8, 3
♦ A, 8, 4	♦ K, 6, 2
♣ 9	♣ 5, 4

Bidding	*Bidding*
1 ♠	2 ♠
3 ♥	?

As West rebid at the level of Three, over East's weak response of Two Spades, and when there was no need for him to rebid, he must have a very strong hand, and East must make a further bid. He bids Four Hearts and West passes.

An inferential force is even more pronounced in a sequence such as:

West	East
1 ♥	1 ♠
2 No Trumps	3 ♥
?	

West must not pass because East is very clearly inviting him to choose between playing the hand in Three No Trumps or Four Hearts, whichever contract best suits him.

Bidding slams There are 40 points in the pack and experience has taught that if the combined hands have a total of 25 points game will be made, if 33 the small slam, and if 37 the grand slam. There are, of course, exceptions, but in the long run the rule is to be relied on.

When the bidding of the partners shows that they hold between them the balance of strength, they should consider bidding a slam. As a guide it may be said that prospects of a slam are good when a player holds enough to make a positive response to a forcing bid; or when the point count of the combined hands totals at least 33; or when a player has enough for an opening bid opposite a partner who has opened with a bid of Two, or who has opened the bidding and made a jump rebid.

Before a slam can be bid with a measure of safety, it is essential for the partners to find out if they hold between them control of the vital suits. The Blackwood convention has been designed to enable the partners to learn how many Aces and Kings are held by the partnership.

When the trump suit has been agreed either directly by support or by implication, or if a forcing situation has been set up, a bid of Four No Trumps by either partner asks the other to bid Five Clubs if he lacks an Ace or holds all four, Five Diamonds if he holds one Ace, Five Hearts if he holds two and Five Spades if he holds three. If the player who has bid Four No Trumps, after his partner's response continues with a bid of Five No Trumps, he is showing that he holds all four Aces and is asking his partner to bid Six Clubs if he lacks a King, Six Diamonds if he holds one King, Six Hearts if he holds two, Six Spades if he holds three and Six No Trumps if he holds all four. Look at the hands at the top of page 92. Bidding:

West	East
1 ♠	2 ♥
3 No Trumps	4 ♠
4 No Trumps	5 ♥
6 ♠	No Bid

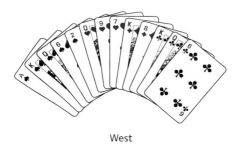

West

East

Once East has shown that he has support for spades, West, with support for hearts, visualizes a slam. His bid of Four No Trumps asks East how many Aces he holds, and East's response of Five Hearts tells West that he holds two. West must bid the slam in spades, because if East plays in hearts and his two Aces are in hearts and clubs, the opening lead of a diamond from South may break Six Hearts out of hand. When West plays in Six Spades, the ♦K is protected against the opening lead and 12 tricks are assured.

As West knows that there is an Ace against the hand the grand slam is out. West has no need to bid Five No Trumps to ask East how many Kings he holds.

The convention is a very useful one, but it must be used with discretion, because if partner lacks the necessary Aces the partnership may find itself carried out of its depth. As a rule, it may be said that if the final contract is to be in clubs the bid of Four No Trumps should not be made unless the bidder holds at least two Aces, and if the contract is to be in diamonds he should hold at least one Ace.

A limit bid is a bid that informs partner of the precise strength of the hand, and so permits him to estimate the combined strength of the partnership, and drop the bidding if he can see no future for it.

No trump bids are limit bids because they are made on an agreed number of points in the hand. A single raise of partner's suit is a limit bid that shows moderate strength and support for the suit; a double raise of partner's suit shows that the hand is too good for a mere simple raise and invites him to bid game if his hand is above average; a triple raise is distributional, it promises good support for the suit and a few scattered points, but no more because with good support for the suit coupled with high-card strength it would be more in order to make a gradual advance to a possible slam.

Responding bids

Suits A jump overcall shows strength, and, though it is not forcing, partner is expected to take action if he holds the values that would justify a response to a bid of One.

An overcall should be based on a five-card or longer suit, though it is reasonable to overcall with A, K, Q, x or K, Q, J, x at the level of One. It is nearly always very unwise to overcall with a broken suit.

In general, when an opponent has opened the bidding with a bid of One of a suit, it is better to counter it with a take-out double than with a weak overcall. A double in this situation shows weakness in the suit doubled and a total of about 13 or 14 points with a balanced hand and 11 or 12 with an unbalanced one. If the doubler's partner has not bid (if he has the double is for a penalty) the doubler invites partner to bid his best suit.

West	East
♠ K, J, 9, 6, 2	♠ 5, 3
♥ K, J, 9, 2	♥ A, Q, 8, 3
♦ 6	♦ K, 7, 2
♣ A, Q, 7	♣ 10, 8, 6, 2

If South has bid One Diamond, West should double. East bids hearts and the good fit has been found. If West bids One Spade over South's One Diamond the heart fit will never be found and a good result will be exchanged for a bad one.

If partner's best suit is the one that has been doubled, either he bids no trumps or passes for a penalty if he holds length in the suit.

A double of One No Trump is made with a balanced hand and a count of about two points more than the no-trump bidder's average. With a weak hand partner will take out into his best suit, but if the combined count totals 23 or more he will pass for a penalty.

The responses to opening Two bids (of suits other than clubs) are not so well defined and clear-cut as the responses to an opening bid of Two Clubs. In general, if partner holds a biddable suit he should bid it at the lowest level. If he lacks a biddable suit, but has a total of from 10 to 12 points, he should bid Three No Trumps. If he lacks a biddable suit and insufficient points to bid Three No Trumps, but has adequate support (i.e. x, x, x or Q, x) for partner's suit and a count of five, he should give a simple raise in partner's suit. If he lacks a biddable suit, insufficient points for Three No Trumps, and insufficient support for partner's suit, he should make the negative response of Two No Trumps.

No trumps The partner of the player who opens the bidding with No Trumps raises on a very precise number of points. The number of points, however, may be reduced slightly if the responder holds a five-card suit. Over a bid of One No Trump, partner holds:

The hand totals eight points and nine points are normally necessary to jump to Three No Trumps. Here, however, the jump to Three No Trumps is justified on the length of the spade suit, and the good intermediate cards. It is unwise to bid spades because if it is assumed that partner holds a balanced 16-point hand he is just as likely to win nine tricks in No Trumps as the responder is to win ten in spades. If Three No Trumps cannot be made there is no reason to suppose that Four Spades can.

A jump take out into a suit is a game force. It does not, however, promise a very strong hand: rather it means that the responder, who knows the precise strength of his partner's bid, can foresee game for the partnership but cannot tell whether the combined hands will play better in No Trumps or in a suit.

West	East
♠ Q, J, 4, 3	♠ K, 10, 9, 7, 2
♥ A, Q, 2	♥ J, 6, 4
♦ K, 9, 3	♦ A, J, 8, 2
♣ A, 7, 6	♣ 8

Bidding	Bidding
1 No Trump	3 ♠
4 ♠	No Bid

Over West's opening bid of One No Trump (16 to 18 points) East who has 9 points has enough to jump to Three No Trumps. He prefers Three Spades, however, which West raises to game, because game in spades can hardly fail, but in No Trumps will be defeated if a club is led.

Another important feature of responding to a No Trump bid is the Stayman convention. It is a bid of Two Clubs over partner's One No Trump, or Three Clubs over his Two No Trumps, made, irrespective of the holding in the suit, to ask partner to bid his better four-card major suit, or, if he lacks one, to bid diamonds.

West	East
♠ K, Q, 2	♠ A, J, 4, 3
♥ A, J, 6, 2	♥ K, Q, 8, 4
♦ Q, 6, 4	♦ 3, 2
♣ A, Q, 4	♣ J, 8, 5

Bidding	Bidding
1 No Trump	2 ♣
2 ♥	4 ♥
No Bid	

Without the convention, East, with 11 points, would have no alternative except to jump his partner's opening bid of One No Trump (16 to 18 points) to Three. The combined total of 29 points is more than adequate for the bid, but Three No Trumps may be defeated if a diamond is led and Four Hearts can hardly fail.

There is a wide range of bids that show weakness and that may be recognized as such by the logic of the situation.

West	East
1 ♠	2 No Trumps
3 ♠	?

East's bid of Two No Trumps shows a count of from 11 to 13 points, and over it West cannot do more than repeat his suit. His hand, therefore, cannot be strong, and his bid of Three Spades no more than the cheapest way of keeping his promise to rebid, which he made when he opened with One Spade.

In the same way, if the bidding is:

West	East
1 No Trump	2 ♠
?	

West should pass. East's bid must be showing a weak hand that he considers will play better in a suit than in No Trumps, otherwise, over an opening bid of One No Trump, it would be impossible for partner ever to play in Two of a suit. Or we may consider the following sequences:

West	East	West	East	West	East
1 ♥	2 ♥	1 ♥	2 ♣	1 ♣	1 ♥
3 ♣	3 ♥	2 ♥	3 ♦	1 ♠	2 ♥
		3 ♥		2 ♠	3 ♥

In all these sequences the bid of Three Hearts shows weakness. A player cannot be holding much of a hand when he cannot do better than rebid his suit at the lowest level, and it is particularly pronounced when he rebids it twice.

If we assume that South deals, a sequence of bidding to illustrate some of the points mentioned might be:

South	West	North	East
1 ♦	No Bid	1 ♥	1 ♠
1 No Trump	2 ♠	3 ♦	No Bid
3 No Trumps	Double	No Bid	No Bid
4 ♦	No Bid	5 ♦	Double
Redouble	No Bid	No Bid	No Bid

The final contract is Five Diamonds, and the hand will be played by South because he was the first on his side to mention diamonds as the trump suit.

How to play

During the playing, the player who has won the contract strives to make it, playing his own hand and that of his partner exposed on the table, against the defenders' striving to prevent him.

The playing period begins by the player on the left of the declarer leading the first trick. As soon as he has done so, the partner of the declarer places his cards face upwards on the table as dummy. He takes no further part in the play except that he has a right to draw his partner's attention to certain irregularities, such as asking him if he has none of a suit when he fails to follow suit, and warning him against leading out of the wrong hand. The declarer plays the dummy hand as well as his own.

The play follows the normal routine of trick-taking games: if a player is able to do so he must follow suit to the card led; otherwise he may either discard or trump. The trick is won by the player who plays the highest card of the suit led, or the highest trump. The player who wins a trick leads the next. If a trick is won in the dummy, the next trick must be led from there.

Declarer's play

After the opening lead has been made, and the dummy hand exposed, it is of first importance for the declarer, before he plays a card from dummy, to take stock of the position and decide upon the best way to play the cards.

In the deal below, against West's contract of Three No Trumps, North leads the ♠Q. At first sight it may seem immaterial whether West wins the trick with the Ace in dummy or with the King in his own hand. In the event, it matters a lot in which hand he wins the trick. If West gives consideration to the position he will appreciate that he must win the first trick with the ♠K in his hand, win the ♣ K, Q, J, reach dummy, by leading the ♠4 to the Ace, to win dummy's Ace

and ♣7, and finally the two red Aces in his own hand. If West wins the first trick with dummy's ♠A, he will lose the contract if the adverse clubs fail to divide three-two, because he has left himself with no side entry to the clubs.

When the declarer is playing a No Trump contract, usually his first aim should be to establish his longest suit. In many cases, however, it is better to develop a short and strong suit rather than a long and weak one.

In the deal at the top of page 97, North leads a club against West's contract of Three No Trumps. Consideration shows that West's best play is to win with the ♣K and play on spades to knock out the Ace. This way, West makes sure of his contract with three tricks in spades, three in hearts, one in diamonds and two in clubs. The diamond suit is longer than the spade suit, but West cannot develop East's diamonds without first losing the lead twice. By then the opponents will have set up the clubs and broken the contract; in any case, only three tricks in diamonds will be developed for eight in all, which is not enough.

West

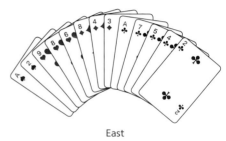

East

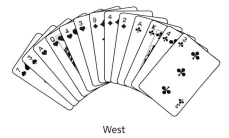

West

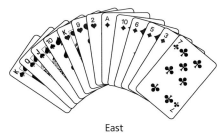

East

In a suit contract, it is usually the right play for the declarer to draw the adverse trumps at the first opportunity. Trumps, however, should not be drawn if there is a better use for them.

In the deal illustrated below, West plays in Four Hearts, and North leads a club. West wins the first trick with the ♣A, and if he draws the trumps at once his contract will depend on the finesse of the ♠Q being successful. It is no more than an even chance. The contract is a certainty if West, after winning the first trick with the ♣A, leads either the 7 or 3 of the suit. It does not matter whether North or South wins the trick, or what card is returned. Declarer wins the next trick and trumps a club in dummy. Now the adverse trumps may be drawn, and

West comes to ten tricks with one spade, five hearts, two diamonds and one club by straight leads, and the ruff (trump) of a club on the table.

A valuable weapon in the armoury of the declarer is the ability to manage a suit to make the most tricks out of it.

West	East
A, 9, 3, 2	*K, Q, 10, 5, 4*

In this position it is vital to play the King first. Then, if either North or South is void of the suit, there is a marked finessing position over the Jack, and five tricks will be made.

The unthinking player who first plays the Ace, on the assumption that it does not matter which high card he

West

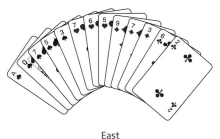

East

plays first because the outstanding cards will normally divide three-one or two-two, will lose a trick in the suit whenever North is void and South holds J, 8, 7, 6. It will occur about five times in every hundred.

West	East
A, K, 10, 5, 3	9, 7, 6

If West cannot afford to lose more than one trick in the suit, his play is to win either the Ace or King; if both opponents follow suit, he enters East's hand in a side suit, leads the 7 from the table and if South plays the 8, plays the 10 from his own hand. This protects him against losing two tricks in the suit if South started with Q, J, 8, x.

There is a percentage play or a safety play for almost every combination of a suit, and it may be found by analysing the division of the remaining cards in the suit.

West	East
♠ A, K, 4, 2	♠ 5, 3
♥ A, 9, 7	♥ 10, 6, 2
♦ A, 9, 4	♦ K, 8, 7
♣ K, 7, 6	♣ A, 10, 5, 4, 3

Against West's contract of Three No Trumps, North leads a spade. West can make his contract only if he wins four tricks in clubs. After winning the first trick with the ♠K, the right play is for West to win the ♣K. If North and South both follow suit, West continues with the

♣7 and plays the 4 from the dummy if North plays an honour, but the 10 if North plays a low card.

If South follows suit, there is only one more outstanding club and it will fall under East's Ace. If North shows out on the second round of clubs, then South started with Q, J, x, x of the suit and West cannot do anything about it. The directed play, however, guarantees that he will win four tricks in the suit if North originally held Q, J, x, x of the suit.

Most important of all, however, is an ability to count the cards. It is not all that difficult, and, in the main, is largely a matter of drawing deductions from the bidding and previous play of the cards, coupled with training oneself to think along the right lines.

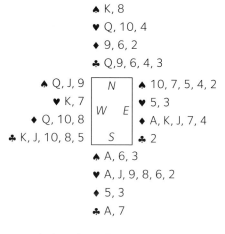

```
              ♠ K, 8
              ♥ Q, 10, 4
              ♦ 9, 6, 2
              ♣ Q, 9, 6, 4, 3
 ♠ Q, J, 9      ┌─────┐   ♠ 10, 7, 5, 4, 2
 ♥ K, 7         │  N  │   ♥ 5, 3
 ♦ Q, 10, 8   W │     │ E ♦ A, K, J, 7, 4
 ♣ K, J, 10, 8, 5 │  S  │   ♣ 2
              └─────┘
              ♠ A, 6, 3
              ♥ A, J, 9, 8, 6, 2
              ♦ 5, 3
              ♣ A, 7
```

West deals at love all, and the auction is:

West	North	East	South
1 ♣	No Bid	1 ♦	1 ♥
2 ♦	2 ♥	2 ♠	4 ♥
No Bid	No Bid	No Bid	

West leads diamonds and East wins the first two tricks with the Ace and King of the suit. A third round of diamonds is ruffed (trumped) by South with the ♥8.

As South has lost two tricks, it would seem that his contract is doomed, because West, by reason of his opening bid and lacking either the Ace or King of diamonds, must surely be holding the Kings of hearts and clubs.

South, however, has a partial count of the hand that will enable him to make his contract if he knows how to take advantage of it. On the assumption that West almost certainly started with three diamonds and probably five clubs, he cannot have more than five cards in spades and hearts. South, therefore, wins the ♥A (in case the King is singleton) and when the ♥K does not come down, he leads a spade to dummy's King, a spade from dummy to the Ace in the closed hand, and then trumps his last spade with dummy's ♥10. As West played the ♥7 under South's Ace and followed to the three rounds of spades, South may reconstruct the position as:

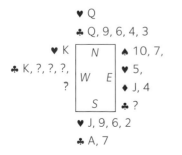

♥ Q
♣ Q, 9, 6, 4, 3

♥ K   ♠ 10, 7,
♣ K, ?, ?, ?,   ♥ 5,
?   ♦ J, 4
        ♣ ?

♥ J, 9, 6, 2
♣ A, 7

Now, by leading the ♥Q from dummy, West is put on lead with the King, and as he must return a club, South wins two tricks in the suit.

Defenders' play

Leading When the bidding period ends, and the playing period begins, the player on the left of the declarer leads to the first trick. It is only after he has led that the partner of the declarer exposes his hand on the table as dummy. It follows, therefore, that the opening lead has to be made in the dark, since the player can see only his own hand and is left to judge the best lead from it, coupled with the information that he has obtained from the bidding. The opening lead must be chosen with care. It is of great importance, because quite often the choice of a good or bad lead will decide whether or not the declarer's contract will be made.

Against a No Trump contract, if partner has bid a suit, leading it usually offers the best chance of defeating the contract, unless the player on lead holds only a singleton in the suit or he has a good suit of his own.

With two cards of partner's suit the higher should be led; with three cards the highest should be led, unless the suit is headed by the Ace, King, Queen or Jack, when the lowest should be preferred. With two honours in partner's suit the higher should be led; with a sequence (a combination of three or more cards of adjacent rank) the highest should be led. In all other cases the fourth highest should be led.

When a player leads his own suit, he should lead the fourth highest of his longest suit, unless he holds a sequence (when he should lead the highest), a long suit headed by the Ace and King and an entry in another suit (when he should lead the King), or an intermediate honour sequence, e.g. A, Q, J, x or K, J, 10, x (when the higher of the two touching honours should be led).

The reason for leading the fourth highest card of a suit is that if partner subtracts the number of the card from eleven, the remainder will be the number of higher cards held by the other three players. The Rule of Eleven.

Q, 9, 7

	Dummy		
5 led	W	E	K, 10, 8
	Declarer		

West leads the 5. As 11 - 5 = 6, and East can see six cards higher than the 5 in dummy and in his own hand, he will know that the declarer cannot hold a card higher than the 4, so that whichever card is played from dummy he can win the trick with the card just higher.

Against a suit contract it is usually best to lead partner's suit, if he has bid one. If he has not, and the player on lead has to lead from his own suit, he should give preference to leading the top card of an honour sequence. He should avoid leading a card that may cost a trick, e.g. leading the King from K, Q, x, or a card that might enable the declarer to win a trick with a card that might have been captured, e.g. leading the Ace from A, Q, x. The lead of a trump is a good lead if the bidding has suggested that the dummy will be able to trump side suits.

Defender play The play of the defenders is more difficult than that of the declarer, because a defender has to combine his hand with that of the unseen one held by his partner. They have the slight advantage of a partnership language that enables them to exchange information and advice, but, for the most part, success in defence comes mainly from drawing the right deductions from the bidding, and the cards that have been played to previous tricks.

To lead the highest card of a sequence, to win with the lowest, and to follow suit as the situation dictates, is a general rule that does not need to be enlarged on. Most of the general rules for defence play, however, have been handed down from the days when whist was the fashionable game. At Bridge reservations have to be made, because the bidding and the exposed dummy hand allow for modifications.

To return the suit that partner has led is not always the best play. At times it is better to take time by the forelock.

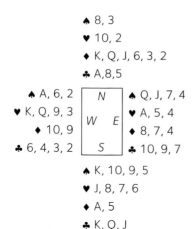

    ♠ 8, 3
    ♥ 10, 2
    ♦ K, Q, J, 6, 3, 2
    ♣ A,8,5

♠ A, 6, 2   ♠ Q, J, 7, 4
♥ K, Q, 9, 3   ♥ A, 5, 4
    ♦ 10, 9   W   E   ♦ 8, 7, 4
♣ 6, 4, 3, 2   S   ♣ 10, 9, 7

    ♠ K, 10, 9, 5
    ♥ J, 8, 7, 6
    ♦ A, 5
    ♣ K, Q, J

South deals and opens the auction with One No Trump (12 to 14 points) and North jumps him to Three.

West leads the ♥3 and East wins with the Ace. If East returns a heart, South has no difficulty in making nine tricks, because dummy's ♥10 protects the Jack in the closed hand and the defenders cannot win more than one trick in spades and three in hearts. With the ♥2 on the table, East should appreciate that his partner cannot hold more than four hearts and that they cannot be better than K, Q, 9, 3, because if they were K, Q, J, 3 he would have led the King and not the 3. As once East gives up the lead he can never regain it, he must take advantage of the time factor, the tempo, and lead the ♠Q. The only chance of defeating the contract is to find West holding the ♠A, and as South's bid of One No Trump postulates a maximum of 14 points, East, who holds seven points and can count 10 on the table, can count

West with just enough room for the ♠A as well as for the ♥ K, Q.

To cover an honour with an honour may be good play in many cases, but it is not when the honour has been led from a sequence.

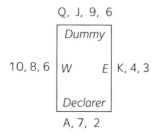

            Q, J, 9, 6
        ┌─────────────┐
        │ Dummy   │
10, 8, 6 │ W   E │ K, 4, 3
        │   │
        │ Declarer   │
        └─────────────┘
            A, 7, 2

The Queen is led from dummy. If East covers with the King, the declarer will win four tricks in the suit by winning with the Ace and returning the suit to finesse against West's 10. East, therefore, should not cover. The Queen will win, but now the defenders will always win a trick in the suit because if the declarer continues with dummy's Jack, the lead is no longer from a sequence and East covers it with the King. With K, x only, East should cover the Queen, otherwise the declarer, after winning dummy's Queen may continue with a low spade (not the Jack) from the table and East's King will be wasted.

Second hand plays low; third hand plays high, is another general rule that has been handed down from the past. It is, perhaps, a rule worth remembering, because exceptions when second hand should play high are few and far between, and when third hand sees only low cards on his right, there are virtually no exceptions to his playing high.

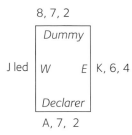

8, 7, 2

Dummy

J led | W   E | K, 6, 4

Declarer

A, 7, 2

West leads the Jack. East should play the King. He knows that the declarer holds the Queen (otherwise West would have led it in preference to the Jack) and if declarer holds the Ace as well the King is doomed. East, therefore, must play on the chance that West has led from A, J, 10, x and that declarer holds Q, x, x.

A very important weapon in the armoury of the defenders is the echo or peter, sometimes called the come-on or high-low signal. Reduced to its simplest terms, when a defender plays a higher card followed by a lower one of the same suit, it is a request to partner to play the suit. In many cases a defender can afford to play the suit only once. In such a case to play a 7 or a higher card is an urge to partner, and to play a lower card is a discouragement to him. Against a trump contract, the high-low play in a side suit shows that a doubleton is held and that the third round can be trumped. If the play is made in the trump suit itself, it shows that three trumps are held. Against a No Trump contract, the echo shows length in the suit, usually four cards.

The defenders are frequently compelled to discard and, nearly always, discarding presents them with a problem. The general rules to follow are not to retain the same suit as partner; not to discard from a suit in which you have the same length as dummy or suspect the declarer has in his hand; and never to discard so that the declarer is given any information.

Counting the cards is, of course, as important to the defenders as it is to the declarer. In some ways, however, the defenders have it a bit easier. If the declarer is in a No Trump contract he will have limited his hand to an agreed number of points. It follows, therefore, that if the declarer's limit is 16 to 18 points and he has shown up with 15 points, the defenders know that he has left in his hand no more than a King or its equivalent. In much the same way, in a suit contract the declarer and his dummy will rarely hold less than eight trumps between them. It follows, therefore, that if a defender holds three trumps, he knows that his partner is probably holding not more than two.

In conclusion, it may be said that good defence consists in playing those cards that give as much information as possible to partner, and making things as easy as possible for him; and on the contrary, in playing those cards that give as little information as possible to the declarer and making things as difficult as possible for him. Whenever it is possible to do so, a defender should play the cards that the declarer knows are in his hand, and retain those of which he knows nothing. If all this comes as a counsel of perfection – the best Bridge players are perfectionists.

Scoring

When all 13 tricks have been played, the players record their scores, and those of their opponents, on a marker, or sheet of paper, as illustrated to the right.

The main object is to win a rubber, which is the best out of three games. When a player makes his contract, the score for tricks won is entered below the horizontal line. All other scores are entered above this line.

A game is won when a partnership scores 100 points below the horizontal line, either in one or more deals.

A partnership that wins a game becomes vulnerable and is subject to higher bonuses if it makes its contract, and increased penalties if it fails. However, vulnerability does not affect the points for winning the tricks contracted for.

If a partnership scores less than game in one deal, it is said to have a part-score and if the opponents then score game the part-score cannot be carried forward towards the next game. When a partnership wins a game a line is drawn across the score sheet below it, and both partnerships begin the next game from a love score.

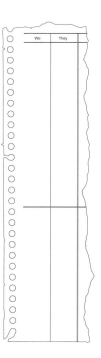

Tricks If a partnership has bid and made its contract, it scores:

In No Trumps:	40 points for the first trick and 30 points for subsequent tricks.
In Spades and Hearts:	30 points for each trick.
In Diamonds and Clubs:	20 points for each trick.

The scores for winning tricks are doubled if the contract has been doubled, and quadrupled if the contract has been redoubled.

103

If a partnership has made tricks in excess of its contract, it scores:

If undoubled: trick value for each trick.

If doubled: 100 points for each trick if not vulnerable. 200 points for each trick if vulnerable.

If redoubled: 200 points for each trick if not vulnerable. 400 points for each trick if vulnerable.

If a partnership has failed to make its contract, it loses:

If undoubled: 50 points for each trick if not vulnerable. 100 points for each trick if vulnerable.

If doubled: 100 points for the first trick; 200 points for each subsequent trick if not vulnerable. 200 points for the first trick; 300 points for each subsequent trick if vulnerable.

If redoubled: 200 points for the first trick; 400 points for each subsequent trick if not vulnerable. 400 points for the first trick; 600 points for each subsequent trick if vulnerable.

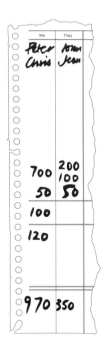

Bonuses

Winning rubber:

in three games 500

in two games 700

Grand slam bid and made: vulnerable 1,500; not vulnerable 1,000.

Small slam bid and made: vulnerable 750; not vulnerable 500.

150 points if either partner holds all four Aces in a No-Trump contract, or all five honours in a suit contract.

100 points if either partner holds any four honours in a suit contract.

50 points if a partnership makes a doubled or redoubled contract.

Brint

Brint was originated by J. B. Chambers in 1929. It is a hybrid of Bridge (see page 85) and Vint, the national card game of Russia.

Number of players

Brint is for four players.

Cards

The full pack of 52 cards is used.

How to play

Brint is played in the same way as Bridge. It has been described as Bridge with Vint scoring, because the score that counts towards game, and recorded below the line, depends entirely upon the level to which the bidding has been carried. No trumps and the suits retain their rank, but each trick (over six) at the level of One is worth 10 points, at the level of Two 20 points, and so on up to Seven when each trick is worth 70 points.

The full scoring table for the game is set out below.

The score for tricks made is unaffected by a double, but if a doubled contract is redoubled the trick score, as well as the bonus and penalty for a

The Scoring Table for Brint

When the contract is at the level of:	Each odd-trick (whether doubled or not) is worth:	When the declarer is not vulnerable:		
		Undoubled	Doubled	
		Penalty for each undertrick	Bonus for contract and each overtrick	Penalty for each undertrick
One	10	50	50	100
Two	20	50	50	100
Three	30	50	50	100
Four	40	100	100	200
Five	50	150	150	300
Six	60	200	200	400
Seven	70	250	250	500

doubled contract, is doubled. The bonuses and penalties are increased by 100 points each if the player is vulnerable.

A game is won by the pair that first reaches a trick score of 160 points. The bonuses for bidding and making slams and games, and for holding honours, recorded above the line as at Bridge, are set out here (see right).

The bonuses in Brint

Successful bid of Seven	1,000
Successful bid of Six	500
Successful bid of Five	250
Successful bid of Four	
vulnerable	500
not vulnerable	250
Four Aces in one hand in no trump contract	150
Five honours in one hand in a suit contract	200
Four honours in one hand in a suit contract	100

They are unaffected by vulnerability, doubling and redoubling.

Calabrasella

Calabrasella, sometimes spelt Calabresella, is also known as Terziglio. It is played with what is now usually called the Spanish pack of 40 cards, but which is also sometimes called the Italian pack. It is an Italian trick-taking card game and is a variation of Tressette. One of the earliest references to the game dates from 1822. It is a game usually played for stakes.

Number of players

Calabrasella is for three players, although four often play in rotation, the dealer giving no cards to himself, and sitting out the hand.

Cards

The Spanish pack of 40 cards is used, made from the standard pack by discarding the 10s, 9s and 8s. The remaining cards rank in the order 3, 2, Ace, King, Queen, Jack, 7, 6, 5, 4. In the game the Ace is worth three points, the 3, 2, King, Queen, Jack one point each.

Players draw for deal, the lowest dealing first. The deal thereafter passes in rotation to the left. Dealer deals 12 cards to each hand in twos. The four cards remaining are set aside face down to form a widow.

How to play

The object is to make tricks containing cards of a counting value (see above). Players study their hands, and the player to the left of the dealer announces either 'I play' or 'I pass'. Should he pass, the

next player has the same option, and if he passes, the dealer. Should all pass, the hand is abandoned, but if any player announces 'I play', the play begins.

The player electing to play is called the Player. He first specifies by suit any 3 not held in his hand. If either of the other players hold that 3 he must pass it to the Player, who may exchange for it any card he wishes from his own hand, not showing it to the third player. If the Player holds all four 3s, he may specify any 2, and so on. If the card he specifies is in the widow, no exchange takes place.

The Player next discards face down any number of cards from his hand from one to four (he must discard at least one). The widow is then exposed, and the Player selects from it sufficient cards to restore his hand to 12 cards. The remainder, plus the Player's discards, are set aside, and are later claimed by the winner of the last trick.

The game now becomes a trick-taking game, with the other two combining in a temporary partnership against the Player. He to the left of the

Player makes the opening lead, and may lead any card he likes. The others follow in a clockwise direction, and are obliged to follow suit to the card led if they are able; if unable to they may discard. There are no trumps. The winner of a trick leads to the next.

The winner of the last trick takes the four cards not used in the trick-taking phase, and is also awarded a bonus of three points. As there are eight points in each suit, the total points available in each deal are 35.

The side which wins the majority of the points (18 or more) collects from the other side the difference in the two totals. If the Player scores 20 points and his opponents 15, the Player receives five units from both opponents. If the opponents had scored the 20 points, each would receive five units from the Player. If there are stakes, the amount to be paid per point must obviously be agreed beforehand. The game can be played for recreation only by keeping a running profit and loss score with pencil and paper.

Calabrasella offers opportunities for skill. Much depends on the decision as to whether or not to play. Of prime importance are stoppers in all suits. Should one of the opponents be able to run off a long suit, the other will be able to discard high-scoring cards (Aces) on it. Should the Player win all the cards in one suit, he might score only eight points from the tricks, whereas an opponent with the same cards will get scoring discards from his partner. The Player can gain the advantage of calling in a 3, but should not rely on much from the widow. In order to keep guards in each suit, he might not be able to discard more than two cards. It is important for him to remember which cards he discards, since only the Player knows which cards are not in play, and thus which suits are short. The disadvantage of playing against two players is a big one, and the commonest mistake is to play with too weak a hand.

Calypso

Calypso was invented by R. W. Willis of Trinidad. It dates from the mid-1950s, and though designed on entirely new lines, inevitably borrows some of the best features of Bridge (see page 85) and Canasta (see page 111).

Number of players

Calypso is for four players playing in two partnerships.

Cards

The game is played with four packs of cards (with identical backs) shuffled together, but the cards are shuffled only at the start of a game, and a player holds only 13 of them at a time.

It is a novel feature of the game that each player has his own trump suit. Spades and hearts play in partnership against diamonds and clubs. The players cut for seats and trump suits. The highest has the choice of both, and his partner takes the corresponding suit and sits facing him. The choice of a trump suit conveys no advantage; it is purely a matter of personal preference.

Thirteen cards are dealt to each player, and the dealer places the rest of the pack to his left, ready for the next dealer after the hand has been played.

How to play

The object of the game is to build calypsos. A calypso is a complete suit (from Ace to 2) in a player's trump suit.

The player on the left of the dealer leads the first trick. Thereafter the lead is made by the player who wins a trick. When playing to a trick a player must follow suit if he can; otherwise he may either discard or trump by playing a card of his own trump suit.

A trick is won by the player who has played the highest card of the suit led, or by the player who has trumped it, or over-trumped it by playing a higher trump of his own trump suit. If two or more players play identical cards, the first played takes priority for the purpose of winning tricks, and perhaps the most important feature of the game is that if a player leads a card of his own trump suit, he wins the trick automatically unless it is trumped by another player or overtrumped by another. To illustrate:

North ♣	East ♠	South ♦	West ♥
♥8	♥J	♥10	♥3

North has led the ♥ 8, and East wins the trick because he has played the highest heart.

♦4	♠6	♦7	♦3

North has led the ♦4, and East wins the trick because he has trumped. South has merely followed suit to North's lead.

| ♥3 | ♠4 | ♦6 | ♥J |

North has led the ♥3, and South wins the trick, because although East has trumped, South has over-trumped. West has merely followed suit to North's lead.

| ♣9 | ♣J | ♣6 | ♣5 |

North has led the ♣9 and wins the trick because clubs is his own trump suit. That East has played a higher club does not score.

| ♣6 | ♠7 | ♦9 | ♣5 |

North has led the ♣6, East has trumped, but South wins the trick because he has over-trumped.

| ♥6 | ♥Q | ♥Q | ♥10 |

North has led the ♥6, and the trick is won by East as his ♥Q was played before South's.

When a player wins a trick, he leaves exposed on the table, in front of him, any cards from the trick that will help him to build a calypso, passes to his partner any cards that will help him to build a calypso, and then discards the others, face downwards, on his right.

North (whose trump suit is clubs) leads the ♣4 and wins the trick:

| ♣4 | ♣6 | ♣J | ♣6 |

North places the ♣4, ♣6 and ♣J face upwards on the table in front of him, and discards the second ♣6. He then leads the ♣8 and the trick is:

| ♣8 | ♣J | ♣7 | ♦8 |

Again North wins the trick. He keeps the ♣7 and ♣8 for his calypso, passes the ♦8 to his partner for his calypso, and

discards the ♣J because he already has one.

The play continues until all 13 tricks have been played; the next player then deals another hand of 13 cards each.

A player may build only one calypso at a time, but once a calypso has been built the player may begin another. He may use any cards in the trick with which a calypso has been completed, but he cannot use any cards from his discard pile. These cards are dead and one object of his opponents will be to give him duplicate cards while he is building his calypso to prevent him building a second or third calypso.

The game ends when each player has dealt once. The score is then made up of the following points:

For the first calypso: 500
For the second calypso*: 750
For subsequent calypsos*: 1,000
For each card in an incomplete calypso: 20
For each card in the discard pile: 10
(* when obtained by individual players)

Partners add their totals together, and stakes are paid on the difference between the totals of the two sides.

A serious view is taken of revoking. A revoke does not become established until a player of the offending side has played to the next trick, and a revoke made in the 12th never becomes established, but if established a revoke suffers a penalty of 260 points.

Canasta

Canasta (Spanish for 'basket') was invented by Segundo Santos and Alberto Serrato in Montevideo, Uruguay, in 1939, and it spread rapidly round the world soon after World War II. Recently it has declined somewhat in popularity, but it remains an entertaining game and is easy to learn.

Number of players

Canasta is best for four players, but can be played by two or three, though not so satisfactorily.

Cards

Two standard packs are used, together with four Jokers, making 108 cards in all.

If there are four players, each receives 11 cards. With three players, each gets 13 cards, and if there are only two players, they get 15 cards each. Cards are dealt one at a time, clockwise round the table starting on the dealer's left. The top card of the remaining pack is then turned over to start the discard pile, and the player on the dealer's left plays first. Before that, however, all the players holding red 3s put them down and draw replacement cards. The deal moves round to the left in subsequent hands.

If the card turned over by the dealer is a wild card (a Joker or a 2) or a red 3, then he turns another card to cover it, and the pack is frozen (so that wild cards and cards on the table may not be used to capture it – see overleaf).

How to play

Canasta is a 'draw and discard' game, like Gin Rummy – each player in turn draws a new card from the pack, and then discards one card, trying to form his hand into matching sets while doing so. It is sometimes possible, instead of drawing a new card from the pack, to capture the entire discard pile, and much of the skill in the game goes towards manoeuvring so as to be able to do this.

If a player is able to form a legal combination including the top card (that most recently discarded) of the discard pile, then he may do so instead of drawing a new card from the pack, and having done so he takes the rest of the discard pile into his hand. The combination may involve the last discard, cards in the player's hand and combinations previously played on the table by him, but may not involve any of the previous discards. Having made his capture, and picked up the discard pile, the player may put down any further cards he wishes – these may include some of the cards he just picked up – and then discards to complete his turn.

There is no restriction on discarding captured cards immediately.

It is illegal to make a capture using a wild card unless the player already has a wild card on the table before the start of his turn – otherwise the last discard must be matched with at least two plain cards of the same rank.

If a black 3 is discarded, it is always illegal for the next player to capture the pile – the main function of black 3s in the game is to act as safe discards.

If a wild card is discarded, then the pile is said to be 'frozen'. It is illegal for the next player to capture the pile, as with black 3s, but there are two additional restrictions which continue to apply while the pile is frozen (i.e. until it is next captured): it becomes illegal to combine the top discard with cards already played on the table – the combination must be with cards from the hand; and it becomes illegal to capture the pile using a wild card, even if a wild card has already been used.

It is normally illegal to put down a set of black 3s, but this may be done by a player on the turn in which he goes out. A set of black 3s may never contain any wild cards (see page 113).

If the last card in the pack is a red 3, then the player drawing it does not discard on that turn.

Wild cards may be added to completed canastas, provided that they do not break the law that no more than three wild cards should appear in one combination. If wild cards are added to a natural canasta, though, it becomes a mixed canasta and only scores 300 points (it may sometimes be necessary to do this in order to go out).

In the early part of the game, the main objective is to be the first to capture the discard pile. Having done this, a player can often continue capturing the pile for the rest of the hand – each time he picks up he recycles the safe discards that he has already used.

When a player has succeeded in making the first capture, and has the chance to go out, it is often good not to do so, but to keep going and make a really huge score. If, on the other hand, his opponent has made the first capture, he will often be stuck simply feeding him cards, and it is usually best to try to go out as soon as possible. Going out is a defensive tactic.

Black 3s should not be discarded too early. Capturing a pile of three of four cards is not very devastating, and it is usually better to hang on to black 3s until the pile gets bigger and a safe discard is really needed.

Scoring

The object of the game is to be the first to 5,000 points.

In order to score, a combination of cards must be laid face up on the table. The only combinations allowed are sets of cards of the same rank – there are no sequences in Canasta. A combination must contain at least three cards. Jokers may be used to substitute for 'plain' cards, and 2s may also be used like Jokers in this way. We refer to 2s and Jokers collectively as 'wild cards'. However, a set may never contain more than three wild cards, or fewer than two plain cards.

A set of seven or more cards is called a canasta, and scores a large bonus. 'Natural' canastas (containing no wild cards) score more than 'mixed' ones. Examples are illustrated in the top illustration on page 114.

The 3s are covered by special rules. Black 3s may not normally be used for anything constructive – but are nevertheless good cards to hold – (see page 112). Red 3s are bonus cards - a player holding one should immediately lay it face up in front of him and draw another card to replace it.

The first time a player puts scoring cards on the table, they must add up to at least a minimum value, which depends on how close that player's side is to the target of 5,000 points. This total may be achieved using several combinations, for example a total of 50 can be achieved with a set of three 5s (15) and a set of two Kings with a 2 (40). If (as usually happens) the first scoring cards are played while capturing the discard pile, this total must be achieved using only the last discard and cards in the player's hand.

The requirements depend on the side's score as follows:

Negative score	No restriction
0–1,495	50 points required
1,500–2,995	90
3,000–4,995	120

This requirement is quite independent of any red 3s laid down. Examples of sets giving the points required are shown in the lower illustration on page 114.

When the game ends, each side adds up the value of their cards face up on the table, then subtracts the value of any cards remaining in their hand. Scores are as follows:

7, 6, 5, 4 or black 3	5
K, Q, J, 10, 9 or 8	10
Ace	20
2	20
Joker	50
Red 3	100
All four red 3s	800
Mixed canasta	300
Natural canasta	500
Going out	100
Going out 'concealed'	200

Canasta for four players

With two or three players, each plays individually, but four players play as two pairs of partners. Partners sit opposite each other. In this case partners keep their scoring cards separately, and they

A natural canasta, top (this one worth 535 points) and a mixed canasta, lower row (worth 430)

must meet the requirements to score a certain number of points with their first combinations and to make one canasta before going out separately, but they can add cards to each other's combinations The end of the game comes when both partners on one side are out (or when the pack runs out). It is usual for partners to go out in immediate succession, one saying 'Shall I go out, partner?' before discarding. If your partner says 'Yes' you are obliged to go out.

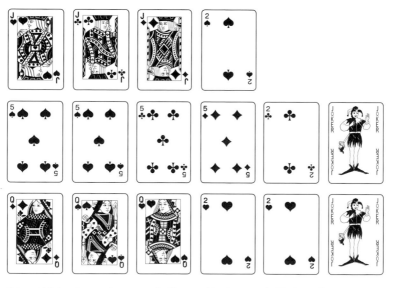

Sets satisfying the requirements of a first combination, worth 50, 90 and 120 points

Cinch

Cinch is a game from the All Fours family which was very fashionable in the USA before Bridge began to oust most other card games of the type. It has some of the attractions of Bridge, like the bidding, without all the conventions, and is a game of skill well worth playing. It is also called Double Pedro and High Five.

Number of players

Cinch is best as a game for four players, as described first here, playing in two partnerships, with the partners sitting opposite each other. It can be played by two to six players, and there are variants such as Auction Cinch, described later.

Cards

The full pack of 52 cards is used. Cards rank from Ace (high) to 2 (low), with the exception of the 5 of the same colour as the trump suit, which is also regarded as a trump and ranks between the 5 and 4. For example, if clubs are trumps, the trump suit ranks as follows:

♣ A, K, Q, J, 10, 9, 8, 7, 6, 5; ♠5; ♣ 4, 3, 2

The 5 of the trump suit is called Right Pedro and the 5 of the same colour is called Left Pedro. Cards in the trump suit have values to players winning them in tricks as follows: Right Pedro five points, Left Pedro five points, Ace (known as 'high') one point, 2 (known as 'low') one point, Jack one point and 10 (known as 'game') one point. On each deal there are thus 14 points at stake.

Players draw cards to determine partners, the two highest playing against the two lowest, the highest being dealer. The dealer shuffles, and the player to his right cuts. The dealer deals nine cards to each player in threes, clockwise from his left. The remaining cards are set aside face down for the moment - they will be used later.

How to play

The object is to take tricks containing the scoring cards, and the trump suit is decided by the side which undertakes to make the most tricks, so the next stage is a round of bidding.

Beginning with eldest hand (to dealer's left), each player in turn makes a bid, or passes. Each player is allowed only one bid. A bid consists of the number of points that the player proposes to make in play, with his partner's help. He can decide which suit is to be trumps, but at the bidding stage he does not announce the suit. The minimum bid is one, and the maximum is 14 (the total points available). Once a player has bid, any subsequent bid must be for a higher number of points. When the round of bidding has finished, the player who bid the highest names the trump suit (he is not allowed to consult his partner, and no signals must pass between them). The side bidding highest has now contracted to make the stated number of points with the trump suit as specified.

As with Bridge, expert players have certain systems of bidding, of which the following is an example:

With a Pedro, bid five to show it.
With A, x, x, or A, x, x, x, bid six.
With A, K, bid seven.
With A, K, J, x, x, bid 11.
With A, K, Q, x or better, bid 12.

Should the first three players all pass, the dealer names the trump suit, but he is not obliged to contract to make a certain number of points.

The trick-taking part of the game starts with each player holding six cards, so the next stage is one of discarding, but each player is given the opportunity to improve his hand by drawing new cards from the remaining pack.

Beginning with the eldest hand, each player discards as many cards as he wishes, face up, and is given by the dealer, face down, enough cards from the top of the pack to bring his hand up to six cards. A player must make at least three discards (if he discards only three, he draws no new cards). No player may discard a trump, unless he is dealt with seven or more, in which case he must discard at least one to bring his hand to six cards.

When it is dealer's turn to discard, he simply 'robs the pack'. He is entitled to look at all the remaining cards and decide which he wishes to take into his hand and to discard accordingly. He announces how many cards he is taking but need not show his discards except that, should there be more than six trumps in his hand and the pack, he must show the other players the trumps that he is forced to discard or not to take into his hand.

In practice, each player will keep all his trumps and usually discard all his non-trumps, because, as all the point-scoring cards are trumps, it is impossible to win any points with a plain card.

With all the players reduced to six cards, the trick-taking phase begins. The player who named the trump suit is called the maker. The maker leads the first trick. Subsequently the winner of a trick leads the next.

When a trump is led, each player must follow suit if able, and must discard if unable. When a plain suit is led, a player able to follow suit may do so or trump, but may not discard. A player unable to follow suit may discard or trump.

The object of each side is to take as many tricks containing point-scoring cards as possible, with particular reference to the contract.

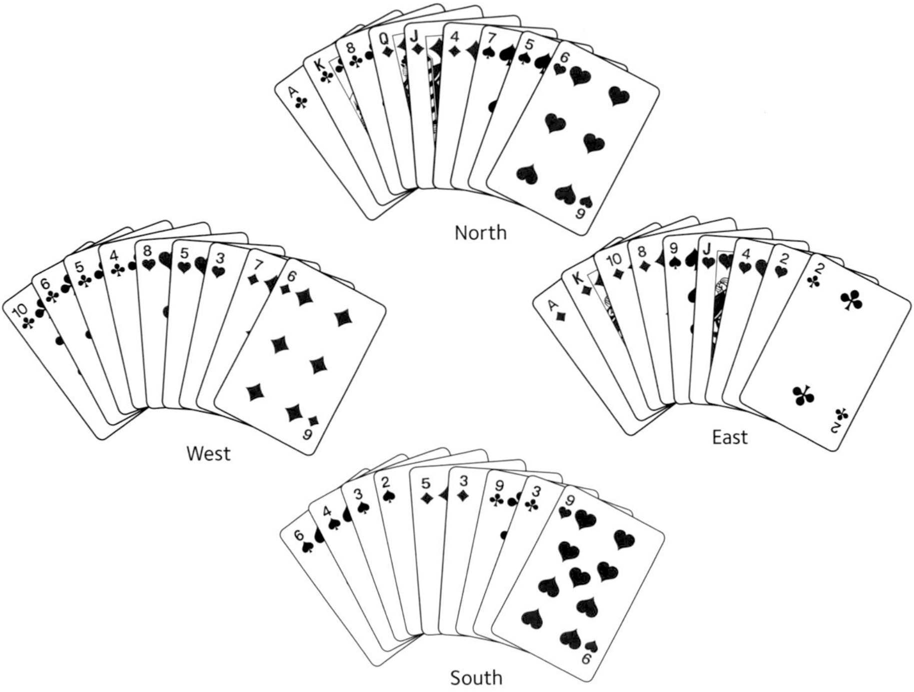

North

West

East

South

When all six tricks have been played, each side counts the number of points won. If the making side has made its contract, i.e. has scored at least the number of points bid by the maker, the side with the higher total of points wins the difference. For example, if the maker bids six and scores nine against the opponents' five, his side scores four points (the difference between the two scores). Notice that even when the maker achieves his contract, it is not necessarily his side which scores. If he bids six and makes six, his opponents having scored eight, his opponents score two points for the difference.

If the making side fails to make its contract, the opponents score the number of points they made, plus the value of the contract. For example, if a side contracts to make ten points, and makes only eight, the opponents score the six points they made plus the ten points of the contract, i.e. 16 points.

When all players have passed, and the dealer names trumps without bidding, the side scoring the more points scores the difference.

Game is to 51 points.

The illustration above shows the nine cards dealt to each hand by the dealer (which is South).

West bids five (to tell his partner he holds a pedro); North, with ♣A, K bids seven; East, with his strong diamonds, bids eight (if his partner's 5 is red, he is certain to make seven, and almost certain to make eight, even without any cards he might draw), while South can only pass.

East announces diamonds as trumps, much to the satisfaction of West, whose ♥5 is now certainly worth five points.

West, North and East each discard all their non-trumps, and draw three, three and two cards respectively. South robbed the pack, finding only one trump, the ♦2, and drawing two cards.

The new hands are shown opposite (see opposite, top).

Play might proceed as follows:

East	South	West	North
♠8	♠2	♦6	♠10
♦A	♦3	♥5	♦4
♠A	♥9	♦7	♣Q
♦10	♣3	♠J	♦9
♦K	♦2	♥Q	♦Q
♦8	♦5	♣J	♦J

East led low and his partner West played ♦6 to prevent North winning the trick and five points should he hold a Right Pedro (West knows he himself has Left Pedro). This play, of third player playing a trump higher than 5 is known as 'cinching the trick'. Knowing that his partner held ♦A, West led Left Pedro for East to take, and West cinched again at

trick 3. East played ♦10 at trick 4, because he would not mind losing it to either ♦Q or ♦J in the South hand, as he would be sure then of taking the last two tricks and capturing Right Pedro.

It would not have helped North to play ♦Q or ♦J at trick four – East would play low and win the last two tricks, conceding no more than six points. At trick 5 East led the ♦K knowing he would lose the last trick but that his opponents could not contribute more than six points to it. East/West thus take eight points, achieve their contract, and score the difference between the two totals, i.e. two points.

It is as well to remember that of the 24 cards in play, 14 will be trumps, and that a player holding four trumps will find at least one other player holding as many. However, it is more important to hold the high trumps than length. A player whose hand consists of six low trumps might not win a point. It is necessary to win at least one Pedro to take the balance of points, and a player can lead a Pedro to a partner holding the master trump, as was shown in the second trick in the hand just described.

It frequently does not pay to draw trumps, a tactic that is frequently used in other trick-taking games, including Bridge. Had East, with his strong trumps, attempted to do so in the example hand, then the play might have proceeded as follows:

North

West

East

South

East	South	West	North
♦A	♦3	♥5	♦4
♦K	♦2	♦6	♦9
♠8	♠2	<u>♦7</u>	♠10
♦8	♥9	♠J	♣Q
♠A	♣3	♥Q	<u>♦J</u>
♦10	♦5	♣J	<u>♦Q</u>

Here, each side took seven points, meaning East/West failed to make their contract, and North/South therefore scored their points, seven, plus the value of the contract, eight, making 15.

It is as well to note that a side failing to make a contract must lose at least 15 points, while if it makes the contract it cannot score more than 14. This suggests bids should be made with caution. On the other hand, naming the trump suit is a big advantage.

CINCH WITH A WIDOW

In this variation of the game, after the first three cards to each player, the dealer deals each player a widow of four cards, which remains on the table before them. Players bid as before, whereupon each player picks up his widow. The maker then names the trump suit, and each player discards seven cards to bring his hand to six. Any player who discards a trump or trumps must show them to the other players. Play then proceeds as before.

CUT-THROAT CINCH

Cinch can be played by two, three, five or six players, each playing for himself. With two or three players, the dealer does not rob the pack, but discards and draws like the other players. Obviously not all the trumps will be in play, which makes the bidding and play more of a gamble. With five or six players, each player is dealt six cards only, so draws the same number of cards as he discards.

In Cut-throat Cinch, the maker plays against the other players. With two players, scoring is as in the parent game, which has two sides. With three to six players, if the contract is made, the side with the most tricks (either the maker or the combined opponents) scores the difference between the two totals (each opponent of the maker scores the difference if his side wins). If the contract is not made, each opponent scores the amount of the bid plus the number of points that he has scored himself personally.

AUCTION CINCH

Auction Cinch, also called Razzle Dazzle, is for five or six players, each playing for himself. Six cards are dealt to each player in bundles of three. Bidding is as in the parent game described, and when the highest bidder has named trumps, each player in turn discards all his non-trumps, and takes cards sufficient to bring his hand back to six cards. The maker then specifies a card not in his hand (usually the highest trump he is missing). The holder of the card acknowledges that he has it, and the two play in opposition against the others. The partner does not change seats, even if sitting next to the maker. The scoring of the points in play is as in the parent game. If the maker and his partner make their contract, the side with most points scores the difference between the two totals. Each player on the winning side scores the difference. If the contract fails, each player on the noncontracting side scores the points specified in the contract plus the points he himself took in tricks.

Some schools prefer that the partner of the maker does not acknowledge that he holds the specified card. This brings surprise and uncertainty to the play while detracting from the skill factor.

Crazy Eights

Crazy Eights is a very simple game, not to be confused with the game of Eights. It is an easy form of gambling game and is considered to be a pre-extension of Switch and Mau Mau, which were highly popular during the 1970s.

Number of players

The game can be played by any number of players from two to eight, but is best suited to four or more, each player playing for himself.

Cards

The full pack of 52 cards is used. The ranking of the cards is immaterial, but cards have a point-scoring value, as described below.

Any player picks up the cards, shuffles, and begins dealing them one to each player face up – the first player to be dealt a Jack becomes first dealer. Subsequently the deal passes clockwise to the left.

Before the deal, each player puts a stake into the centre. The dealer then deals five cards to each player, one at a time to the left, then lays out eight cards face up in the centre of the table, arranged in two rows of four. The remainder of the pack is set aside.

How to play

Beginning with the player on the dealer's left, each player in turn may lay a card from his hand face up on one of the eight cards in the centre. The card must match in rank the card onto which it is played. A card in the centre may be played as many times as required, i.e. if two players are dealt an 8, and there is an 8 in the centre, each player can play his 8 onto it in turn. A player who cannot go says 'pass'.

Should a player get rid of all his cards, he shouts 'crazy eights' and collects the whole pool of stakes. Frequently the game ends with every player being forced to pass while still holding a card or two. In this case, every player counts the points still held in his hand according to the following scale: Aces count as 15 points, Kings, Queens and Jacks count as 10 points, and all other cards their pip value.

The pool is then divided between the high player (whose points total is highest) and the low player (whose points total is lowest).

In the illustration on page 122, players A, B, C, D, E and F have each contributed two chips to a pool of 12 chips. Player A dealt the hands as shown, and placed the eight cards in the centre of the table.

Player B plays first and lays his ♦J on the ♣J, player C plays his ♠8 on ♣8 and so on. All players can play to the first round, but player D must pass in the second, players C and A in the third, players B and F in the fourth, and finally player E passes on the fifth round.

Player A is left with K, 5, 3 = 18 points; B with K, 7 = 17 points; C with K, 9, 5 = 24 points; D with 7, 5, 3, 3 = 18 points; E with the ♠9 only = 9 points; and F with K, 10 = 20 points. So player C collects six chips for high, and player E six chips for low.

A

B

C

D

E

F

Cut-throat Bridge

Many suggestions have been made to make Bridge (see page 85) suitable for three players. There is a variation called Towie but what has become known as Cut-throat Bridge is the original and the simplest of the three-handed variations.

Number of players

This game is specifically designed for three players who are unable to find a fourth for Bridge.

Cards

The full pack of 52 cards is used to play Cut-throat Bridge. The players take seats at random and after drawing for deal, shuffling and cutting in the usual way, the dealer deals 13 cards each to the three players and also to a fourth hand that is temporarily set aside.

How to play

The auction, beginning with the dealer, is conducted as in Bridge (see pages 85–104), and when a player's bid, double or redouble has been passed by the other two players, the player on his left leads the first trick. The player who has obtained the final contract then sorts the fourth hand, spreads it in front of him on the table, and plays it as his dummy, against the other two players in partnership with each other.

The play and scoring are the same as in the parent game, with the exception that if a player loses his contract both his opponents score the penalty points. The winner of a rubber receives a bonus of 700 points if neither opponent has won a game, but 500 points if either has.

Very clearly the game is a gamble, because the players must bid in the hope of finding the cards they need in the dummy hand.

A variation designed to make the game less speculative is for every player to be dealt 17 cards and the 52nd card is dealt face downwards to the dummy. After looking at their cards, and before bidding them, every player contributes four of them, face downwards, to the dummy. This way every player knows four out of the 13 cards that he is bidding for.

In another variation, instead of bidding for the dummy, an agreed number of deals (that must be divisible by three) is played, and, in turn, every player plays the dummy against the other two playing in partnership.

In this variation rubbers are not played, but the player who bids and makes game scores a bonus of 300 points. There is no vulnerability.

Double Rum

'Double Rum' is not a bad name for this game, because it is a variation of Rummy (see page 148), played with two packs of cards shuffled together with two Jokers.

Number of players

The game may be played by up to eight players; each plays for himself.

Cards

Two identical packs are used with two Jokers, making 106 cards. Aces rank either high or low, but not round-the-corner (K–A–2), and Jokers are wild.

Ten cards are dealt face downwards to each player. The rest (the stock) is placed face downwards in the centre, with the top card placed face upwards alongside it to start the discard pile.

How to play

The object of the game is to get rid of all cards held, by melding them face upwards on the table, either in sets of three or more of the same rank, or in sequences of three or more of the same suit.

The player to the left of the dealer starts. He is under no obligation to meld, but he must take either the top card of the stock or the top card of the discard pile, and discard a card to reduce his hand to ten cards. If he chooses to meld he must do so between drawing a card and discarding one, and as well as melding, at the same time he may add cards to melds that he has already made, and to those of his opponents.

A Joker may be moved from one end of a meld to the other, provided the player has the card to replace it. If, for example, a sequence is: ♠ 6, 7 8, Joker, a player who holds a ♠9 may play it in place of the Joker and transfer the Joker to represent the ♠5. However, a Joker cannot be moved a second time and a player who holds a ♠5 cannot play it in place of the Joker and place the Joker elsewhere. Nor can a Joker be moved or replaced if it is in the interior of a sequence, as in ♠ 4, 5, 6, Joker, ♠8. When a Joker cannot be moved it is customary to place it crosswise, as a reminder to the other players.

The game is won by the player who is first to meld all his cards. The other players pay him the same number of units as the pip value of the unmelded cards left in their hands – a Joker counts 15, an Ace 11, the court cards 10 each, and all other cards their pip values.

If the stock is exhausted before the game has been won, the game continues and the players draw cards from the discard pile, discarding a different card to that drawn.

Euchre

Euchre is a game that has always been more popular in the New World than in the Old. It was made famous by Bret Harte's witty *Plain Language from Truthful James*, published in 1870.

Number of players

The standard game is suitable for two to six players, but is best for four, two playing in partnership against the other two, as described first here.

Cards

The game is played with a 32-card or short pack, that is the standard pack from which the 6s and lower cards have been removed. The cards rank in the order from Ace (high) to 7 (low) with the exception that the Jack of the trump suit (Right Bower) takes precedence over all other trump cards, and the Jack of the suit of the same colour (Left Bower) ranks as the second highest trump.

There is some advantage in dealing. The players, therefore, must draw cards to decide who shall deal. The highest takes first deal, which, thereafter, passes round the table clockwise.

The dealer gives five cards to each player either in bundles of two then three, or three then two. It does not matter which, but he must be consistent throughout the game. The rest of the pack is placed face downwards in the centre of the table, and the top card is turned face upwards.

How to play

The turned up card is the potential trump suit, and, beginning with the player on the left of the dealer, each player in turn has the option of either refusing or accepting it.

To accept it as the trump suit the opponents of the dealer say: 'I order it up'; the dealer's partner says: 'I assist'; and the dealer himself says nothing, but accepts by making his discard. To refuse the card as the trump suit, the opponents and partner of the dealer say: 'I pass'; the dealer signifies refusal by taking the card from the top of the pack and placing it, face upwards, partly underneath the pack.

If all four players pass on the first round, there is a second round. Beginning with the player on the left of the dealer, each player in turn may now either pass, or name any suit he likes (other than that of the turned up card) as trumps. If all four players pass on the second round, the hand is abandoned and the deal passes.

When the trump suit has been settled, the player who has named it (the maker) has the right to go it alone, but he must announce his intention to do so before a

125

card has been led. His partner places his cards face downwards on the table, and takes no active part in the hand. The maker (he is the only one of the four who can go it alone) plays his hand against the two opponents in partnership. If he wins the march (all five tricks) he scores four points; if he wins three or four tricks he scores one point; if he is euchred (i.e. fails to win at least three tricks) the opponents score two points each.

Euchre is a trick-taking game. The player on the left of the dealer (or the player on the left of the maker if he is going it alone) leads to the first trick. Thereafter the player who wins a trick leads to the next. A player must follow suit to the card led if he can, if not he may either discard or trump.

If the partnership that made the trump suit wins the march it scores two points; if it wins three or four tricks it scores one point; if it is euchred the opposing side scores two points. The side that is first to score five points wins.

TWO-HANDED EUCHRE

The game is played in exactly the same way as the parent game except that the pack is reduced to 24 cards by removing the 8s and all the lower cards. There is also no declaration of going it alone.

THREE-HANDED EUCHRE

The game is played in the same way as the parent game except that the maker of the trump suit plays against the other

two in partnership. If the maker wins the march he scores three points; if he wins three or four tricks he scores one point; and if he is euchred each of his opponents scores two points.

CALL-ACE EUCHRE

This is a variation that may be played by four, five or six players, each playing for himself. It is played in the same way as the parent game with the exception that the maker has the option of either playing for himself or calling for a partner by saying: 'I call on the Ace of...' and he names a suit. The player who holds the Ace of this suit then plays in partnership with the maker against the other players, but he does not reveal himself. It follows, therefore, that until the Ace is played, and it may not be in the deal, everyone except the holder of the Ace (if it is in play) is left to guess where his interest lies.

The scoring is rather different from that of the other variations as fundamentally the game is all against all. For winning the march a lone player scores one point for every player in the game; in a partnership hand the score is two points each if three or four players are in the game, and three points each if five or six players are in the game. For winning three or four tricks a lone player scores one point; in a partnership hand both players score one point. If a lone player or a partnership is euchred the other players score two points each.

Five Hundred

Five Hundred is a trick-taking game that was invented early in the 20th century. It was particularly popular in the USA.

Number of players

The game is designed for three players, but may be played by more.

Cards

A short pack of 32 is required, plus the Joker, making a pack of 33, so from a standard pack the 6s, 5s, 4s, 3s and 2s are removed.

The game is played with a trump suit, and the cards in the trump suit rank as follows: Joker, Jack (called right bower), Jack of the same colour as the trump suit (called left bower), Ace, King, Queen, 10, 9, 8, 7.

The cards in the plain suits rank normally: Ace, King, Queen, Jack, 10, 9, 8, 7, except that the suit of the same colour as the trump suit will not contain a Jack. Therefore the suits have an unequal number of cards: the trump suit has ten cards, the suit of the same colour has seven cards and the other two suits have eight cards.

In addition, the suits are ranked: hearts (high), diamonds, clubs, spades.

Players draw for deal, the lowest dealing. For this purpose the cards rank in their usual order, but Ace counts low, and Joker lowest of all. The dealer shuffles, the player on his right cuts, and

the dealer deals three cards to each hand, beginning on his left, then three to the centre to form a widow, then four to each hand, then three to each hand. Each player therefore has ten cards, with the other three in the deck being in the widow.

How to play

The players examine their cards and bidding begins. A bid is an offer by a player to make a stated number of tricks with a specified trump suit or without a trump suit (a bid in 'no trumps'). Each bid must be higher than the previous bid. The values of the bids are as follows:

	Six	Seven	Eight	Nine	Ten
Spades	40	140	240	340	440
Clubs	60	160	260	360	460
Diamonds	80	180	280	380	480
Hearts	100	200	300	400	500
No trumps	120	220	320	420	520

Eldest (left of dealer) begins and may bid or pass, and bidding continues until two players in succession pass, whereupon the last bid made constitutes the contract. (In some schools the bidding is not continuous, and each player is allowed one bid only, while in other schools the bidding is progressive but a player who passes cannot re-enter the bidding.) Should none of the players bid, the deal is abandoned, and passes to the next player.

Once a player has won the contract, he picks up the widow, and discards three cards face down to keep his hand to ten cards.

The ten tricks are now played out, with the player with the contract leading the first trick. The winner of a trick leads the next. The normal rules apply: each player must follow suit to the lead, and if unable to follow suit he may trump or discard. A trick is won by the highest trump played, or if there is none by the highest card in the suit led.

In a no-trump contract, the Joker remains a trump – the only one. It can be played only if its holder cannot follow suit. If the Joker is led in a no-trump contract, its player specifies the suit it

represents, and the other players must play cards of that suit if they are able to. The Joker always wins the trick.

For the declarer, the object is to make at least as many tricks as he contracted to do. His opponents score individually for the tricks they make, so they are playing for themselves, but they should also play in partnership, because defeating the contract will cost the declarer more than the points they can make individually for themselves.

If the declarer makes his contract, he scores its value as set out in the table on page 127. There is no bonus for overtricks, with one possible exception, which is that a player who takes all ten tricks scores a minimum of 250 points. So if a player's contract is worth less than 250 (i.e. eight spades or less), he will earn a bonus by taking all ten tricks.

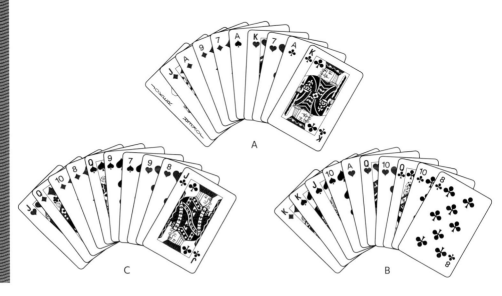

A

C

B

If the declarer fails to make his contract, he loses the value of his bid. A player can thus have a minus score, which is recorded with a circle round it, and the player is said to be 'in the hole'.

Each of the two players opposing the declarer scores separately for the tricks they make – ten points per trick, and there is no bonus for defeating the declarer. Game is to 500 points (hence the name). It is rare for a player to win without making at least one contract, so, as stated earlier, the ten points per trick are of less significance than the making or defeating of contracts.

Should the declarer and an opponent pass 500 on the same deal, the declarer is the winner. Should the two opponents pass 500, the one who took the trick to take his score to 500 first is the winner.

It is customary to set a limit to the 'hole', say 500. Should a player reach 500 in the hole, the opponent who is leading at the end of the deal is the winner. This is to prevent a player in the hole bidding recklessly and preventing his opponents from making a contract, and in effect spoiling the game.

To outline the mechanics of the game, suppose hands are held as in the illustration opposite. Player A has bid seven diamonds, and has been lucky enough to find ♣ A in the widow. He decides to lead trumps immediately, hoping to lose one only, to ♥ J (left bower), which will ensure his contract. Play proceeds as follows:

	Player A	Player B	Player C
1	Joker	♦K	♦8
2	♦J	♣8	♦10
3	♣A	♣10	♣J
4	♣K	♣Q	♦Q
5	♥K	♥A	♥8
6	♥7	♥Q	♥9
7	♦7	♥10	♠7
8	♦A	♠10	♥J
9	♠A	♠J	♠9
10	♦9	♠K	♠Q

From trick 2, when ♦J (right bower) failed to drop ♥J, Player A knew that his best chances were that Player C held the ♥A, which would give him a chance of making ♥K, or that Player C could be forced to lead his remaining trumps (in which case Player A would lose only one trump) or that the defenders would make a mistake with their discards. As it happened, the defenders played well, and Player A was forced to lose both hearts and two trumps.

Player A therefore failed to make his contract of seven diamonds, and scored 180 points in the hole. Players B and C each made two tricks, so each scored 20 points.

Strategy in playing the cards is similar to most trick-taking games. The main skill in Five Hundred lies in the bidding. As the trump suit consists of ten cards, one player must hold at least four, so four trumps is the minimum requirement for a bid, and even then they must be good ones and supported by side Aces. Unless six or more trumps are held in the deal, the chances are slightly in favour of at least one more being in the widow, but this should not be relied upon. As a rough guide, a player might count any of the top four trumps (Joker, Right and Left Bower, Ace) as one point each, all trumps held in excess of three as one point each, all master cards in side suits as one point each, and a guarded King in a side suit as half a point, and bid accordingly. In the example hands on page 128, Player A held three points in top trumps, two more with the ♦ 9, 7, one more with ♠A, and two half-points with guarded Kings, the ♥K and ♣K (he found ♣A in the widow). He therefore had seven points and bid seven diamonds. The ♣A would usually have made his contract a good one, but as it happened the outstanding trumps were badly split for him, and the ♥A was badly placed.

A variation often played is to allow an extra bid, called nullo. This is a contract to win no tricks at all. There are no trumps. The value of the bid is 250, placing it between eight spades and eight clubs. A player holding the Joker can play it only when he has no cards of the suit led. If the Joker is led, its player specifies the suit it represents. The Joker always wins the trick in which it is played. When the declarer makes nullo, he scores 250 and his opponents score nothing. If he fails, he is debited 250, and his opponents score ten points each for each trick he has made.

Five Hundred for four players

With four players the pack must be enlarged to allow each player to have ten cards. The 6s, 5s, and two red 4s are added to the 33-card pack. Play is in partnerships, partners sitting opposite each other. Bidding proceeds as before, and the player making the highest bid leads the first trick. Each side keeps its tricks separately, and scoring is as before.

Five Hundred for five players

The full pack is used, plus the Joker, so that each player receives ten cards and there are three in the widow as before. Each player plays for himself, but the player who wins the contract calls upon one of the others to be his temporary partner, and the two play that hand against the other three. In some schools the declarer names the player he wants as his partner, who will possibly be a player who has bid, and who therefore is known to have a good hand. More usually, the declarer calls upon the holder of a specific card to be his partner. This will usually be the highest missing trump, but it might be an Ace in a side suit. The holder of the card does not announce it, so until he plays the card only he knows that he is partnering the declarer. Players never change their seats.

Each partner trying to make a contract scores the relevant points if successful and is debited with them if unsuccessful. The opponents each score ten points for each trick taken.

Hearts

Hearts and its several variations are very similar in principle to Black Maria (see page 83) because the object of the game is to avoid taking tricks that contain certain specified cards. It originated with a family of related games called Reversis, which became popular around 1750 in Spain. Hearts itself was established in its own right around 1850. Today it is popular among school students in the USA.

Number of players

The game may be played by any reasonable number of players, but it is at its most interesting and skilful as a game when played by four, each playing for himself.

Cards

The full pack of 52 cards is used. However, when the game is played by three players or by more than four, low cards are removed from the pack to reduce it to a number that allows every player to be dealt the same number of cards.

All the cards are dealt out one at a time, and clockwise.

How to play

The play follows the general principles of trick-taking games: the player on the left of the dealer leads to the first trick, and thereafter the winner of a trick leads to the next; a player must follow suit to the card led if he can, and if he cannot he may discard any card that suits him.

The ♠Q and all cards of the heart suit are penalty cards. Every deal is a separate event, and the usual method of settling is to debit the player who wins the ♠Q 13 points, and those who win hearts one point for each card.

A revoke is heavily penalized. A player may correct a revoke if he does so before a card is led to the next trick; otherwise the revoke is established, the hand is abandoned, and the revoking player is debited all 26 points.

The game is not a difficult one, but it calls for an ability to count the cards, read the distribution and visualize possibilities. It is instructive to consider the play in the deal illustrated overleaf on page 133.

West has to make the opening lead and assumes that the best lead is the ♥2 because one of the other players will certainly have to win the trick.

Against West's opening lead of the ♥2 the play will be short and sharp, and West will come off worst of all because good play by his opponents will saddle him with the ♠Q.

West	North	East	South
♥2	♥4	♥3	♥8
♥6	♥7	♥10	♥9
♥Q	♥K	♥J	♦A
♥A	♥5	♠Q	♦Q

A more experienced West would have kept off leading a heart. It is probable that his best lead is the singleton diamond, because he has nothing to fear in the spade suit, and, once he has got rid of his diamond, he gives himself the best chance to get rid of the dangerous ♥A and ♥Q.

DOMINO HEARTS

In this version of the game, the players are dealt only six cards each, and the rest of the pack is placed face downwards in the centre of the table. The player on the left of the dealer leads the first trick, and the game is played in the same way as the parent game except that if a player cannot follow suit to a card that has been led he must draw a card from the stock, and continue to do so until he draws a card of the suit led. Only after the stock has been exhausted may a player discard from his hand if he cannot follow suit to a lead.

Play continues until all the cards have been taken in tricks, each player dropping out as his hand is exhausted. If a player wins a trick with the last card in his hand, the next active player on his left leads to the next trick. The last player to be left in the game retains all the cards left in his hand, and takes into it any cards that may be left in the stock.

The ♠Q is not a penalty card; only cards of the heart suit are, and one point is lost for each one taken in a trick or left in the hand of the surviving player.

GREEK HEARTS

In this version, as in Black Maria (see page 83) each player, before the opening lead is made, passes three cards to his right-hand opponent and receives three from his left-hand opponent.

As in the parent game the penalty cards are the ♠Q and all cards of the heart suit, and the penalties for winning them are the same; if, however, a player wins all the hearts and the ♠Q, instead of losing 26 points, he receives 26 points from each of the other players.

The game calls for some considerable skill, because, before passing on his cards, a player has to decide whether he will take the easy road and play to avoid winning penalty cards, or try for the big prize by winning them all. The decision is never an easy one, because in discarding a high heart one may be helping an opponentgain a better score, and oneself to lose a good score if one receives the ♠Q and a couple of high hearts from one's left-hand opponent.

HEARTSETTE

This variation is played in the same way as the parent game, but with a widow hand, dealt face down. If three or four

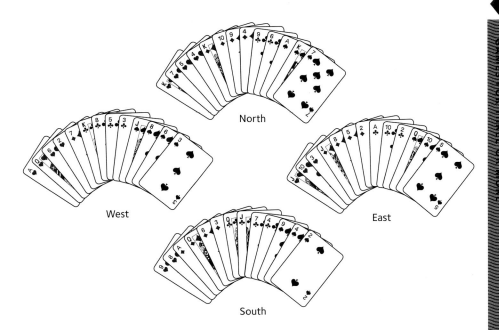

North

West

East

South

take part in the game the ♠2 is removed from the pack, and if five or six take part the full pack is used.

When there are three players, each one is dealt 16 cards; when four, 12 cards; when five, ten cards and when six, eight cards. The remaining cards are placed face downwards in the centre of the table.

The player on the left of the dealer leads to the first trick and whoever wins it takes the widow and discards from his hand to reduce it to the proper number of cards. No one else sees the widow nor the cards that have been discarded.

The play continues in the same way as in the parent game with the same penalty cards and the same penalties for winning them.

OMNIBUS HEARTS

Also called Hit the Moon, this version combines most of the features that have been added to the parent game. Like it, it is at its best when played by four people, each playing for himself.

Thirteen cards are dealt to each player, and before the opening lead is made each player passes three cards to his right-hand opponent and receives three from his left-hand opponent.

The play is the same as in the parent game. All the hearts and the ♠Q are penalty cards, but a novel feature is that the ♦10 is a bonus card. A player loses one point for every heart that he wins and 13 points if he wins the ♠Q. By contrast, he wins 10 points if he takes the ♦10, and if he wins all the hearts, the ♠Q and the ♦10 (known as hitting the moon – no longer such a feat as it once was) he wins 26 points instead of losing 16.

The game is won by the player who has the highest plus score, or lowest minus score, when one player reaches a score of –100.

The game calls for skill both in discarding to the right-hand opponent and in the play. Good discarding is dictated by the fact that only the club suit is neutral and harmless. Every heart is a liability and top spades are dangerous (unless adequately supported by low cards) and though top diamonds are advantageous the low ones may simply be liabilities.

In play it is necessary to aim at forcing the lead into the hand of the least dangerous opponent. All the time temporary partnerships must be formed. If the score stands at: North –83, East –41, South +32, West +47, it is obvious that West will be doing his best to win the game by driving North to –100 as quickly as possible. A skilful South, therefore, will enter into a tacit partnership with North to try and save him by prolonging the game and so give himself more time to pull ahead of West. The strategy is perfectly proper because both players are acting in their own interests.

PIP HEARTS

This version is played in the same way as the parent game, but the ♠Q is not a penalty card and the penalty for winning a heart is increased to the pip value of the card, the court cards counting Jack 11, Queen 12, King 13 and Ace 14.

Knaves

Knaves is so called because the four Knaves (or Jacks) are penalty cards and the object of the players is to avoid winning tricks that contain them.

Number of players

Knaves is a game for three players.

Cards

The full pack of 52 cards is used, cards ranking from Ace (high) to 2 (low).

Seventeen cards are dealt to each player and the last card is turned face up on the table to denote the trump suit. It takes no other part in the game.

How to play

The player on the left of the dealer leads the first trick; thereafter the player who wins a trick leads the next. A player must follow suit, if he can, to the card led. If he cannot he may either use a trump card if he has one in hand, or discard a card of a plain suit.

The player who wins a trick scores one point for it, but four points are deducted from a player's score if he wins the Knave of hearts, three points if he wins the Knave of diamonds, two points if he wins the Knave of clubs, and one point if he wins the Knave of spades. The aggregate score for each deal, therefore, is seven points (i.e. 17 points for tricks minus 10 points for Knaves) unless one of the Knaves is the card turned up to denote the trump suit. Game is won by the first player to score 20 points.

The players play all against all, but skilful play introduces temporary partnerships that add much to the interest of the game. If, for example, one player is in the lead and the other two are trailing behind, they will combine with the aim of preventing the leading player from winning still more, even if they cannot reduce his score by forcing him to win tricks that contain Knaves. In the same way, if two players have an advanced score, and the third is down the course, the two who are ahead will so play that such points as they cannot themselves win will go to the player with the low score rather than to the one with the high score.

The game, therefore, gives ample scope for clever play. Until the last Knave has been played, a player has to strike a balance between the incentive to take a trick, and so score a point, and the fear of being saddled with a Knave, resulting in a loss.

There is much more in the game than appears on the surface. Consider the hands in the illustration shown overleaf (see page 136).

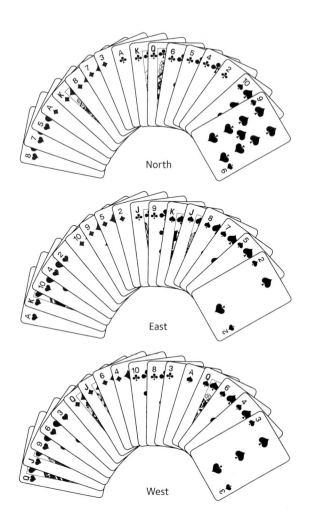

No score to anyone.

East deals and the ♣7 is turned up. With his many trumps, North appears to be in a position to score well. In reality, however, his hand is not good, because although the trumps give him the advantage of winning tricks, this is more than offset by the fact that he is in the dangerous position of being forced to take Knaves. Indeed, North is very likely to come out with a poor score; against good play by West he will be hard put to avoid taking the Knaves of both hearts and diamonds – for a loss of seven points – and, in any case, he can hardly avoid taking one of them.

Loo

The modern player may be forgiven for mistaking the meaning of the name which has been attached to this game! In fact it is a truncation of the now obsolete 'lanterloo', from the French *lanturlu*, a word best translated by our word 'fiddlesticks'. There are several variations of the game, of which Three-card Loo, Five-card Loo and Irish Loo are described here.

Number of players

Loo is suitable for any number of players, though the best number is six or seven.

Cards

The standard 52-card pack is used, with the cards ranking from Ace (high) to 2 (low), except in Five-card Loo, in which the ♣J is the highest ranking card (see Five-card Loo on page 138).

The first player to deal puts into a pool an agreed number of units. It may be any number divisible by three. Three cards are then dealt, one card at a time, to each player, and to an extra hand that is known as 'miss'. The top card of the remainder of the pack is turned up to denote the trump suit.

How to play

The dealer offers the player on his immediate left the choice of refusing to play, playing with the cards dealt to him, or exchanging his cards for 'miss' and playing with those. In turn, each player is offered the same choice, though, of course, once a player has chosen to exchange his hand for miss, a subsequent player is reduced to choosing between playing with the cards dealt to him or not playing the hand. Once a player has made a decision he must stand by it, and if he has chosen not to play he throws his cards face downwards to the centre of the table, and waits for the next round of play.

The player who first chooses to play leads to the first trick. Thereafter, the usual rules apply whereby the player who wins a trick leads to the next. The play is governed by the following rules:

- A player must follow suit if he can, and must head the trick if he can.
- If a player cannot follow suit he must trump if he can, and if the trick has already been trumped he must overtrump if he can.
- If the player on lead holds the Ace of trumps (or the King if the Ace has been turned up) he must lead it.
- If the player on lead holds two or more trumps he must lead one of them, and if there are only two players in the game he must lead the highest.

- A player who fails to comply with any of these rules, when able to do so, is deemed to have revoked; the pool is divided among the non-offenders, and the offender pays the full amount back to the pool.
- When the hand has been played those who have won tricks divide the pool between them: one-third of the amount in it to the winner of each trick.
- Those who have not won a trick are looed, and must put into the pool as many units as there were in it at the beginning of the deal. Unlimited loo, however, can come very expensive, and in practice it is essential for the players to agree upon limiting the losses of looed players.
- If no player is looed, the next dealer replenishes the pool as at the beginning of the game.
- If every player refuses to play, the dealer takes the entire pool and the next dealer replenishes it.
- If only one player chooses to play the dealer must come into the game against him, but if he holds a weak hand, he may protect himself against loss by announcing that he will play for the pool. In this event he is not looed if he fails to win a trick, and, in return for the concession, he leaves in the pool any amount to which he may be entitled by reason of his having won tricks.

FIVE-CARD LOO

This is a variation of the parent game that differs from it in the following ways:

- Every player is dealt five cards, and as there are five tricks to be won the number of units paid into the pool must be divisible by five.
- There is no miss.
- A player may exchange cards by drawing them from the stock. He may exchange any number of cards that he chooses, and once he has exchanged a card he must enter the game.
- The highest card in the pack is the ♣J. It is known as Pam. It ranks as a trump and takes precedence even over the Ace; if, however, a player leads the Ace of trumps and announces 'Pam be civil' the holder of Pam is debarred from playing it to the trick.
- If a player holds five cards of a suit, or four cards of a suit and Pam, he is said to hold a flush and must expose his hand at once. He wins the pool and all the other players, except those who may hold flushes or Pam, are looed.
- If one or more players hold flushes, one in the trump suit wins over one in a plain suit, and between two or more in a plain suit, the one with the highest card is the winner. If two or more in plain suits are exactly equal the pool is divided.

IRISH LOO

This game is a combination of the three-card and five-card games, and is considered by competent players to be the best of the several variations.

Every player is dealt three cards, there is no Pam and no miss, but a player is allowed to exchange cards by drawing from the stock. The game is played in the same way as the parent game, with the novelty that if clubs are trumps everyone must enter the game. It is known as Club Law and makes it imperative that the penalty for being looed must be limited to a reasonable amount.

Strategy

Loo, in all its variations, is so bound up by hard and fast rules of play, already mentioned, that there is very little to be said about the play of the cards. At best one can only say that the most successful player is not he who knows how to play, but he who knows when to elect and when to refuse to play.

The most important point to note is that, apart from Pam at Five-card Loo, there are only three certain tricks, i.e. the Ace, the King-Queen combination and the Queen-Jack-10 combination of trumps. Usually the player who holds the Queen, Jack and 9 of trumps will win a trick, but it is not certain, and he may be looed if in an unfavourable position at the table. It is the same if a player holds the King and 3 of the trump suit. He will certainly win a trick if the suit is led and

he is the last to play, but if he is not, he may not win a trick, because if the 4 is played he is compelled to play the King and a later player may win with the Ace. It leaves him only with the remote possibility of winning a trick with the lone 3 of trumps.

Perhaps in practice the picture is not so depressing as it appears in theory, because, even if there are seven players in the game, a large number of cards remain in the stock. Some of the high cards, therefore, may not be active and a combination such as a Jack and 10 of trumps, or even a Jack, 10 and a card in a plain suit, may win a trick.

In general a player is advised not to be too cautious about electing to play if he holds a weak hand, but he is advised to be careful. In practice he should keep a close watch on the number of units in the pool and weigh up the possible loss against the possible gain. If, for example, there are 15 units in the pool at Five-card Loo and the cost of being looed is 10 units it is not worth entering the play with a weak hand because, look at it which way you like, the cost of being looed is three times more than the possible gain that will accrue by winning one trick. It is not a good bet.

Napoleon

Napoleon, usually called Nap, is one of the simplest of all card games. It is essentially an easy betting game for up to six players.

Number of players

Any number up to six may play, each playing for himself.

Cards

The full pack of 52 cards is used, cards ranking from Ace (high) to 2 (low).

Each player is dealt five cards.

How to play

Beginning with the player on the left of the dealer, every player in turn must either pass or declare to win a specified number of tricks in the ascending order: Two, Three, Four and Nap (a declaration to win all five tricks).

The player who has contracted to win most tricks leads to the first trick and the card that he leads determines the trump suit. Play follows the usual routine of trick-taking games: a player must follow suit if he can, otherwise he may discard a card or trump if he has one in hand. The player who wins a trick leads to the next.

Stakes are paid only on the number of tricks contracted for. Those won above, or lost below, the number contracted for are ignored. The usual method of settlement is by means of a level-money transaction:

Declaration	Declarer wins	Declarer loses
Two	2 units	2 units
Three	3 units	3 units
Four	4 units	4 units
Nap	10 units	5 units

Payment is made to, and received from, all players at the table.

Nap(oleon) is such an elementary game that in some circles interest is added to it by introducing a number of extraordinary declarations by way of adding variations:

Misery is the opposite to Napoleon, in that each player must make a declaration to lose every trick. It ranks between the declaration of Three and Four, and though normally it is played without a trump suit, some play it with a trump suit, determined as in the parent game by the opening lead. It pays and wins three units.

Wellington is a declaration to win all five tricks at double stakes. It can only be declared, however, once a declaration of Nap has been made.

Blücher takes this one stage further and is a declaration to win all five tricks at triple stakes. It can only be declared, however, once a declaration of Wellington has been made.

Peep Nap sanctions the player who has declared Nap (or Wellington or Blücher if these declarations are permitted) to exchange the top card of the pack for one in his own hand.

Purchase nap sanctions each player before declaring to exchange any number of cards in his hand for fresh cards, by paying into a pool one unit for every card exchanged. The pool is carried forward from deal to deal and taken by the first player to win Nap (or Wellington or Blücher if these declarations are permitted).

Sir Garnet allows an extra hand of five cards to be dealt in the usual way and placed in the centre of the table. Instead of making the usual bid, each player in turn, to the left of the dealer, has the opportunity to pick up the five extra cards, adding it to his original hand so that he now holds ten cards. He then discards five cards, without revealing them. The player is then obliged to bid Nap, but if he fails to make the bid, he must pay double the normal penalty.

SEVEN-CARD NAPOLEON

In this variation seven cards are dealt to each player, and a player cannot contract to win fewer than three tricks. There is no Wellington and no Blücher. Misery is optional and, if permitted, ranks between Nap and Six.

Apart from these amendments, the game is played in the same way as the parent game.

Settlement is made as follows:

Declaration	Declarer wins	Declarer loses
Three	3 units	3 units
Four	4 units	4 units
Nap	10 units	5 units
Misery	10 units	5 units
Six	18 units	9 units
Seven	28 units	14 units

Payment is made to, and received from, all players at the table.

Oklahoma

Oklahoma is a game of the Rummy family, not unlike Canasta. It is less complex than Canasta but satisfying to those who like to make lots of melds and hold plenty of cards in their hands.

Number of players

Oklahoma is best for three players, as described here, but can be played by two, four or five players with the same rules.

Cards

Two standard packs are joined together and a Joker added, making a pack of 105 cards in all. The cards rank from Ace (high) to 2 (low), but all eight 2s and the Joker are wild cards (representing any card the player wishes). Ace in a sequence can be either high or low but cannot be used 'round the corner (King, Ace, 2). The cards have special values in scoring, as detailed later.

Players draw to decide dealer, the lowest card drawn denoting the dealer (the Joker counts low). Thereafter the winner of a hand deals the next.

Each player is dealt 13 cards, one at a time. The remaining cards are placed face down in the centre to form the stock. The top card is placed face up beside the stock to begin a discard pile.

How to play

The object is to form sequences or sets. The player to the dealer's left may take the turned-up card into his hand or refuse it. If he refuses it the second player has the option and if he refuses it the dealer has the option. The card can be taken only by a player who can meld, i.e. use it to complete a set of three or more cards of the same rank, or a sequence of three or more cards of the same suit, which he lays down on the table in front of him. A player who takes the card and melds completes his turn by discarding another card face up in its place, the turn passing to the next player clockwise. Play then proceeds normally as described below.

Should the turn pass round the table and back to dealer's left again, eldest takes the top card from stock into his hand. He may now meld or not, but completes his turn by discarding a card onto the discard pile. Play now proceeds with each player having the option of taking the top card of the discard pile into his hand, or the top card of the stock.

There are two obligations for a player taking the top card of the discard pile. He must immediately meld with it, either by using it to form a new meld or by adding it to a meld he already has on the table. Players may at any time on their turn add cards to their own melds (but not to their opponents'). Having melded with the top card, the player is obliged to take the rest of the discard pile into his hand. He may then make as many melds with these cards as he pleases. His turn does not end until he discards, which he does by beginning a fresh discard pile.

A melded sequence can be as long as 14 cards (a complete suit with an Ace at each end), but a set of cards of the same rank cannot be of more than four cards, whether or not it includes wild cards.

When a wild card (2 or Joker) is used in a sequence, its user must announce the card that it represents, and it cannot be changed. So a player using a 2 to form a meld of, say, ♥9, ♥8, ♣2, specifying the ♣2 as being the ♥7, cannot later add the ♥7 to the meld and use the ♣2 as the ♥6 or ♥10. However, the Joker has a special property. If a player uses one in a meld, and later acquires the card that the Joker represents, he can, on his turn, replace the Joker with the card and take the Joker into his hand for use a second time. A player can take the discard pile if it is headed by the card his Joker represents, by taking the card to replace his Joker. When discarding, a player is not allowed to discard the ♠Q, unless it is the only card left in his hand.

The deal ends either when one player goes out (i.e. melds all his cards and discards) or when the stock is exhausted. A player taking the last card of the stock is allowed to meld, if able, and discard, whereupon the deal ends, and no further melds are allowed.

A player cannot go out without discarding. It follows that a player with two cards only in his hand cannot go out by drawing a card from stock to form a set or sequence with them, because this would leave him with no card to discard, so his only chance is to acquire cards to add to his existing melds. When a player goes out, his opponents cannot add cards from their hands to their melds.

At the end of the deal, each player scores for the cards in his melds, with the cards still held in his hand debited against him. Cards value as follows:

Joker: melded 100; in hand -200.
♠Q: melded 50; in hand -100.
Ace: melded 20; in hand -20.
K, Q, J, 10, 9, 8 (excluding ♠Q): melded 10; in hand -20.
7, 6, 5, 4, 3: melded 5; in hand -5.
2: melded, the value of the card it represents (except ♠Q, when it is worth 10); unmelded -20.

A player who goes out is given a bonus score of 100 points, but not if he goes out on his first turn. A player who goes out who has not previously melded is said to go out 'concealed', and gets an additional bonus of 250 (this does not count towards his running game score). The game score is 1,000 points, the game ending with the deal on which a player passes that score. If two or three pass 1,000 on the same deal, the highest score wins. The winner receives a bonus of 200 for game.

Panguingue

Panguingue is similar to Rummy (see page 148) and arises from the Mexican game of Conquian. It retains the characteristics of using the Spanish 40-card pack and of play rotating to the right.

Number of players

Any reasonable number may play – perhaps six to eight is best.

Cards

Eight of the 40-card packs are used, making a pack of 320 cards. The 40-card pack is formed by removing from a standard pack the 10s, 9s and 8s. It is possible to use fewer packs, but fewer than five should not be used. The cards rank in the order: King, Queen, Jack, 7, 6, 5, 4, 3, 2, Ace. The 320-card pack is shuffled by many hands and amalgamated. Each player draws a card, and the lowest becomes eldest hand. The second lowest becomes dealer and sits on eldest's left (this is because the dealing and the play rotates anti-clockwise).

The final shuffle before the deal is made by the player at the dealer's left. It is unusual for all the cards to be used during one hand, and after the first deal the practice between deals is to shuffle only the cards which have been used together with a batch from the unused cards, these going to the bottom of the total pack. The deal does not rotate – the player to the left of the winner deals the next hand.

Without holding the whole pack in his hand, the dealer deals ten cards to each player in bundles of five. The remaining cards are placed face down to form the stock. It is usual to divide the pack in two so that the stock is not unmanageable. The upper part, called the 'head', is used while the lower part, the 'foot', is put to one side to be used if necessary.

How to play

The top card of the stock is turned face up to begin a discard pile. Beginning with eldest (the player to the dealer's right) and proceeding anti-clockwise, each player in turn announces whether he will stay in the game or drop out. A player who drops out says that he is 'going on top' and pays a forfeit of two chips. The chips are placed on that part of the stock called the foot. His cards are placed face down below the foot, but crosswise, because they do not become part of the stock and must not be used in the hand.

Those players remaining, in turn anti-clockwise, draw a card either from the top of the discard pile or from the top of the stock. The card from the discard pile can be taken only if it can be melded with immediately. A meld, usually called a 'spread', is either of a group or of a sequence, as in the more familiar Rummy, and consists of three cards.

A group consists of three cards of the same rank, but to be valid there are restrictions as to suits. If the rank is King or Ace (called 'non-comoquers') there are no restrictions; any three cards are valid. However, for other ranks, the cards must be either all of the same suit or all of different suits.

A sequence (called a 'stringer') consists of three cards of the same suit in sequence (remembering that a sequence continues from 7 to Jack).

A player may lay down any melds on his turn (if taking the card from the top of the discard pile, he must meld with it, as stated). Subsequently, on his turn, he may add to any of his melds, called 'laying off'. A player may lay off on his own melds only – not on his opponents'. A sequence may be added to by laying off additional cards in sequence. A group of the same suit may be added to by laying off cards of the same rank and suit. A group in different suits may be added to by laying off cards of the same rank in any suit (this means that such a meld is not restricted to four cards only).

A player may take the top of the discard pile to lay off on one of his melds.

Certain melds are called 'conditions', and a player who makes one immediately collects chips from all other players. So far as groups are concerned, certain ranks (7s, 5s and 3s) are called 'valle cards' or value cards. The five classes of condition melds are as follows:

- A group of valle cards of different suits (worth one chip from each player).
- A group of valle cards in the same suit (worth four chips in spades, two in other suits).
- A group of non-valle cards in the same suit (worth two chips in spades, one in other suits).
- A sequence of Ace, 2, 3 (worth two chips in spades and one in other suits).
- A sequence of King, Queen, Jack (worth two chips in spades and one in other suits).

A player who lays off on a condition collects again from each player its value, except for three valle cards in the same suit he collects only two chips in spades and one in other suits. A player collects each time he lays off on a condition. If a player lays off three or more cards on a meld, he may split it into two separate melds, provided that each half is valid. By doing so he may create a condition. For example, if he adds to a sequence of ♦ 5, 4, 3 the ♦2, the ♦6 and the ♦A, he may split the sequence of six cards into two sequences: ♦ A, 2, 3 and ♦ 6, 5, 4. This creates a condition (Ace, 2, 3) and the player collects one chip from every other player (or two if it is in spades).

A player may also take a card or cards from a meld to which he has laid off to form a new meld, provided that he leaves a valid meld. This is called 'borrowing'. For example, if he makes a meld of ♥ J, 7, 6 to which he adds ♥5, 4, he may later borrow the ♥ 5, 4 to make a new meld with ♥3 or another ♥6. Or he may borrow the ♥J to make, for example, a meld of ♥J, ♣J, ♠J. But he could not borrow the ♥7, or ♥6, or ♥5, because to take one of those cards would not leave a valid meld.

The object of each player is to meld all his cards ('go out') – whereupon he wins the game.

A player's turn consists of taking either the top card of the discard pile or stock, melding or laying off, if he wishes, and, except when going out, discarding. A player who goes out may not discard; thus to go out a player needs 11 cards melded on the table.

If the top card of the discard pile can be laid off on a meld of the player whose turn it is, any other player can demand that he take the card and lay it off. This might be done to disrupt the hand of the player in play, since having laid off the card he is forced to discard.

It follows that a player with nine cards melded and one in his hand still requires to find two cards to lay off. Should he draw a card from stock which he lays off on his melds, he must still discard the card in his hand. This leaves him with ten cards melded and none in his hand, but he has not gone out. He must continue to draw, on his turn, until he draws a card which he can lay off, and

thus go out with 11 cards melded.

If a player is in the situation of having ten cards melded, the previous player must not discard a card which would allow him to go out (unless the previous player has no alternative).

The winner of the game (i.e. the player who goes out) wins one chip from all the others remaining in the game (in some schools he collects two chips from any player who has not melded). He also collects from each player chips representing the values of his conditions. (As a player collects for conditions as he melds them, the winner therefore collects twice for his conditions.) The winner also takes the chips of those players who dropped out, i.e. those chips stacked on the foot of the stock.

In the unlikely event of the stock (both head and foot) being exhausted before any player has gone out, the discard pile is turned over and becomes the stock, play continuing as usual.

So far as strategy is concerned, a player should try to hold cards giving multiple options of melding rather than isolated pairs or possible sequences with gaps in the middle. As the number and rank of cards held in the hand are immaterial in the settling when an opponent goes out, there is no point in laying down melds prematurely. However, a player should lay down and collect for conditions and get down a first meld if there is a double payment to the winner by players who have failed to meld.

Polignac

Polignac is a French, 18th-century, trick-taking game with its roots in Hearts (see page 131) and Black Maria (see page 83). It is sometimes called Quatre Valets or Four Jacks.

Number of players

Polignac is for four players.

Cards

A 32-card pack is used, i.e. a standard pack with 6s, 5s, 4s, 3s and 2s removed.

Eight cards are dealt face downwards to each player.

How to play

The player on the left of the dealer leads the first trick. Thereafter the player who wins a trick leads the next. A player must follow suit to the card led, if he can, otherwise he may discard.

The object of the game is to avoid taking tricks that contain a Jack, and one point is lost for every Jack taken, with the exception of the ♠J (Polignac) which costs the winner two points.

The usual method of scoring is to play a pre-arranged number of deals (that should be a multiple of four) and he who loses the least number of points is the winner.

It is a very simple game, but some skill is called for, particularly when it comes to choosing the best card to lead after a trick has been won, correct discarding when unable to follow suit,

and deciding whether or not to win a trick when the choice is available.

SLOBBERHANNES

If we may judge by its name, Slobberhannes is either of Dutch or German origin. It is a very simple game played in the same way as Polignac. The only difference is that a player loses one point if he wins the first trick, one point if he wins the last, one point if he wins the trick containing the ♣Q, and a further one point (making four points in all) if he wins all three penalty tricks.

Rummy

Rummy, or Rum, as the name is often abbreviated to, is one of the most popular card games. Derivatives include Gin Rummy (see page 60) and Canasta (see page 111). The Mexican game of Conquian is considered to be ancestral to all rummy games.

Number of players

Any number up to six may play.

Cards

The full pack of 52 cards is used. They rank from King (high) to Ace (low).

Ten cards are dealt to each player if only two play; seven cards if three or four play; and six cards if five or six play. The rest of the pack (the stock) is placed face downwards in the centre of the table, and the top card of it is turned face upwards and laid alongside it to start the discard pile.

How to play

The object of the game is for a player to make sets of three or more cards of the same rank, or sequences of three or more cards of the same suit (the Ace being low) and declare them by exposing them on the table, after drawing a card from the stock or discard pile and before discarding a card from the hand.

At the same time a player may add one or more proper cards to sequences and sets already declared either by himself or the other players. Each player in turn, beginning with the one on the

left of the dealer, must take into his hand either the top card of the stock or the top card of the discard pile, and discard a card from his hand, but if he has drawn the top card of the discard pile he must not discard it in the same turn.

If the stock is exhausted before any player declares all his hand, the discard pile is turned face downwards and becomes the stock.

The player who is first to declare all his cards wins the hand, and the other players pay him ten points each for every court card left in their hands, one point for every Ace, and its pip value for every other card. If a player declares all his cards in one turn he scores rummy and is paid double.

Rummy is a simple game that has acquired a number of improvements and many variations.

BOATHOUSE RUMMY

In this version, a player may draw the top card of the stock; or he may draw the top card of the discard pile and then either the top card of the stock or the next card of the discard pile. He may, however, discard only one card.

In a sequence the Ace may be either high, low, or round the corner.

The play does not come to an end until a player can declare his entire hand in one turn.

A losing player pays only for the unmatched cards in his hand, but Aces are paid for at 11 points each.

CONTINENTAL RUMMY

This variation of the parent game is suitable for any number of players up to 12. If two to five play then two packs with two Jokers are used; if six to eight play then three packs with three Jokers are used; and if nine to 12 play four packs with four Jokers are used.

Each player receives 15 cards. A player may not declare until all 15 of his cards are melded either in five three-card sequences, or in three four-card sequences and one three-card sequence, or in one five-card, one four-card and two three-card sequences. Sets of three or more cards of the same rank are of no value. A Joker may be used as any card. The Ace may be high or low, but not round the corner.

There are many ways of scoring, but generally the following rules apply: the winner collects from all the other players one unit from each for winning, and two units from each for every Joker in his hand.

Stock

Discard pile

A good rummy player will maximize his opportunities. With the hand above the player should take the ♠5 and discard ♣9, as ♠5 offers alternative chances of melding: either with ♥5 or ♠6

GAMBLER'S RUMMY

This version is so called because it is the variation of the parent game that is most frequently played for high stakes.

Only four players can play in this version of Rummy and each is dealt seven cards. The Ace is low and, as in the parent game, counts only one point in the settlement. A player is not allowed to declare all his hand in one turn. He must declare it in at least two turns, but he is not debarred from going out during his second turn even if on his previous turn he played off only one card on another player's declaration.

The stock is gone through only once. When it is exhausted the players must draw the top card of the discard pile, and the game ends when a player refuses it.

KNOCK RUMMY OR POKER RUM

This version is played in the same way as the parent game, but a player does not expose his sequences and sets on the table. Instead, after drawing a card, he knocks on the table, and then discards. Play comes to an end. Players separate their matched cards from their unmatched ones, and each announces the count of his unmatched cards. The player with the lowest count wins the difference in counts from all the other players. If a player ties with the knocker for the lowest count he wins over the knocker. If the knocker does not have the lowest count he pays a penalty of ten points to the player with the lowest count. If the knocker has all his cards matched when he knocks and wins, he receives an extra 25 points from all the other players.

Scotch Whist

Scotch Whist is sometimes called Catch the Ten because one of the objects of the game is to win the trick that contains the 10 of the trump suit. It first appeared in *The American Hoyle* (or *Gentleman's Handbook of Games*) of 1868.

Number of players

Any number from two to eight may play. If two, three, five or seven play, each plays for himself. If four, six or eight play they may either play each for himself, or form into partnerships.

Cards

Scotch Whist is played with a pack of 36 cards. The deck is reduced by removing the 2s, 3s, 4s, and 5s from the standard pack. The cards rank from Ace (high) to 6 (low) with the exception that the Jack of the trump suit is promoted to rank above the Ace. Every player must begin with the same number of cards: if five or seven players take part, the ♠6 is removed from the pack; and if eight players take part, all four 6s are taken out.

Dealing varies with the number of players taking part in the game. If two play, each receives 18 cards that are dealt in three separate hands of six cards each, to be played independently; if three play, each receives 12 cards that are dealt in two separate hands of six cards each, to be played independently; if four or more play, the cards are dealt out in the normal clockwise rotation. In every case the dealer turns up the last card to indicate the trump suit.

How to play

The player on the left of the dealer leads the first trick. Thereafter the player who wins a trick leads the next. Play follows the usual routine of trick-taking games: a player must follow suit, if he can, to the suit led and if he cannot he may either trump the trick or discard on it.

The object of the game is to win tricks containing the five top trump cards, and the player, or partnership, that does so scores 11 points for the Jack, four points for the Ace, three points for the King, two points for the Queen, and ten points for the 10. Over and above this, each player, or partnership, counts the number of cards taken in tricks, and scores one point for every card in excess of the number

originally dealt to him, or them. The game ends when a player, or partnership, has reached an agreed total, usually 41 points.

It stands to reason that a player must direct his play towards winning tricks that contain the top cards of the trump suit, particularly that which contains the 10, since the Jack can only go to the player to whom it has been dealt, and usually the luck of the deal determines who will win the tricks that contain the Ace, King and Queen.

In a partnership game the player who has been dealt the 10, either singleton or doubleton, would be well advised to lead it. It gives a good score if his partner is able to win with the Jack; if an opponent wins the trick the partnership must hope to recover by aiming to win as many tricks as possible. If the game is being played all against all, the player who has been dealt the 10 should try and get rid of all the cards in his shortest suit, so that he can win the 10 by trumping with it.

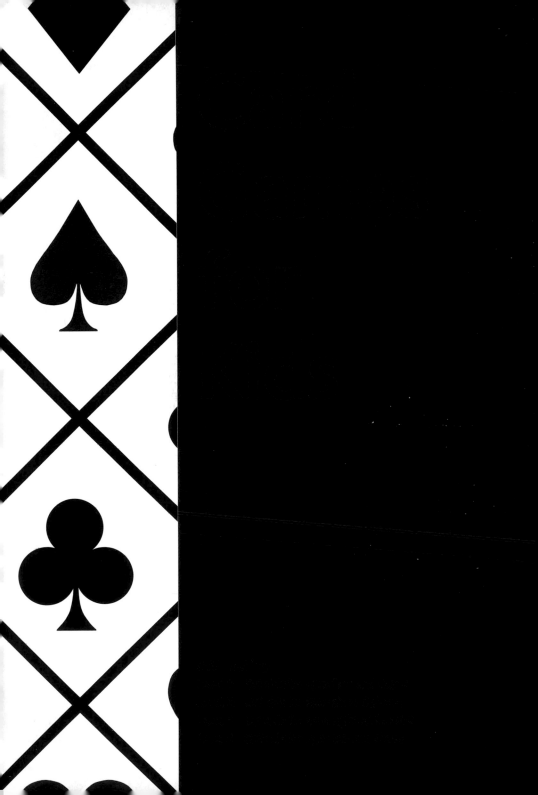

Beat my Neighbour

Also known as Beat my Neighbour out of Doors, and Beggar my Neighbour, this is one of the all-time favourite card games for children. It's very relaxing, as it requires no decision-making at all.

Number of players

This is a game for two players.

Age and skill level

For ages six and above; level 2.

Cards

A standard 52-card deck is shuffled and dealt between the two players so that each has half the pack. The players hold their cards in a face-down stack.

How to play

The player who is not dealing starts the game, turning over the top card of his or her stack and placing it in the middle of the table.

The rank of card played determines how many cards the next player must lay. If the card was a numbered pip card, the second player need only lay one card. However, if the card was a 'pay card' (that is to say, either an Ace or a court card), he or she must lay the following cards in compensation:

> **For an Ace** – four pip cards
> **For a King** – three pip cards
> **For a Queen** – two pip cards
> **For a Jack** – one pip card

When payment is complete, the player who laid the pay card collects up the cards from the waste pile and adds them to his or her hand. They then restart the play by laying another card in the centre of the table as before.

If a player turns up a pay card when they are in the midst of paying their opponent for a card, the earlier pay card is void and the opponent must compensate the other player. For example, John puts down a King and Anna begins paying him three, turning over a four, a five, then a Jack. The Jack means that John must now compensate Anna by putting down one card. He plays a five and Anna collects the waste pile and restarts the game.

Jacks are the most valuable cards as they give a player the chance to win the waste pile while offering only a minimal chance to their opponent of turning up a pay card in the midst of their compensation.

The winner is the player who collects all the cards, leaving their opponent with none. However, this situation can take hours, days or weeks to achieve. In many cases, it is the player who gives up last who wins the game by default!

Bisley

Bisley is a patience classic which will test the brainpower of adults and children alike.

Number of players

This is a game for one player.

Age and skill level

For ages ten and above; level 4.

Cards

Remove the Aces from the pack and lay them out, face up, as the first four cards in a row of 13. Add three further rows of 13, as per the illustration below.

How to play

The bottom card in each column is active and can be moved either onto the foundation piles (the Aces), building upwards by suit, or it can be built on other columns, either up or down, providing the card moved is of the same suit as the one it joins.

The player's first objective should be to free the Kings from the layout. When a King is exposed, it is moved to the top of the board and positioned directly above the corresponding Ace. The King becomes a second foundation card and can be built on in descending order.

Only single cards can be moved. Shifting whole or part of a column is not allowed. The space left vacant by the removal of the last card in a column is not filled.

Success arrives when you have removed all the cards from the layout onto the foundation piles. It doesn't matter whether you build more cards onto the Ace or the King of a particular suit and it is irrelevant where the two sequences meet. If there are no cards left in the layout, you've won.

Active cards

Cardgo

This is a card game that harnesses the inexplicable addictiveness of bingo. The opportunity to win prizes will prove irresistible for any pre-teen partygoer.

Number of players

This is a game for two or more players.

Age and skill level

For ages five and above; level 1.

Cards

This is definitely a game that requires supervision, so appoint an adult to act as dealer and game caller. Once the dealer has all the players seated around a table, he or she deals five cards to each and places the remainder of the pack face down at his or her side.

Each player holds their five cards in their hand, so their opponents cannot see.

How to play

The game begins when the dealer turns over the top card of his or her stack and announces its value; so, for example, if the top card is a four of diamonds, they will simply say 'Four'. The dealer continues to turn the cards over, announcing them at a steady and unbroken pace until the game ends.

The players check each newly revealed card against those they hold in their hand. If they have a card of matching value, they must place it face down in front of them. The flow of the game must be continuous; tell the players that if they are distracted and miss a card, you will not hold the game up for them to backtrack. Concentration is the essence of this game.

The winner is the first player to turn all their cards face down. When this feat is achieved, the victorious player must shout 'Cardgo'. If two players put their cards down at the same time, it is the first to call 'Cardgo' who wins the game.

SUITS IN THE HOUSE

If you want to get specific and make things a little harder, you can play the game with a divided pack. Simply split the pack by colour, separating the red cards from the black. Deal the reds to the players and keep the black cards as the stock. If you have more than five players, you will need two packs of cards.

Dealer's card

Player's hand

Cheat

With minimal rules and scope to bluff, cheat, shout and accuse, this is the perfect game with which to kick off the card playing at any family gathering.

Number of players

This is a game for two or more players.

Age and skill level

For ages five and above; level 2.

Cards

Seat players around a table, spacing them so that their cards are out of view of their opponents. If you have more than four players, you may like to use two decks of cards shuffled together.

The players pick a card from the deck. The person with the lowest card is the dealer, who then distributes the entire deck between the players as evenly as possible. Cards are dealt individually and face down.

How to play

The player to the left of the dealer starts the game by placing a card face down in the centre of the table and naming its value. For example, saying 'Four'.

The turn now passes around the table in a clockwise direction, and players must build on the previously played card by playing one higher, one lower or the same. So, for example, the next player must now lay a card face down on top of the four and say 'Three', 'Four' or 'Five'. They can also play more than one card; so they could say 'Two threes' or 'Three fives'. Of course, they may not have any fives, let alone three of them, but in this game that doesn't matter. There is no option to pass or take any kind of penalty. If you haven't got a playable card, you simply have to play another card and bluff.

If a player suspects that an opponent is bluffing and has laid a card that is not what they said it was, the player can accuse their opponent of cheating. The accuser shouts 'Cheat' and the card (or cards) played is revealed. If the accuser has made a good call, the pile of cards on the table passes to the bluffer as punishment. However, if the call of cheat was wrong and the card played is correct, the accuser has to take up all the cards in the centre. The player who picks up the cards restarts the game.

The person who gets rid of all his or her cards first is the winner. For second and third places, players need to add up the numbers on their cards. Picture cards count as ten points and an Ace counts as 15. The person with the least points is second, and so on.

Colonel

A compulsive and addictive Rummy variant (see page 148), Colonel will have the noisiest of children and teenagers enraptured. The rules are simple, the game play is slick and the victory is always sweet.

Number of players

This is a game for two players.

Age and skill level

For ages nine and above; level 3.

Cards

Both players are dealt ten cards, which are placed face down in front of them. The remainder of the cards are placed face down in a neat stock pile in the centre of the table and the top card is turned over and placed to one side.

How to play

The non-dealer leads off and can take either the exposed face-up card (which is called the option card) or the unseen top card from the stock pile. Whichever they choose, they must then discard one of their cards, which is placed face up and becomes the new option card.

At the end of their turn the player may now declare any sequences or sets of cards they have completed. They do not have to do this, but if they want to, the sets are placed face up on the table.

Either player can add to a declared three-of-a-kind or sequence during the game, provided they do so during their turn. So, for example, if Sarah declares three Kings during her turn, her opponent, Joe, can put down the odd King he holds when it is his turn.

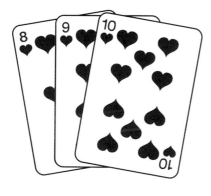

Sequence

Three-of-a-kind

Players take turns alternately, with each free to take either the stock or option card. The first player to empty their hand and play out all their cards is the winner. Of course, this situation does not always arise, so if the stock pile is emptied before either player can play out their cards, the game is decided on points. The players count up the value of the cards held in hand, with court cards and Aces counting ten and all others the value of their pips. The player with the lowest total is the winner.

Rising to the challenge

An optional twist on Colonel sees the introduction of a challenge. At any point during the game prior to the stock pile running out, one of the players can challenge their opponent to put down their cards and have a count-up. If the player challenged declines, the game continues as normal; however, if they accept, play is brought to a halt and the cards are scored in the same way as when the stock pile runs out.

Scoring

Colonel can be played on a game-by-game basis, with the first to win a set number of hands declared the champion, or it can be played using a more complicated but traditional points system. In the latter scenario, the winning player receives points commensurate with the difference between the value of the cards held

at the end of the game compared to their opponent's closing hand. So, for example, if Alice holds two Kings (value = 20) when the stock runs out but Max has two Queens and a Jack (value = 30 points), Alice wins the game and adds the score of ten (30 − 20 = 10) to her total. The first player to reach an agreed figure is the champion.

Winning way

As in Rummy, the key to success is to keep your options open for as long as possible and to note the cards collected and ignored by your opponent. Avoid pursuing sets that can be completed by only one card, and instead go after those that offer a greater probability of success.

Demon

Demon is a demanding game that calls for concentration in abundance and a large helping of brainpower.

Number of players

This is a game for one player.

Age and skill level

For ages ten and above; level 4.

Cards

Deal 13 cards from a well-shuffled deck into a stack. The cards are placed face down on the table and become 'the heel'. The top card of the heel is turned over. To the right of the heel, deal out one card to establish the foundation card for the hand. Unlike many patience games, Demon does not use Aces or Kings as its foundations but instead uses this variable card which is defined by the deal. Cards of the same suit are built onto the foundations in ascending order and go 'round the corner'. For example, if the foundation card is a three, players must next play a four onto it, then a five and so on. They carry on building upwards until they get to the King, then complete the suit by playing the Ace and, lastly, the two.

Finally, deal out four face-up cards from the deck beneath the foundation row to start the layout.

Foundation card

The heel

How to play

The object of the game is to play all the cards from the stock and the heel onto the foundation cards. When you have built all 52 cards onto the foundations, you've won.

Start by seeing if any of the cards in the layout can be built onto one another or the foundations. Single cards can be moved from the bottom of one column providing they are of alternating colour and descending sequence to the bottom card of the column they join. Entire columns can also be moved, but fragments of columns cannot.

Any spaces made in the layout must be immediately filled by the top card from the heel. Once a card has been played from the heel, the next card in line is turned over. When the heel is exhausted, players may fill gaps in the layout from the waste pile but they are no longer obliged to fill these gaps immediately and can, instead, wait for an opportune moment or card, if they would rather do so.

The remaining undealt 34 cards form a stock, which is held in hand. The stock is dealt to a waste pile three cards at a time, although at the end of the deal you may find there are fewer than three cards, in which case you should turn the cards one by one. Cards from the stock can be played either onto the foundation cards or onto the layout. The stock is dealt and re-dealt until either the game is won or becomes blocked.

Be warned – this game is far from easy and it make take you many deals before you make it 'out'.

Winning way

Many youngsters will struggle initially to summon up the powers of concentration needed to succeed at Demon. However, you should encourage them to persevere and, most importantly, to take their time. Only by checking each card carefully against both the layout and the foundations does a player stand any chance of success.

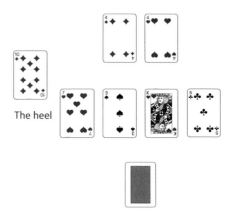

The heel

The stock

As soon as a card of the same rank as the first foundation card appears, it should be moved to the foundation and replaced with the top card of the heel. The next card in the heel is then turned face up.

Dominoes

Dominoes, or Sevens, offers a rarely found combination of speed and strategy, making it a firm favourite with youngsters eager to move on from more frivolous games of fun and fortune.

Number of players

This is a game for two or more players.

Age and skill level

For ages six and above; level 2.

Cards

Cut the cards to select a dealer; the player who draws the lowest card deals. The entire deck of 52 cards is distributed as evenly as possible between the players. Any inequity will be redressed providing the deal rotates for each hand.

The player to the left of the dealer leads but must play a seven to start the game. If he or she doesn't have a seven,

they must 'knock' and the turn passes around the table in a clockwise direction.

How to play

Once a seven has been played, the next player must try to play onto that card and build up the layout. If the game had commenced with the first player laying a seven of diamonds, the next player has three choices: build in suit sequence (playing the six of diamonds to the left of the seven or the eight to the right); play another seven of a different suit above the opening card; or 'knock'. A knock occurs when a player is unable to add to the layout in any direction, in which case he or she says 'Knock!' and the turn passes on.

As the game develops, there will be four rows of cards building to the left and right, and players can build on any of these rows in either ascending or descending sequence.

The first player to get rid of all of his or her cards is the winner. Play continues until only one player is left holding cards; that unlucky soul collects the wooden spoon and is the Dominoes dunce.

Foundation
cards (7s)

Dundee

Dundee is a compelling game of chance which will keep kids occupied for hours, and what's more, it's simple and can be played almost anywhere. It is also known as Second Guess.

Number of players

This is a game for one player.

Age and skill level

For ages six and above; level 2.

Cards

Shuffle the cards and settle down – you will be playing for some time!

How to play

Hold the shuffled deck face down. Before turning over the first card, you must announce a rank of card, for example, 'Five'. Say the word out loud and be clear – you will only cheat yourself if you mumble or kid yourself that you've forgotten what you said.

You must try to avoid predicting the card you are about to turn over. If your announcement coincides with the rank of card revealed, your turn reaches an immediate end. So, back to our example, if you'd announced 'Four' and then turned over the four of hearts, the game's up. The cards must then be shuffled again and the game recommences.

The game continues in this way until either you predict a card or you get through the entire deck. This latter situation is extremely rare. The game is also made harder by the rule that you cannot make the same prediction in consecutive turns.

You have won the game when you've turned over the entire deck and so have no more cards held in your hand. If you don't make it to the end of the pack, you can count up the remaining cards and make a mental note of how close you got. Keep trying to beat your personal best and, if you've got a sibling to play against, see if you can outperform them.

Go Boom!

This classic is a favourite among children and a great introduction to cards for youngsters. But don't be fooled – easy doesn't mean boring!

Number of players

This is a game for four players. More can play with a second pack of cards.

Age and skill level

For ages eight and above; level 3.

Cards

All the players pick a card from the deck. The person with the highest card deals. Seven cards are dealt face down to each player. All other cards are collected into a stack in the middle and the top card is turned over and put face up next to it to start the game. This is the widow.

How to play

The aim is to cover up the widow with one of the seven cards in your hand. The card you play must be of the same rank or suit as the widow. If you don't have a card that you can put down, you must take a card from the stack. It is now the next person's turn.

It's better to put down higher cards if you have the choice. Once all the cards from the stack are gone, everyone carries on playing from the cards in their hands, and if you can't put a card down, then you miss a turn.

The person who runs out of cards first is the winner. To find out who comes second and third, turn all the cards over and add up the numbers on your cards. Picture cards count as ten points and an Ace counts as 15 points. The person with the most points is the loser and the person with the least points is second.

Winning way

Try to get rid of your higher-value cards as early as possible. To this end, when you cover the widow with a card of matching suit (rather than rank), you should try to put down an Ace, a court card or the highest-valued pip card you can. That way, if you don't get rid of all of your cards, your deficit total won't be too high and you'll have a chance of coming second.

Widow   Stack

Go Fish

Go Fish is an uncomplicated gem that will entertain youngsters and encourage a little skulduggery and much excitement.

Number of players

This is a game for three to six players.

Age and skill level

For ages six and above; level 2.

Cards

Each player is dealt five cards. The remaining cards are set face-down on the table in a stock.

How to play

The player to the dealer's left (let's call him Arthur) takes the first turn. He asks a specific player for a particular rank (though not suit) of card; for example, 'Martha, give me your Kings'. Arthur can only ask Martha for a rank of card that he already owns (so he can only ask for Kings if he holds a King).

If Martha has any Kings, she must hand them all over to Arthur, who then takes another turn. As long as he continues to ask opponents for cards that they have, Arthur continues to have extra turns.

When Arthur asks an opponent for a rank of card that they do not hold, the opponent shouts 'Go fish'. Arthur must then take the top card from the stock; if that card is of the rank he asked for, he

takes another turn. He must, however, reveal the card to the group before taking another turn.

If the card Arthur drew from the stock is not of the rank he had asked for, his turn ends and the game continues with the player who had shouted 'Go fish' then taking a turn.

When a player collects a complete set of four cards of the same rank, he or she must show them to the other players and set them face down in front of him or her.

There are two ways to win and whichever scenario occurs first brings the game to an end:

1. The person who gets rid of all their cards first is the winner.

2. The stock of cards runs out and the winner is the player who has discarded the most sets of four cards.

The winner announces their win with a shout of 'Got my wish!'.

Winning way

Try to make a mental note of the cards your opponents seek. Also, consider keeping quiet about pairs of cards you hold; wait until another player asks for those cards from a third party, thereby revealing that they hold the other pair.

Golf

Easy to set up, addictive and with the option of a head-to-head, two-player version, Golf with cards is more fun than hitting a small ball around a park in the cold.

Number of players

This is a game for one player, although can be played by two (see page 167).

Age and skill level

For ages eight and above; level 3.

Cards

Shuffle the pack and deal out seven rows of five cards overlapping and face up. This 35-card layout is called the links. The remainder of the cards are held in hand (face down) and dealt one by one onto a waste pile. The objective of the game is to move the cards in the links onto the waste pile.

How to play

1. Turn over the first card held in hand. The card revealed is used to start the waste pile and this can be built on with any of the exposed cards (the bottom card in each column) in the links.

2. Place the cards moved from the links face up on top of the waste pile. You can play cards out of the layout in either ascending or descending order and irrespective of suit. So, for example, if the card on top of the waste pile is an eight of spades, you could add either a seven or a nine of any suit on top of it from the links.

3. When a card has been removed from the bottom row of the links, the card beneath it becomes available for play.

4. Continue adding to the pile by moving cards from the links until there are no cards left that you can play. The sequence can go up and down at will, so just because the first card added to that eight of spades was a nine, you don't have to keep going up. A nine can be followed by a ten and then another nine, and so on.

5. Aces are low (that is, they count as one), and they can only be built on by a two; Kings, similarly, can only be built on by a Queen. In other words, you can't take the sequence 'round the corner' (King-Ace-two).

6. When you've exhausted all the available moves, turn over the next card held in hand and add it to the waste pile.

7. Continue playing until either the links are empty or your stock of cards in hand has run out.

Scoring

You calculate your score for the hole (hand) by counting up the cards left in

The links

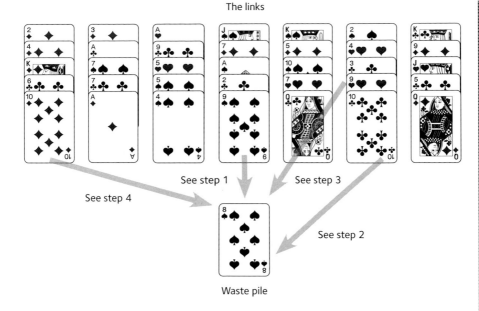

See step 1

See step 3

See step 4

8 ♠

See step 2

Waste pile

the links at the end of play. If, however, you manage to empty the layout, you count up the cards left in hand and award yourself a minus score. Just as in real golf, low scores are best. Ideally, you should aim to play 18 holes for a complete round. Keep a note of your score and see if you can get a score of less than 72 strokes for the round.

Two-player option

The great thing about Golf patience is that it can also be played competitively as a two-player game. You'll need to play with two packs of cards, and have access to a large table with a couple of hours spare! But it's a fun game and the

rewards are worthwhile. The rules for the two-player version are as follows: Each player deals out his or her cards as above and the two hands are played simultaneously.

You can either record the scores for each hole, and the player with the lowest aggregate score at the end of '18 holes' is the winner, or you can adopt 'match play' scoring.

Under match play rules, each hole is either won, lost or halved (drawn), so at any stage a player is 'two up', 'four down' or a similar score as in the real match play game. The round continues until one player has an unassailable lead.

GOPS

GOPS (or Game Of Pure Strategy) has simple rules and is a popular game with younger children, while its strategic qualities hold the interest of older players. This is definitely one for all the siblings.

Number of players

This is a game for two players, although there is also a three-player version (see opposite).

Age and skill level

For ages six and above; level 2.

Cards

Separate a standard 52-card pack into its four suits. Player 1 is given the 13 club cards and player 2 takes the diamonds. The 13 hearts are put to one side, and the 13 spades are shuffled and placed face down in the middle of the playing table.

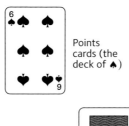

Points cards (the deck of ♠)

Player 1 (all the ♣)

Player 2 (all the ♦)

How to play

The deck of spades are called the points cards and to kick off the game the top card is turned over by player 1. The two players must now bid to win the card that has been revealed. If they win it, the points value of the card is added to their score (Ace = 1; Jack = 11, Queen = 12, King = 13).

The players bid with the cards they hold in hand and can put down any card at any time. All they must do to win is put down a card of higher value than their opponent. Ideally, they must try to put down a card with a value of only one more than that which their rival plays.

The two players place the card they wish to play face down in front of them before simultaneously revealing them. That way there can be no cheating or hesitating to gain an advantage.

The player who plays the highest card wins the hand and claims the value of the point card (spades) to his or her score. If the two players put down cards of equal value, they each take half the value of the point card. Once a hand has been played, the three cards used are discarded. The second player now turns over a points

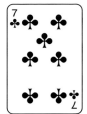

Player 2 (right) wins this hand

card and the game continues for a maximum of 13 hands. The first player to reach or exceed 46 points has an unassailable lead and is the winner.

Keep a written running total of your scores and make sure that each player agrees with what has been recorded. Disagreement over scores can lead to abandoned games and arguments!

Three-player GOPS

A three-player version of GOPS can be played by simply including the discarded set of 13 hearts cards in the game. Player 3 is given the hearts and the spades are placed face down in the middle of the table as before.

The only other modification required is that if all three players bid with cards of equal value, the points for the hand are now shared three ways.

Winning way

Impulsive youngsters can enjoy reasonable success by simply playing high cards to win high cards and vice versa. Of course, that approach will not always work and teenagers may want to think more strategically about their GOPS playing. The game itself takes its name from an acronym which stands for Game Of Pure Strategy, and there are many pages of theory about tactics for GOPS that can be found on the Internet. Unfortunately, these complicated algebraic ramblings, complete with Greek characters and probability symbols, make for impenetrable reading to anybody who has not taken the trouble to get a mathematics doctorate.

I Promise

Whether played for stakes or fun, I Promise is an engaging trick-based game that is a favourite with kids and adults alike.

Number of players

This is a game for two or more players.

Age and skill level

For ages ten and above; level 4.

Cards

Cut the cards to select a dealer; the player who draws the lowest card deals. The dealer distributes the cards until there are not enough to make another complete round of the table. Each player must have the same number of cards. Spare cards are put to one side.

Before the players look at their cards, the dealer turns over the last card dealt to himself or herself as this card indicates the trump suit for the deal.

The players now assess their cards and begin making their 'promises'. The player to the left of the dealer starts the process and must declare how many tricks they 'promise' to win during the hand. The number announced is recorded by the dealer.

How to play

When all players have made their predictions, the trick playing begins, with the player sitting to the left of the dealer laying the first card.

All players must either follow suit or, if they can't, play a trump. If they can do neither, they discard a card. The player laying the highest trump, or if no trumps are played, the highest card that follows in suit, wins that particular trick.

At the end of each trick, the dealer records who won. The trick winner gets to lead off the next trick.

Play continues until the cards run out. The scores are then counted up and players are awarded one point for each winning trick, plus a bonus of ten points if they successfully predicted the number of winning tricks they would make. So, for example, if Tom said he'd win three and did so, he'd earn 13 points for the hand, but if Meryl had said she'd win five but only won four, her total would be four points. Players continue playing hands in this way and the first person to reach a total of 100 points is the winner.

Winning way

Avoid reaching your predicted total too early in the hand, as you may find that your opponents gang up on you to ensure you win an additional trick that will mean you lose your ten-point bonus. For example, if you predict you will win

This player could bid three tricks fairly safely

With only two high cards, this player would be
safer bidding two tricks – or three if spades
or diamonds were trumps

three tricks and take the first two of
eight, you would be unwise to play a
high-ranking trump at the next hand. It
is very likely that you'll take the trick, but
with five hands remaining you cannot
afford to win any more, and you may find
yourself vulnerable should your
opponents decide to conspire against
you. If they all play low-ranking cards,
you may be forced to take an unwanted
victory, taking you over the amount of
tricks that you predicted you'd win .

I PROMISE NOT TO

Variations on the game include reducing
the number of cards by one each time,
moving the deal around the table and
predicting how many tricks you won't
win. In this version, a player has all his
or her points deducted for that round
if they end up winning the amount of
tricks they said that they wouldn't win.

King Albert

This demanding patience game is simple to play. Unfortunately, winning is not quite so straightforward!

Number of players

This is a game for one player.

Age and skill level

For ages ten and above; level 4.

Cards

Shuffle the pack and deal out 45 cards in rows of nine cards, then eight, seven and so on, down to a single card. The cards should be placed overlapping and face up on a table or board.

You should have seven cards left (if you haven't, you've either lost some cards or you're not very good at counting). The seven cards in hand are your 'reserve' and should be placed face up on the board. That's the easy bit done.

How to play

Your first objective is to release the Aces from the layout and establish them as your foundation piles; to do this, you must move other cards out of the way and onto other columns or foundation piles.

You can only move cards onto other columns in descending sequences of alternating colour, and you can only move single cards or complete columns – nothing in between. If you move an entire column, you will be left with a gap in your layout which can be filled with any active card (the bottom one in a column). This is a critical part of the game as your decision on which card to move may have a profound impact upon the shape of the game.

The seven reserve cards are used for building on the foundations or for 'packing' on the exposed cards in the layout. The reserve cards are a critical part of King Albert, providing the player with the chance to get things moving if the game stalls.

Victory is yours when you've managed to build complete suits of 13 cards on each of the foundation piles. Enjoy the smug, warm glow of triumph as you place the final King on the last foundation pile... it won't happen too often.

Old Maid

'Pairs with added tension' would be a fair description of this time-honoured classic, which has long been beloved by young card players.

Number of players

This is a game for two or more players.

Age and skill level

For ages six and above; level 2.

Cards

Remove one Queen from a standard deck to ensure that there will be a single 'old maid' left who cannot be paired during the game.

The cards are shuffled and all 51 are dealt individually around the table. Unless you have three players, the cards will not divide evenly, so it is likely that some players will have one card more than the others. This inequity will be redressed if the deal rotates around the table in the usual fashion with each hand.

The players pick up their hand and immediately discard any pairs of cards they hold, putting them face down into the centre of the table (see right).

With the completed pairs discarded, each player now fans his or her cards and places them face down on the table.

How to play

The dealer goes first, offering his or her cards to the player immediately to their left, who must take one card without seeing it. The player adds the card to their hand and if it completes a pair they can discard the matched cards onto the waste pile. If it is another singleton, they must keep it.

The player now fans his or her cards and offers them to their left-hand neighbour, who must take one. The game continues in the same way moving around the table in a clockwise direction, with players either discarding pairs or adding to their hand.

When a player has successfully paired all his or her cards and has emptied their hand, they are safe. Play continues until one player is left with the odd Queen or 'old maid'. That player is the loser.

Pairs

As simple as Snap! but with less noise, Pairs is the perfect way to get youngsters using their brains rather than their mouths.

Number of players

This is a game for two or more players.

Age and skill level

For ages six and above; level 2.

Cards

For this game to run smoothly, it is imperative that the cards are laid out properly at the start of the game. The cards (which must be shuffled) are placed face down on a flat surface (for example, a table) and spaced evenly in a grid made up of four rows of 13 cards, as shown in the illustration below.

How to play

The game begins when the youngest player turns over two cards in the layout. If the cards revealed are of equal value, the player picks them up (see opposite) and puts them to one side. He or she may now reveal another pair of cards, and their turn continues until they choose two cards that do not match.

When two unmatched cards are revealed, they remain in the layout and are turned face down once more before the next player takes their turn.

Players must take great care not to mess up the layout. If cards move out of line and start overlapping, the game can easily descend into chaos and it is harder for players to remember where the cards are. Players take alternate turns until there are no cards left to play.

At the end of the game, each player counts up how many pairs of cards they have each collected. The player with the most cards is the winner.

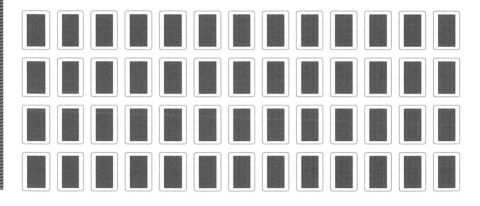

Too easy

If matching cards by their face value becomes too easy, you can also make the game colour-specific. So, for example, if you reveal the Ace of hearts, you will only complete a match if you locate the Ace of diamonds next.

Winning way

Pairs is essentially a game that tests the players' ability to memorize card positions. To improve their chances of winning, they must endeavour to employ strategies that will help them recall the positions of the cards revealed during the game. Some people use repetition, chanting to themselves as if they were saying a mantra (for example, 'top left Ace, bottom right Queen'), while others try to visualize the cards they have seen.

More sophisticated memory systems like 'chunking' can be researched through self-help books if you're feeling very competitive. Be warned, though – children often have very good memories compared to those found in the addled brains of adults, so this game suits them perfectly. If you're not careful, your six-year-old might well give you a sound thrashing at Pairs.

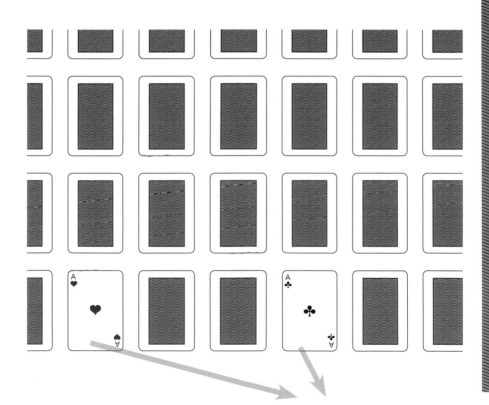

Puss in the Corner

This solo card game is challenging without being impossible, which makes it a rare and precious gem indeed.

Number of players

This is a game for one player.

Age and skill level

For ages eight and above; level 3.

Cards

Separate out the four Aces from a standard deck of cards and place them in a square in the centre of a large table (see illustration, right). The Aces are the foundation cards in this game and are built upon in ascending order. The remaining 48 cards are shuffled and placed face down in the player's hand.

How to play

Turn over the cards held in hand, one by one. Cards can be played onto the layout if they follow in sequence and are matched in colour, so, for example, a two of hearts can be played onto either the Ace of hearts or the Ace of diamonds.

If the card revealed cannot be added to the layout, it is placed face up into one of four waste piles positioned at the corners of the four Aces (see the illustration opposite, top).

When the opportunity arises, the top card from any of the waste piles can be played onto the layout.

Players should try to play cards of similar rank onto particular waste piles. One pile should be reserved for cards ranked two to four; the next for cards five to seven; the next for cards ranked eight, nine and ten; and the last for court cards. By adopting this approach, players reduce the likelihood of finding themselves blocked later in the game.

Foundation cards

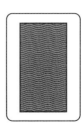

Hand

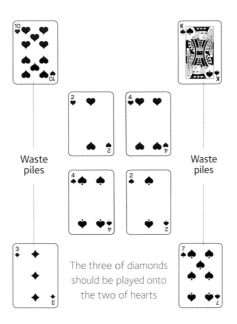

Waste piles

Waste piles

The three of diamonds should be played onto the two of hearts

Play continues in this fashion until the stock of cards runs out. The cards are then gathered up from the four waste piles (take care to place the lowest-rank pile at the top of the stack). Cards from the new stack are turned over one by one and are either played onto the layout or a single waste pile. The top card from the waste pile can be played onto the layout at any time.

If you have grouped your cards sensibly, it should be possible to get the remainder of the cards into the layout without too much effort. But you only get one deal, so when the stack of cards has been emptied onto the layout and the waste pile, that's your lot.

When all 52 cards in the deck have made it onto the layout, the game is complete. You should win more games than not. If you can't bear losing, however, you can always give yourself one more chance to go through the waste pile.

Winning way

The key to success in this game is to make sure you organize your waste piles properly. Group the cards as outlined in 'How to Play' to start with, but as the game develops you will need to think more tactically. If you empty a waste pile, for example, you may want to fill the space with a card that you will soon be needing. Similarly, you may want to avoid covering a card that will soon become playable. Think ahead and try to keep your options open.

Snap!

Simple, fast and noisy – this is the perfect card game for young ones!

Number of players

This is a game for two players but can be played by three (see below).

Age and skill level

For ages four and above; level 1.

Cards

Shuffle a standard 52-card deck and deal out all the cards between the two players.

How to play

Players hold their cards (face down) in their hand. The game begins when both players simultaneously turn over their top cards and place them on the table face up in front of them.

If the two cards revealed are of different values, the two players each turn over the next card in their stack (placing it on top of the previously played card) as before. The game continues in this way until cards of equal value appear together. Upon sight of a matching pair, the players must shout 'Snap!' The first player to utter the word takes their opponent's cards. The person who snaps up all the cards and sits smugly with a hand full of 52 cards is the winner. The loser is the player complaining passionately that he or she has been cheated.

Changing the style

Younger players often struggle to master the concept of playing cards simultaneously and their hesitancy can often lead to allegations of cheating, scuffling and (worst of all) snivelling. If you have this problem, an alternative way of playing can be employed. Players simply play their cards alternately onto a central waste pile and shout 'Snap!' when the card played matches the value of the one on top of the pile.

More players

If you want to play Snap! with three or more players, you will need to use two decks of cards. The rules remain the same; just make sure that you properly shuffle all 104 cards.

Speed

A fantastic game for those with quick brains and even quicker hands.

Number of players

This is a game for two players.

Age and skill level

For ages eight and above; level 3.

Cards

Shuffle a standard 52-card deck and deal out all the cards between the two players. Each player must now deal 15 of their own cards into a 'patience'-style layout. The cards are placed in five stock piles: the first contains one card, the second two ... down to the fifth pile of five cards. The cards are set face down, with the exception of the bottom card in each pile, which is turned over.

The remaining 11 cards are called the 'spit' cards and they are held face down in a pile in the player's hand. Players are not allowed to look at the spit cards in advance of them being played.

How to play

When both players are ready to play, they each turn over their top spit card and place it in the middle of the table (between the two layouts).

The game, which begins as soon as the two cards are turned over, is played like a rapidfire version of patience. The basic objective is to play all your cards out of your layout and onto the spit piles. Players play continuously (they do not take consecutive turns) and continue until they can make no more moves.

Cards are played from the bottom of the stock piles in the layout onto either of the two spit piles and turned face up. A card moved to a spit pile must be the next in sequence (either up or down), irrespective of suit.

Players are only allowed to use one hand to move their cards and can only play one card at a time. As cards are played from the layout, the bottom card in each stock pile is turned over. If a stock pile is emptied, the gap in the layout can be filled by moving the bottom card of another stock pile into the space. As soon as a card touches a spit pile or a space in the layout, it is deemed to have been played. There is no going back, and as soon as the card touches down, your opponent is free to play onto it.

When neither player can make any more moves, both shout 'Spit!' and turn over the top cards from the spit cards held in hand. The two cards are placed on top of the respective spit piles and play resumes. The first player to empty the cards from their layout onto the spit piles is the undisputed Spit King.

Storehouse

This Demon (see page 160) variant is recommended for children not yet ready for the rigours of the more demanding original.

Number of players

This is a game for one player.

Age and skill level

For ages eight and above; level 3.

Cards

Remove the four Aces from a 52-card deck and shuffle the remaining cards. Deal 13 cards face down into a stack. These cards become the 'heel'. To the right of the heel, place the four Aces in a row – these will be the foundation cards for the hand. Cards are built onto the foundations in ascending order and carry on building upwards until they get to the King, when the suit is completed.

Finally, deal out four face-up cards from the deck beneath the foundation row to start the layout.

How to play

Storehouse employs the same rules on how to play as Demon (see page 160).

Foundation piles

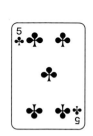

The heel

   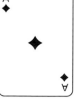

Layout

Three-stake Brag

With three times the opportunity for stake laying, this is a Brag variant that is sure to delight those with a penchant for bluff and bravado.

Number of players

This is a game for up to 10 players.

Age and skill level

For ages ten and above; level 4.

Cards

The preliminaries of Three-stake Brag are the same as for the single-stake variant (see page 211). However, in this game, stakes are placed after each card is dealt.

How to play

After the dealer has dealt one card to each player, the play is temporarily halted while stakes are placed. The players look at their card and bid as before. The players continue staking until they wish to go no further. The cards are revealed and the player with the highest-ranked card takes the pot. If two players have cards of equal status, the winnings are shared. There are no braggers (wild cards) in this first round.

The players leave their first card face up on the table and the dealer now hands them a second card. Another round of stake laying takes place, and when it reaches its conclusion cards are revealed. Braggers are now effective, so, for example, the Jack of clubs and the Queen of hearts count as a pair of Queens. The player with the highest-ranked pair wins the hand (natural pairs always beat an equally ranked pair that includes a bragger). If there are no pairs, the same rules apply as for the first round.

The two played cards are now left on the table and the dealer passes out a third card to each player. The now-familiar stake laying follows before the cards are revealed. This time, however, the rules change about the best hand: now the player whose cards total closest to 31 (either above or below) takes the kitty. Aces count as 11 and court cards are worth ten; all other cards have a value commensurate with their pips. Braggers are of no additional significance.

In Three-stake Brag, this hand is impossible to beat

10 pts   10 pts   11 pts

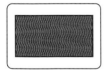

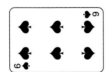

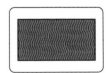

War

The name alone will get most kids queuing up for a game, while its instant playability will appeal to even the most pacifist among them.

Number of players

This is a game for two players.

Age and skill level

For ages six and above; level 2.

Cards

Shuffle a standard 52-card pack and deal all the cards equally between the two players.

Players do not look at their cards, which are placed face down in a pile in front of them. They are now on the brink of War.

How to play

Both players simultaneously turn over the top card in their respective piles and place it face up in the middle of the table (see illustration below).

The highest-ranking card wins the hand and collects the cards, placing them face down at the bottom of his or her pack. Aces are high and suits are ignored. If the two cards played are of equal value, the two players must now go to War. They both now place the top cards of their packs face down in the middle of the table. These cards are not revealed; instead, the players return to their packs and take the new top card; they turn this over and place it face up on the table (see illustration opposite, top).

Whoever plays the highest card wins the hand and collects all six cards from the middle of the table. These are then placed face down at the bottom of his or her pack. If, however, the turned-up cards are of equal value, the War continues. Each player puts down another face-down card before turning over the next card in their stack. Should a player run out of cards during a War, the game comes to an end.

Player 1   Turned-up cards   Player 2

Turned-down
cards

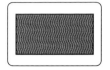 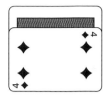 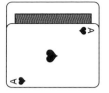 

New turned-up cards

Just like Snap!, the winner is the person who collects all 52 cards, leaving their opponent with nothing. It can take quite some time for the game to reach a conclusion … but that's not necessarily a bad thing.

Helping younger children

War is the perfect game to help your children understand and remember the traditional ranking system for playing cards. Each hand requires the players to make a decision about whether one card is higher than another, so after three or four games they should soon start picking things up. To help them get started, you might want to make them a simple reference chart, which will also help to prevent too many noisy arguments about whether a Jack is higher than an Ace. All you need to do is arrange a suit of cards in order and stick them to a piece of cardboard, or simply write down the following sequence on a piece of paper: (highest) **A K Q J 10 9 8 7 6 5 4 3 2** (lowest).

Authors

Lively, interactive and demanding, Authors is the perfect game with which to start the card playing at a children's party or family gathering.

Number of players

This game is for three to nine players.

Cards

Each player draws a card from a shuffled deck. Whoever draws the highest-ranking card is appointed dealer; thereafter the job of dealer moves around the table in a clockwise fashion.

The whole pack is dealt one at a time to each player, starting with the person seated to the left of the dealer. Some players may end up with more cards than others, but this inequity will even itself out providing the deal rotates. Players should keep their cards concealed.

How to play

The player to the left of the dealer (let's call her Maya) starts the game by asking any other player (in this case Liam) to give her a particular card, say, for example, the Ace of diamonds. If Liam has the Ace of diamonds, he must give it to Maya.

Players can only ask for a card if they already hold another card of the same rank. So, back to our example, for Maya to ask for the Ace of diamonds, she must already hold an Ace from one of the other three suits.

If Maya's bid is successful, her turn continues until she asks for a card from a player who doesn't hold the card she seeks. When this happens, the turn passes to the player asked.

When a player has collected all four cards of a particular rank, he or she must place the cards face down in front of them.

If a player runs out of cards, he or she can take no further part in the current deal. If their hand is emptied by the completion of a set of cards (rather than by another player successfully bidding for his or her final card), the turn passes to the player from whom they collected their last card.

When all the cards have been played, the players count up the number of completed sets of cards they have collected. The player with the most is the winner of that hand and is given a bonus of ten points. Each player is also awarded a point for every set of cards gathered during the deal. Scores are recorded and the player with the highest aggregate total over a set number of deals is the winner. Alternatively, the game can be played in a 'first past the post' style, with the first to exceed 25 points crowned champion.

Chase the Ace

One card, no complicated rules and little scope for ponderous tactical play make Chase the Ace the perfect party warm-up game.

Number of players

Any number can play.

Cards

Players are each given three tokens – sweets or coins for example – which represent the three lives they have in Chase the Ace. A standard 52-card deck is required. The deck is shuffled and each player takes a card, with the player drawing the lowest card appointed dealer for the game. The dealer places one card face down in front of each player. At this stage the players do not look at their cards.

How to play

The game starts with the player to the left of the dealer. He or she picks up their card and looks at it. Their aim is to hold the highest card possible: Kings are high, Aces are low and the suits rank with spades the highest, then hearts, then diamonds and lastly clubs.

If the player holds a King, he or she must place it face up in front of them. If they hold any other card, they can either stand (in other words stick with the card they hold), or exchange the card with the player to their left. The player cannot refuse and must hand over their card. The turn passes around the table in a clockwise direction. When it reaches the dealer, he or she can elect to either stand or exchange their card with the top card from the remaining stack of cards.

When all players have had their turn, the cards are turned over. The player with the lowest card puts one of their sweets into the centre of the table; they now have only two lives left. The cards are gathered up, shuffled and dealt once again. The deal moves around the table clockwise and the game continues until all but one player has run out of sweets.

Winning way

The only way to improve your chances of winning at Chase the Ace is to make sure you make a sensible decision about whether to hold or exchange your original card. Play the percentages and bear in mind that you do not have to win the hand – you just have to avoid coming last. There are no prizes for the player with the highest-ranking card, only penalties for the player left holding the lowest.

Donkey

This game is a simplified version of Pig (see page 197) that is sure to delight fans of the original and newcomers alike.

Number of players
This game is for four to 13 players.

Cards
The rules of Donkey are similar to those of Pig (see page 197) and the cards are sorted in the same way prior to playing the game. Players cut for the deal, the drawer of the highest card being first dealer. The cards are sorted by rank as in Pig to match the number of players, then shuffled and four cards are dealt to each player. Prizes for the game are laid out for all but one of the players (so, if there are six players in the game, there will be only five prizes).

How to play
The dealer calls 'Swap' and the game starts with the players discarding a card to their left-hand neighbour and picking up the card which, by the same process, arrives at their right.

When all players are ready, the dealer calls 'Swap' again and the process is repeated. The game continues, with players discarding and receiving cards one by one, until they complete a four-of-a-kind hand. When this feat is achieved, the player puts down his cards and takes a prize. With this player out,

the game contiues until there are no prizes left. The winner of the game is the first player to complete a four-of-a-kind hand. However, there is no additional prize for coming first. Coming last, though, is something to be avoided, as there is no prize for the player who fails to complete a set.

Winning way
Donkey, like Pig, is for the most part a game of chance. Players should be encouraged to keep their options open for as long as possible and should try to remember the cards they have already passed on, but aside from that, it's all down to luck!

This card moves to the next player   This card joins the hand, completing four-of-a-kind

Fan Tan

Fan Tan is also known as Card Dominoes, Parliament and Sevens, and must not be confused with the well-known gambling game that is played in China under the same name. In fact, the Chinese game is not a card game at all.

Number of players

Any reasonable number may play, with perhaps four to six being the best.

Cards

The standard 52-card pack is used, with cards ranking from King (high) to Ace (low).

Players cut for the deal, the drawer of the highest card being first dealer. Thereafter the deal passes to the left.

This game can be played with sweets or coins to make it more fun. Before each deal each player should place the number of coins or sweets (let's call them 'units') that they want to play for into a pool. The cards are then dealt one by one, face downwards, until the pack is exhausted.

How to play

Play begins by the player on the left of the dealer placing a 7 face upwards in the centre of the table. If he has no 7 he contributes one unit to the pool, and the player on his left now has to play a 7 to the centre of the table or contribute one unit to the pool, and so on.

As soon as a 7 has been played to the centre of the table, the next player must play either the 6 of the same suit on its left, or the 8 of the same suit on its right, or the 7 of another suit below it. The game continues clockwise round the table, the players building up to the Kings on the right of the 7s and down to the Aces on the left of them.

Any player who is unable to play in his turn contributes one unit to the pool, and if he revokes, by failing to play when he could do so, he forfeits three units to the pool, and five units each to the holders of the 6 and 8 if he fails to play a 7 when he could and should have played it.

The game is won by the player who is first to get rid of all his cards. He receives all that is in the pool and from each of the other players one unit for every card that that player holds.

Skill comes into the game by holding up the opponents. As a general rule a 7, unless it is accompanied by several cards of the same suit, should be kept in hand for as long as possible; and, if a player has a choice, he should choose the card that will allow him later to play a lower or higher one of the same suit, rather than one that can only help the opponents.

In the illustration below, the player should play the ♣10, because when the ♣J is played he can follow with the ♣Q. It would be an error of judgement to play the ♥6, because it doesn't help him, but might help the opponents.

The game can, of course, be enjoyed by adults or children without the need for a pool.

Play or pay

The original version of Fan Tan was called Play or Pay and may still be enjoyed. The eldest hand may lead any card (not necessarily a 7). The next player must play the next higher card in the same suit, or, if unable to, pay a chip to a pool. The sequence is built upwards only, and is regarded as continuous, i.e. Ace follows

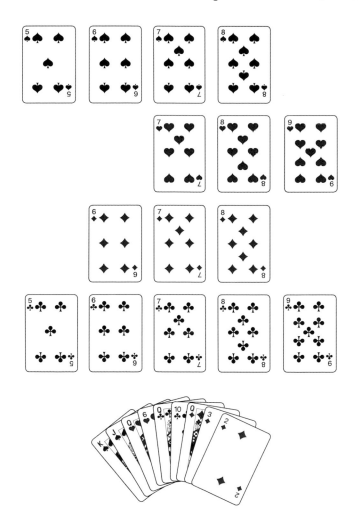

King. Only one suit is played at a time, and only when the first suit is finished is a second begun. The player who lays the last card in the first suit also plays the first card to the next – the suit and the rank are of his choice. The first person to get rid of his cards wins the pool.

The first player to play might choose a suit in which he has two consecutive cards, and lay the higher. By this means he is certain to lay the last card in the suit and thus begin the next. It is clearly an advantage to play first to the final suit, when opposite rules apply, and the player will decide which of his cards provide the biggest gap and lead so that his own cards are played before this gap is filled.

If the hand in the illustration above is held by the player to play first, its holder has an excellent chance of winning. He should begin with ♥K, and will play the last card in the heart suit with ♥Q. He then begins spades with ♠8 and plays the last card with ♠7. He then lays ♣4 and ends the suit with ♣3. Then he plays ♦10 and wins provided each of his opponents holds one of the cards ♦ 9, 8, 7, 6, 5, 4, 3. An alternative plan would be to play the diamond suit second, and hope that the last suit, whether it be spades or clubs, will begin at such a level that he can play his two consecutive cards before any other player has gone out.

It should be pointed out that if players put in chips for each pass, each player might easily pass 40 times in one deal, so stakes should be geared accordingly. An alternative method of settling up debts would be for each loser to pay the winner at the end of the deal one chip for each card remaining in his hand. Like Fan Tan, the game can, of course, be played just for enjoyment.

Fe–Fi–Fo–Fum

With a fairytale chant and prizes on offer, Fe-Fi-Fo-Fum is sure to make any party go with a swing.

Number of players

This is a game for four to six players.

Cards

Deal out a well-shuffled pack between all the players. It doesn't matter if some players have an extra card; this inequity will even itself out if the starting point for the deal rotates with each hand.

How to play

The player to the left of the dealer leads off. He or she can play any card they wish, setting it down face up in the centre of the table. As they lay the card, they say 'Fe'.

The player who has the next card in ascending sequence and matching suit follows, playing the card and announcing it by saying 'Fi'. So, for example, if the game had opened with the four of hearts (Fe), the next card would be the five of hearts (Fi). The play continues with whoever holds the six, seven and eight, each player announcing their cards with calls of 'Fo', 'Fum' and 'Giant's tum' respectively. The sequence ends when a player lays a card and calls 'Giant's tum'.

The player who brought the run to a halt in this way starts the game off again by laying a new Fe card from their hand.

Sequences do not go 'round the corner', so when a King is laid (irrespective of whether it is a Fe, Fi, Fo or Fum card), the sequence stops and another is started by the player who played the King. Aces are low.

As the game develops, more and more cards will become stop cards because the next card in sequence has already been played. For example, following an opening sequence of the four to eight of hearts, the three of hearts would now become a stop card. When it is played, the run ends and the player who laid it starts a new sequence with a fresh Fe card.

The first player to play all their cards is the winner. Continue playing until only one player is left holding cards. If you want to add a little spice to the proceedings, you can lay out prizes. Put out enough for all but one of the players so that the loser gets nothing.

| Fe | Fi | Fo | Fum | Giant's tum |

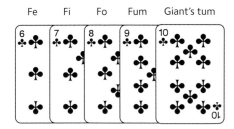

Kemps

Kemps spices up gatherings with a little subterfuge and a whole lot of tension, making it a party classic.

Number of players

Kemps is for four, six, or eight players.

Cards

Players are divided into pairs and each team takes a moment in private to discuss the signals they will use during the game. Once all is agreed, the players reconvene and the cards are cut to decide who will deal; the player with the lowest card becomes the dealer.

Four cards are dealt face down to each player, with an additional widow hand dealt face up to the centre of the table. The remainder of the cards are placed in a stack face down on the table.

How to play

The players pick up their cards and when the dealer says 'Go' they can begin exchanging cards with the widow hand in the centre of the table. Players are looking to collect four-of-a-kind. They can only exchange one card at a time, but may do so continuously; there is no need to wait until an opponent has taken a turn. If two players go for the same card, the first of them to touch it gets it. If children are playing, they may need a little supervision to avoid a fight breaking out!

When the players have taken all the cards they wish from the widow hand, the dealer takes away the four cards and deals out replacements from the stack of unused cards. When the new cards are laid out, the dealer says 'Go' again and the card swapping resumes.

The hand carries on in this fashion until one of the players calls it to a halt or the stock of cards runs out. If the latter situation occurs and the hand reaches a stalemate, it is ruled a draw and has no impact on the outcome of the game. However, a positive outcome for the game can be achieved in two ways:

A call of 'Kemps'

If a player achieves a hand made up of four-of-a-kind, he or she must try to alert their team-mate to the fact, without drawing the attention of their opponents. It is not possible to call the hand to a halt, so each player but must instead rely upon the system of signals agreed between them prior to the game. Signals cannot be verbal and are usually gestures or body movements. Players are also not allowed to deliberately try to confuse opponents by using signals when they do not have four-of-a-kind.

When a player detects that his or her team-mate has completed a set, they should immediately call 'Kemps'. The hand is brought to an end and the player in question reveals his or her cards. If the call is correct, that team wins the hand; however, if the partner misinterpreted the signal and called the game prematurely, the hand goes to the opposing team.

A call of 'Stop Kemps'

A hand can also be won by a player who intercepts a signal and calls 'Stop Kemps' before his or her rival has a chance to halt the hand. So, for example, if a player sees their opponent raise an eyebrow in very deliberate fashion while looking directly at his or her team-mate, they may want to take the risk of calling 'Stop Kemps' on the grounds that they are probably signalling that they have completed a winning hand. If the player calls it correctly, his or her team will win the hand, but if, when the cards are checked, the opposing team has not yet assembled four-of-a-kind, the player who called 'Stop Kemps', and his team-mate, lose.

Each time a team loses a hand, it is given a letter from the word 'kemps' as punishment. The object of the game is to avoid collecting five letters and spelling out the word. The first team to lose five hands is, in effect, the loser of the game. If you are playing with more than two teams, keep going until only one is left.

Winning way

Signals must be clear, simple and should be used at an agreed time during each hand. For example, rubbing the tip of your right index finger when the dealer collects up the cards and re-deals the widow hand. A lingering gesture of this kind is far more likely to be picked up than something more fleeting that might be missed. You should also try to observe the cards other players are going for: if your playing partner picks up a card and you have a matching one, you should think about discarding it. You should also watch what your opponents are picking up and when possible block them by hanging onto sought-after cards.

Cheat

Although it is against the rules to use fake signals to induce other players to call 'Stop Kemps', if you're clever about it, you can definitely get your rivals twitching with a few carefully employed moves. Surely they can't think that you'd sniff and scratch your nose solely to mislead them... perish the thought!

Newmarket

This is a versatile game that can keep things moving at family parties but that can also occupy rowdy youngsters eager for prizes or those in search of a boredom cure on a rainy day.

Number of players

This is a game for three to eight players.

Cards

Players each pick a card from the deck of a standard pack of 52 cards, and whoever chooses the lowest card becomes the dealer.

After shuffling and cutting the deck, the dealer distributes the cards as evenly as possible to the players. He or she also deals out a dummy hand, which they place to one side along with any spare cards left over from the deal.

Before the players look at their cards, the dealer takes four cards from a separate pack and lays them face up on the table. These are called the boodle cards and they must be an Ace, King, Queen and Jack each from different suits; so, for example, the Jack of spades, Queen of diamonds, King of hearts and Ace of clubs.

The players are each given ten counters, which they must place on the boodle cards (they are also given another ten counters, which they keep in reserve). They can place all ten counters on one card, but more often will spread them around.

How to play

With the stakes placed, the player to the left of the dealer leads off. He or she can play a card of any suit, but it must be the lowest card that they hold in that suit.

Play is continuous rather than by turn, and the next player to go is the one who holds the next-highest card in the suit. So, for example, if Player One had laid down the seven of hearts, the player who holds the eight of hearts would take a turn next.

The play continues in this way until either play is blocked because the card needed is tucked away in the dummy hand, or because the run is complete (Aces are high, so the appearance of an Ace will automatically bring the run to an end).

Play is restarted by the person who played the last card, and resumes with them leading the lowest card of another suit. If, however, they do not hold any cards from another suit, the job of leading off passes to the player on their left.

When a player plays a card identical to one of the boodle cards, they receive all the counters that have been staked on that particular card.

Boodle cards

   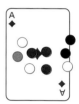

Dummy
hand

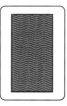

The player who gets rid of all their cards first wins the hand. The victor then receives one counter from each player in respect of every card they still hold. If no player manages to get rid of all their cards, the winner is the player with fewest cards when the game becomes blocked. In these circumstances, the winner is entitled to one counter from each of their rivals in respect of the difference between the cards the winner has left and those the losers still hold in hand. So, for example, if David had three cards left at the end of the game and his rivals Stewart and Sharon each had five, they would both have to pay the victorious David two counters.

Winning way

Consider carefully your options when leading off, as this is your opportunity to control the game. Watch the cards played and try to work out which cards your opponents hold. As the game develops, you may be able to frustrate your rivals by playing high-ranking cards that rid you of a particular suit without allowing them the opportunity to do likewise.

Pig

Whether played for prizes or just for fun, this is a game sure to delight anyone who enjoys letting their hair down and being silly from time to time.

Number of players

This is a game for up to 13 players.

Cards

Take a standard 52-card deck and sort the cards by rank so that you end up with 13 complete sets. You will need one complete set per player. It doesn't matter which rank of cards you choose as the object of the game is to be the first player to assemble four-of-a-kind with no preference given to the value of the cards. Put the remainder of the cards to one side and shuffle the cards you have selected. Each player is dealt four cards face down in front of them.

How to play

The game play in Pig is continuous rather than by taking turns, so instead of one player leading off, the dealer calls 'Start'. The game commences with the players discarding a card to their left-hand neighbour and picking up the card that, by the same process, arrives at their right.

The game continues, with players discarding and receiving cards one by one, until one of the players completes a four-of-a-kind hand. When this feat is achieved, the triumphant player points

to his or her nose without saying anything. All the other players should immediately do likewise. The last player to point to their nose loses the hand

When a player loses a hand, they are given a letter from the word 'pig' as a penalty. The object of the game is to avoid collecting three letters and spelling out the word. If you are playing Pig at a children's party, you may want to avoid confusion and argument by writing the letters on some sticky labels and handing them to the losing player at the end of each hand. Once a player has collected P–I–G they are out. The game continues until only one player is left. Prizes can be given to the victor in the usual fashion – a chocolate pig is an ideal reward.

Twist in the tail

To maintain the interest of players who are 'out' – and thereby avoid that awkward situation where only two are engaged in the game – you can introduce a fun new rule. Tell the redundant pigs that they are allowed to try to distract the active players by talking to them; if any of the players speak back to the ostracized swine, they are out too.

Pip-Pip!

Pip-Pip! can be quite a noisy game, so it's perfect for a party.

Number of players

Any number may play up to about 12, but six to eight players is probably best.

Cards

Two standard packs are shuffled together. The cards rank as usual, except that 2 acts as the top card in each suit.

The players draw cards and the highest deals first, the card they drew determining the trump suit. Thereafter the deal passes to the left, and the trump suit is determined by the player to the right of the dealer cutting the pack.

Seven cards are dealt face down to each player, and the remainder of the pack is placed face downwards in the centre of the table (the stock).

How to play

The object of the game is to win tricks containing 2s, Aces and court cards. Players score as follows: 2 is worth 11 points, Ace 10 points, King five points, Queen four points and Jack three points.

The player on the left of the dealer leads the first trick. Thereafter the player who wins a trick leads the next. A player must follow suit if he can; if not he may either discard or trump. If two players play identical cards, the player of the second takes precedence.

Immediately after a player has played to a trick he draws a card from the stock; if he now holds in his hand the King and Queen of the same suit, other than of the trump suit, he may call 'Pip-Pip', and place the two cards face upwards on the table in front of him, instantly scoring 50 points. At the end of the current trick, the trump suit changes to that of the exposed King and Queen.

'Pip-Pip' may be called and 50 points scored if a player is dealt the King and Queen of a suit – other than of the trump suit. The trump suit is then changed before the first trick is played. If two or more players are dealt the King and Queen of a suit (other than of the trump suit) each scores 50 points if he calls 'Pip-Pip'. The trump suit is changed to that of the player who was first to call. 'Pip-Pip' may be called twice in the same suit provided the player has both Kings and both Queens of it. A King or a Queen once paired cannot be paired a second time.

Drawing cards from the stock continues until there are fewer cards than players. The remaining cards in the stock are then turned face upwards and the players play the last seven tricks with the cards left in their hands.

The game ends when every player has dealt an equal number of times.

Pope Joan

Pope Joan is a very old card game that at one time was exceptionally popular in Scotland. The ♦9 is given the name of 'Pope' and as the Pope was hugely disliked by members of the Scottish Reformation, that might explain why the card was also given the nickname of 'Curse of Scotland'. Pope Joan is a type of gambling game.

Number of players

Any number from three to eight may play, with four to six being best.

Cards

The game is played with a standard pack of 52 cards from which the ♦8 is removed.

How to play

Originally a special board, consisting of a circular tray divided into eight compartments and revolving about a central pillar was used with counters. Today these boards are museum pieces, and modern players must make do with eight saucers labelled: *Game*, *Ace*, *King*, *Queen*, *Jack*, *Matrimony*, *Intrigue*, *Pope*, placed in the centre of the table.

Each player begins with the same number of counters of an agreed value, and the dealer places six in the saucer labelled Pope (♦9), two each in Matrimony and Intrigue, and one each in Game, Ace, King, Queen and Jack. It is called 'dressing the board'.

Cards are dealt to the players and to an extra hand (widow) in the centre of the table. The number of cards dealt to each player and the widow depends on

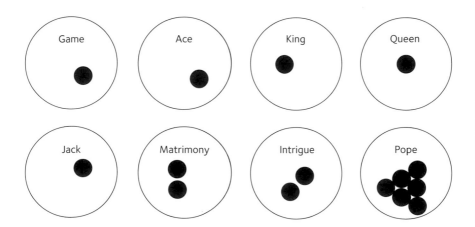

the number of players in the game. The players must each hold the same number of cards, so any over-cards go to the widow. The last card is turned face upwards to denote the trump suit, and if it is either the Pope (♦9) or an Ace, King, Queen or Jack, the dealer wins the counters in the corresponding saucer.

The player on the left of the dealer leads the first trick. He may lead any card he chooses, and at the same time he announces it. Suppose it is the ♣6. Then the player who holds the ♣7 plays it and announces it, the player who holds the ♣8 plays it and announces it, and so on, until the run comes to an end.

The four Kings are stop cards, and in the diamond suit the 7 is as well, because the ♦8 has been removed from the pack. In practice, of course, any card may be a stop card on account of the cards in the widow hand, and because the next higher card may already have been played.

When a run comes to an end, the player of the stop card starts a fresh run by leading any card he likes. In this way the game continues until one of the players has played all his cards. He is then entitled to the counters in the Game saucer, and, in addition, he receives from each player one counter for every card left in his hand. The player who is left with the Pope (♦9), however, is exempt from paying the winner so long as he holds the card in his hand. If he has played it in the course of the game he loses this advantage.

During the course of the game, any player who plays the Ace, King, Queen or Jack of the trump suit, or the Pope (♦9), wins the counters in the corresponding saucers; if the same player plays the King and Queen of the trump suit he wins the counters in Matrimony, and if the same player plays the Queen and Jack of the trump suit he wins those in Intrigue.

The deal passes round the table clockwise, and any counters that have not been won in a deal are carried forward to the next.

Ranter Go Round

Ranter Go Round is an old Cornish game with the more appropriate alternative name of Cuckoo. It is a game that all children enjoy.

Number of players

This can be played by almost any number of players, from six to around 15.

Cards

The full pack of 52 cards is used, cards ranking from 2 (low) to Ace (high).

How to play

Each player begins with an agreed number of tokens, which is usually three (for children, it is fun to use little sweets or coins). The dealer deals one card face downwards to each player, who then looks at it. The object of the game is to avoid being left with the lowest card.

The player on the left of the dealer begins the game. He may either keep his card or offer it to his left-hand neighbour with the command 'Change'. There is no choice about it. The player so commanded must exchange cards with his right-hand neighbour unless he holds a King, when he says 'King', and the game is continued by the player on his left.

When an exchange has been made, the player who has been compelled to do so may pass on the card he has received in the same way, and so on, clockwise round the table, until the card is brought to a halt either by a King or by a player receiving a higher card in exchange, so he has nothing to gain by passing it on.

Any player giving an Ace, 2 or 3 in obedience to the command 'Change' must announce the rank of the card.

The dealer is last to play, and if he wishes to exchange his card, he does so by cutting the remainder of the pack and taking the top card of the cut.

If in doing this he draws a King he loses the hand and contributes one unit to the pool. If he does not draw a King, all the players expose their cards and the one with the lowest contributes one unit to the pool. If two or more tie for lowest card, they all contribute to the pool.

When a player has contributed all his tokens to the pool, he retires from the game. The others continue, and the game is won by he who is left with at least one token in hand.

Red Dog

Red Dog is a game of chance that is best played for sweets or for coins at parties. It is quick, tense and dramatic, and offers a roller-coaster ride that is guaranteed to get your party swinging.

Number of players

This is a game for two to ten players.

Cards

The game is played with a standard pack of 52 cards. Each player should have a pile of tokens to use as stakes, such as coins. For younger players, you could give each child a bag of individually wrapped sweets to use as stakes instead.

Each player should draw cards from a shuffled deck to determine the dealer; the lowest card gets the job.

Before the cards are dealt, the players each put an agreed number of tokens into the centre of the table to establish a pool. It is probably best to start with two per player.

Five cards are now dealt to each player (although if the number of players exceeds eight, each receives only four). The players pick up their cards and assess them. A good hand is one that includes high-ranking cards of all four suits, with the four Kings offering the perfect hand and guaranteed victory. The remaining cards are placed face down in front of the dealer to form a stock pile.

Players must now place their stakes prior to the game commencing. The player to the left of the dealer starts the bidding and must stake at least one token. The maximum bid by any one player must not exceed the total number of tokens held in the pool (so, in our example, if there were five players, no individual could stake more than ten coins or sweets).

How to play

The player to the left of the dealer goes first. The dealer takes the top card of the stock and turns it face up on the table.

If the player can beat it (with a higher-ranked card of the same suit), he or she shows the other players the superior card and collects the tokens from the pool. The winning player keeps their remaining cards and the pool is restocked with another two units from each player.

If the active player cannot beat the card turned over by the dealer, they turn over their hand of cards and their stake is added to the pool.

The game continues until all players have had their turn. If you wish to continue playing, the cards must be gathered up and a fresh deal made.

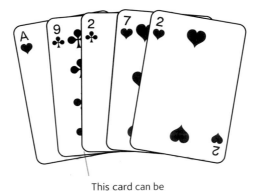

This card can be
played to win the pool

The player with the most coins or sweets is the winner. Of course, if you prefer not to give your children sweets, you can play for counters that can be totalled up at the end of the game, with a non-confectionery prize awarded to the final victor.

Winning way

If you have a great hand with lots of high-ranking cards, you will be tempted to stake big, but you may be wise to play more discreetly. A big stake may discourage your opponents from making a big bid themselves. A couple of overconfident, gung-ho players can soon boost the pool, so let them believe they are going to win and watch them throw their sweets or coins away!

Spinado

Spinado is a less complicated version of Pope Joan (see page 199) with only three pools: Matrimony, Intrigue and Game.

Number of players

Any number from two to seven may play.

Cards

Remove the four 2s and the ♦8 from a standard pack of 52 cards. Cards rank from King (high) to Ace (low). The dealer deals the cards to the players and to an extra hand (widow). As the players must each hold the same number of cards, over-cards go to the widow hand.

How to play

Before dealing the dealer contributes 12 counters to the Matrimony pool, and six each to the Intrigue and Game pools. The other players contribute three counters each to the Game pool. Matrimony is the King and Queen of Diamonds, Intrigue is the Queen and Jack of Diamonds.

The player on the left of the dealer starts the game by playing any card. The other players continue by playing the next higher cards in the chosen suit in succession until a stop is reached. The player who plays the stop card then starts a new run by playing any card he chooses.

The ♦A is known as Spinado and whoever holds it may play it at any time as long as he plays it with the proper card, announcing that he is playing Spinado. It constitutes a stop, and he receives three counters from each opponent.

During the game, the player who plays the ♦K receives two counters from each of the other players, and if he plays the ♦Q as well he wins the Matrimony pool. The player who plays the ♦Q and the ♦J wins the Intrigue pool, and those who play the Kings of spades, hearts and clubs receive one counter from each of the other players.

The game is won by the player who is the first to play all his cards. He takes the counters in the Game pool and is exempt from contributing to the pools in the next deal, unless it is his turn to deal.

A player who is left with Spinado in his hand pays the winner of the game double for each card he is left with. Spinado, therefore, should not be kept back too long. However, it is not always best to play it with one's first card. If, for example, a 10 is led, and the player who holds Spinado also holds the King and Jack, it is best not to play Spinado with the Jack, because if the Jack proves to be a stop there was no need for the play of Spinado, and the King is the natural stop if another player follows with the Queen.

It is better to play Spinado with some card that is not known to be a stop.

Thirty-One

Thirty-One, also known by the French name *Trente et un*, has been played in Europe since the 15th century and is still popular today.

Number of players

Any number of players from two to 15 or so may play.

Cards

This is played with the full pack of 52 cards. Three cards are dealt face downwards to each player, and three cards are placed face upwards in the centre of the table as the widow hand.

How to play

Before each deal the players contribute an agreed amount of tokens to a pool.

In turn each player, beginning with the one on the left of the dealer, must exchange one of his cards (and never more than one) with a card from the widow. He cannot pass. Counting the Ace as 11, the court cards as 10 each and all the other cards at their pip values, the object of the game is to hold three cards of the same suit which add up to 31. Next in value is a hand that contains three cards of the same rank. Failing either, the pool is won by the player who holds the highest total in any one suit.

The exchange of cards with the widow continues until a player has a hand of 31. As soon as a player holds such a hand, he exposes it on the table, claims the pool, and the deal passes. At any stage of the game, however, a player who thinks he has a hand good enough to win may rap the table. The other players now have the right, in turn, either to stick with the cards they hold, or exchange one more card with the widow. The players then expose their cards and the one with the best hand wins the pool.

This player might be advised to exchange his ♦5 with the ♥7 and then rap, because 25 is not a bad score

Widow

Hand

Baccarat

Baccarat, more correctly Baccarat Banque, is a game of chance that is played in casinos everywhere.

Number of players

The game may be played by any number up to 30 or more.

Cards

Six packs of cards are shuffled together (in Las Vegas eight packs are used) cut and placed in an open-ended box known as a shoe, designed to release only one card at a time. The court cards rank in value at 10 points each; all other cards at their pip values.

How to play

The banker sits midway down one of the sides of a long, oval table (see illustration at the top of page 209), and the players sit in equal numbers on both sides of

him. Those for whom there is no room to sit, stand behind them.

The banker, who is also the dealer, puts his stake on the table in front of him, and any player who wishes to bet against the whole of it calls 'Banco'. If two or more call, the one nearest to the banker's left makes the bet. If no one calls, the players combine their bets to equal the stake put up by the banker.

The banker then gives a card face downwards to the player on his right, a card to the player on his left and a card to himself. He repeats the operation so the three of them have two cards each.

The object of the game is to form in two or three cards a combination counting as nearly as possible to 9.

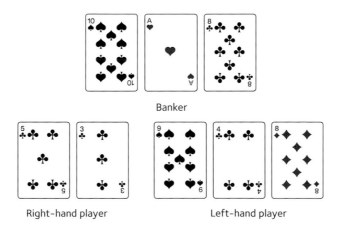

Banker

Right-hand player   Left-hand player

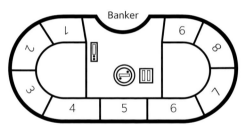

The layout of the staking table used in Baccarat and Chemin de Fer

In counting the total, ten is disregarded; if, for example, a player's two cards total 15 it counts as a point score of 5.

The banker looks at his two cards and if he has a point of 8 or 9 he shows his cards (a natural). If he has not got a point of 8 or 9, he announces that he will give and the player on his right looks at his cards. If he has a point of 8 or 9 he shows his cards and announces his natural. If he has not got a point of 8 or 9 he may ask for one more card which the banker gives to him face upwards. The player on the left of the banker goes through the same performance, and then the banker may, if he chooses, take one more card. Finally, the banker wins or loses to each player according to whose point is nearer to 9; equality neither wins nor loses. A natural beats a three-card hand.

For example (see illustration at the bottom of page 208): the banker holds ♠10 and ♥A, making a point of 1, and he, therefore, must give. The right-hand player holds ♣5 and ♣3. He faces his cards, announces his natural point of 8, and must win. The left-hand player holds ♣9 and ♣4, making a point of 3. He must draw and the banker gives him ♦8, reducing his point to 1. For the moment, however, the left-hand player does not announce his point. The banker faces his cards, and, as he holds no more than a point of 1, he draws a card. It is the ♣8, which raises his point to 9.

The banker, therefore, wins from the left-hand player, but loses to the right-hand player because though the banker has a point of 9, against the point of 8 held by the right-hand player, a natural beats any point made by the addition of a drawn card.

The rules of play are strict and should never be deviated from because the player who is holding the cards is playing for all on his side of the table. If he deviates from the rules, and thereby loses the hand, he is liable to make good all losses incurred through his error.

A player must not look at his cards until the banker has either announced that he holds a natural or that he will give cards. When a player does look at his cards, if he holds a natural he must expose his cards and declare his natural at once. If a player does not hold a natural, he must: draw a card if he holds a point of 4 or less, stand if he holds a point of 6 or 7, and decide whether to draw or stand if he holds a point of 5.

Blind Hookey

Blind Hookey is the simplest of all gambling games.

Number of players

Any number may play.

Cards

The full pack of 52 cards is used. After the pack has been shuffled by one player and cut to the banker, it is passed to the player on the left of the banker, who removes a minimum of four cards from the top of the pack, placing them in a pile face down on the table in front of him. He passes the pack to the neighbour on his left who does the same, and so on until all the players (the banker last) have placed a small pile of cards in front of them.

How to play

Without looking at the cards, all the players (except the banker) stake to an agreed limit and turn their piles face up to expose the bottom card. The banker wins from all whose card is lower than or equal with his and loses to all whose card is higher. Aces may be high or low.

Play continues with the same banker if he wins more than he loses, or finishes level, but passes to the next player if the banker loses more than he wins.

Another way of playing the game is for the banker to cut the pack into three piles. The players place their stakes on either of two piles, and the third pile is taken by the banker. The three piles are turned face upwards and the players receive from the banker or lose to him according to whether the bottom cards of their piles are higher or lower than the bottom card of his pile.

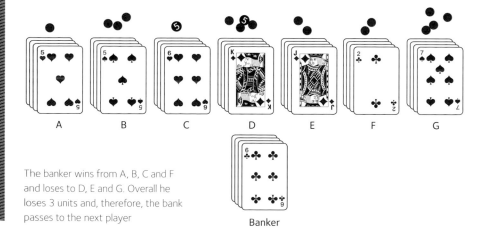

The banker wins from A, B, C and F and loses to D, E and G. Overall he loses 3 units and, therefore, the bank passes to the next player

Banker

Brag

Simpler than Poker, but with all the drama of placing stakes and bluffing plus the opportunity to say 'I will see you', Brag is a teenage card sharp's dream game.

Number of players

This is a game for up to ten players.

Cards

Players agree minimum and maximum stakes (one to five counters per bid is suggested).

After the cards have been cut by all and the player with the lowest card has been appointed dealer, he or she places a minimum stake into the pot (the centre of the table). The dealer then deals out three cards to each player, placing them face down one at a time onto the table. The players collect their cards and assess their hands. The stake laying now begins.

How to play

The player to the left of the dealer starts the bidding. They stake as much or as little as they want (provided they stay within the prescribed minimum and maximum levels). A high bet suggests they are confident that the hand they hold will be a winning one ... although, of course, it might be a bluff.

The turn moves around the table in a clockwise direction, and each player can either match the bet, raise (make a bigger bet) or fold. If a player folds, they do not have to stake any more counters and simply return their cards to the dealer. They will take no further part in the hand.

The betting continues, moving round and round the table for as long as it takes until all players still in the game have bet the same amount and no player wishes to raise the stakes further. Of course, if one player out-stakes all the others and none of his or her opponents are prepared to match them, they win the hand automatically. In this situation they do not have to show their cards to the rest of the players – they will never know if the player was bluffing or had genuine cause for confidence.

With the bidding over, the cards are turned over and the hands assessed. Three cards are wild and can be used to represent any other card to make a winning combination; these three cards – the Ace of diamonds, the Jack of clubs and the nine of diamonds – are called the braggers. Combinations of cards rank in the following order (with the best first):

Trios (three of a kind) will always beat a pair, irrespective of rank.

Three natural Aces (including the Ace of

diamonds but no other braggers)

Three Aces (including any two Aces and one of the other braggers)

Three natural Kings

Three Kings (two Kings plus any of the braggers)

The pattern continues down to the three twos.

Three natural Aces

Pairs

The ranking of pairs is in keeping with the above, so a natural pair will always beat a pair of the same rank that consists of one natural card and a bragger.

Natural pair

Singletons

If there are no pairs, the hand is won by the player who has the highest-ranked single card. Suits have no bearing on the outcome, so if two players have cards of the same rank, the pot is shared.

The player with the best hand – as you might expect – takes the pot.

Although the lower hand has more high cards in Brag, the King singleton beats them

Chemin de Fer

Chemin de Fer, nearly always called Chemmy, is a form of Baccarat (see page 208) modified for social play. In all games of chance the banker has an advantage to a greater or lesser degree, but here it is much less than at Baccarat because the banker plays against one hand instead of against two.

Number of players

Any reasonable number can play.

Cards

The full pack of 52 cards is used, although two or three packs shuffled together is better. In a casino, a number of packs will be used.

How to play

For all practical purposes the difference between Baccarat and Chemin de Fer is that at the latter game the bank passes in rotation round the table, the banker holding the bank until he loses a coup, when it is passed to the player on his left; and the banker deals only one hand, not two, to the players, the hand being held by the one who has made the largest bet.

As the banker plays against only one hand, he may not use his judgement as to whether to draw or stand. The rules for play are precise and strict:

- If his point is 8 or 9 he declares a natural.
- If his point is 7 he stands whether the player draws any card or stands.
- If his point is 6 he draws if the player draws a 6 or a 5, but stands if the player draws any other card or stands.
- If he holds a point of 5 he draws if the player draws a 7, 6, 5, 4, 3 or stands, but stands if he draws any other card.
- If he holds a point of 3 or 4 he draws if the player draws a 7, 6, 5, 4, 3, 2 or Ace or if he stands, but stands if he draws any other card.
- If he holds a point of 0, 1 or 2 he draws whether the player draws any card or stands.

Player   Banker

Top: Banker's point is 6. Player has drawn a 6, so banker must draw
Above: Banker's point is only 4, but as player has drawn a 9 he must stand

Easy Go

Easy Go is a very simple game of chance, requiring no skill or concentration.

Number of players

Any number up to nine may play.

Cards

The full pack of 52 cards is used.

How to play

The banker deals five cards face upwards to every player, except himself. He now turns up a card and any player who holds a card of the same rank pays into a pool two units if it is the same colour and one unit if it is different. In all the banker turns up five cards in turn, and for the second card the players pay into the pool three units if the cards are of the same colour and two if they are different; for the third card they contribute five units if the cards are of the same colour and four if they are different; for the fourth card they contribute nine units if the cards are of the same colour and eight if they are different; for the fifth card they contribute 17 units if the cards are of the same colour and 16 if they are different.

There is now a second show of five cards by the banker, but this time the players take out of the pool at the same rates as they paid into it.

After this, anything left in the pool is taken by the banker, but if there is not enough in the pool to meet the requirements of the players he must make it good.

The bank passes clockwise.

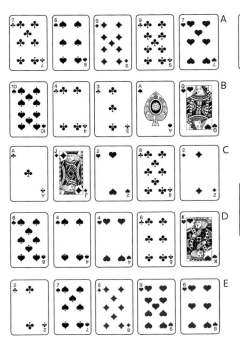

First five cards faced by banker

A pays 0 units to the pool
B pays 1 unit to the pool
C pays 13 units to the pool
D pays 7 units to the pool
E pays 5 units to the pool

Second five cards faced by banker

A receives 1 unit from the pool
B receives 6 units from the pool
C receives 16 units from the pool
D receives 9 units from the pool
E receives 2 units from the pool

Overall result of this game of Easy Go: A wins 1 unit; B wins 5 units; C wins 3 units;
D wins 2 units; E loses 3 units; banker loses 8 units

Hoggenheimer

Hoggenheimer is known as English Roulette, because the bets and staking bear a similarity to the French gambling game.

Number of players

Any number may play.

Cards

Hoggenheimer is played with a pack of cards from which all of the 2s, 3s, 4s, 5s and 6s have been removed, and the Joker (or one of the rejected cards) added. This will leave a pack of 33 cards.

How to play

After the pack has been shuffled and cut, the banker deals the cards, face downwards, in four rows of eight cards each, and places aside, also face downwards, the 33rd card. Great care must be taken when dealing that no one sees the face of any of the cards.

The top row is for spades, from Ace down to 7; the second row for hearts, from Ace o 7; the third row for diamonds, from Ace to 7; the bottom row for clubs, from Ace to 7.

The players now stake their money. They may stake on a single card being turned up (even chance), or two touching cards being turned up (2 to 1 chance), or all four cards in a column or any group of four touching cards being turned up (4 to 1 chance), or all eight cards in a row being turned up (8 to 1 chance). All of the cards

in a bet must be exposed during the game before the Joker appears and stops play.

When the players have placed their bets, the banker picks up the 33rd card and shows it. If it is the Joker he wins all the money on the table and there is a redeal. If, as is more likely, it is another card, he places it in its appropriate place in the layout, exposes the card that it replaces and transfers this card to its place in the layout; and so on until the game is brought to an end when he exposes the Joker.

The banker then collects the money on the chances that have not materialized in full, and pays out on those that have.

Hoggenheimer in progress. Stake 1 is on ♠10 being turned up; Stake 2 on ♠9, ♠8; Stake 3 on all four Queens; Stake 4 on ♦10, ♦9, ♣10, ♣9; Stake 5 on all clubs; Stake 6 on ♥7 and ♦7

Lift Smoke

Lift Smoke is a simple English game. It can be played for stakes by each player putting an agreed amount into a kitty before each deal.

Number of players

The game is for four to six players, six perhaps being the best. Each player plays for himself.

Cards

The full pack of 52 cards is used. The cards rank from Ace (high) to 2 (low). One player picks up the cards and deals them round face up – the first player to be dealt a Jack becomes the first dealer. Thereafter the winner of each game deals for the next.

The dealer deals the cards one at a time in a clockwise direction to each player, beginning with the player on his left. Each player receives the same number of cards as there are players in the game, i.e. with six players each player receives six cards. The last card dealt to the dealer is turned face up to establish the trump suit. The cards not dealt are placed in the centre of the table to form a stock.

How to play

When all players have seen the trump suit, the dealer takes his cards into his hand, and the trick-taking phase of the game begins. The player to the left of dealer leads the first trick, with any card he likes. Subsequent players must follow suit if able, and if unable may trump or discard. The trick is won by the highest trump, or failing a trump by the highest card in the suit led.

When a trick is won, it is placed face down to one side, and the winner of the trick takes into his hand the top card of the stock. No other player takes a card, so the hands are now unequal. The winner of a trick leads the next trick.

Each time a player fails to win a trick, his hand will diminish by one card. When a player is reduced to no cards, he drops out of the game. The last player remaining wins the game and takes the kitty.

If the last card is taken from the stock while two or more players still have cards, the winner is the player who takes the next trick.

Monte Bank

Monte Bank, also known as Monte, is the national card game of Mexico.

Number of players

Any number may play.

Cards

The game is played with a pack of cards with the 8s, 9s and 10s removed.

After the cards have been shuffled and the pack cut by one of the players, the banker draws the two cards from the bottom of the pack and places them face upwards on the table (the bottom layout), and then the two cards from the top of the pack and places them face upwards on the table (the top layout).

How to play

The players place their bets up to an agreed maximum on whichever layout they choose. The banker then turns the pack face upwards and if the exposed bottom card (known as the gate) is of the same suit as any of the four cards in the layouts, he pays all bets on that layout, and collects all bets on a layout that shows no cards of the same suit as the gate.

The layouts and gate are then discarded, the game continuing with new layouts and another gate. The bank passes clockwise after five deals.

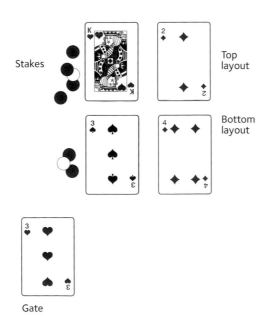

Stakes

Top layout

Bottom layout

Gate

Racing

Racing is a simple gambling game.

Number of players
Any number may play.

Cards
Racing is played with the standard pack of 52 cards.

How to play
The four Aces are placed in a row on the table. The remainder of the pack is shuffled and cut, and the banker draws the top seven cards from the pack and lays them in a vertical column immediately below the Aces, so that the layout takes the form of a T (see illustration, right).

The banker deals the remaining cards one at a time, and each time that the card of a suit is dealt the Ace of the same suit is moved one card forward, the winner being the Ace that is first to pass the seventh card.

Players may place their stakes on whichever Ace they choose, the race ending when an Ace passes the seventh card.

Racing layout. The banker might offer evens on a suit if there are no cards in the column to match the Ace; 2-1 if there is one card (as with clubs and hearts here); 3-1 if there are two cards (diamonds here); 5-1 if there are three cards (spades here); and 10-1 if there are four cards. If there are five or more cards of a suit in the layout, it is impossible for that suit to win, and there must be a redeal.

Slippery Sam

Slippery Sam is probably the only banking game that favours the player rather than the banker, because the player has the advantage of seeing his cards before he bets and, therefore, can calculate whether the odds are in his favour or against him.

Number of players
Any number up to ten may play, with six to eight the best.

Cards
The full pack of 52 is used, the cards ranking from Aces (high) to 2s (low).

How to play
The banker places an agreed sum in a pool and then deals three cards, one at a time, face downwards, to each player. The remainder of the pack (the stock) he places face downwards on the table in front of him and topples it over to make it easier to slide off the top card.

The player on the left of the dealer, after looking at his cards, bets that at least one of them will be in the same suit as, and higher than, the top card of the stock. He may bet all that is in the pool or any part of it, but he may not bet less than an agreed minimum. When he has made his bet, the banker turns over the top card of the stock. If the player has won his bet he exposes his card and takes his winnings out of the pool. If he has lost his bet he pays the amount that he betted into the pool and does not expose his card. The four cards are then thrown into a discard pile, and the opportunity to bet passes to the next player.

A player must not look at his cards until it is his turn to bet; if the pool is exhausted the bank immediately passes to the next player, otherwise the banker holds the bank for three full deals round the table, and then he may either pass the bank to the player on his left or hold the bank for one more deal round the table.

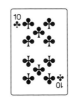

Since the player wins if a red card or a club lower than the 10 is exposed, and loses only if a spade or the Ace, King, Queen or Jack of clubs is exposed, he has 32 chances of winning and 17 of losing: he should stake heavily!

Sweet Sixteen

Two cards, a banker and a simple target – this game is as sweet as its name.

Number of players

This game is for two to ten players.

Cards

Before the game can start, the players must agree upon stakes and upon the number of deals over which the game will be played. It's probably best to play for five deals and to award points according to the scoring guide outlined below. Counters can be used to aid scoring. Each player should start with ten counters, but don't forget that the bank will need to be well stocked too!

Next, a banker must be appointed; the players each cut the deck and whoever gets the lowest card gets the job. The banker removes the eights and sixes (with the exception of the eight of diamonds) from the deck. The remaining 45 cards are shuffled and passed to the player seated to the left of the banker.

How to play

The first player to start takes the top two cards from the deck, which is positioned face down in front of him or her. Their aim is to hold two cards with a value of 16 (Aces are low and court cards each count ten). They can swap their cards one at a time, discarding one of the cards held onto a waste pile and taking the top card from the deck.

The player can continue changing cards to get closer to the grail of 16. However, if they exceed 16, their hand will 'bust' and their turn comes to an end. They may choose to avoid this situation by electing safely to stick on any total under 16.

A player does not tell his or her opponents what they have scored – even if they have bust – but instead simply puts their cards face-down in front of them. They now shuffle the deck, mixing in the cards from the waste pile, and pass it to the player seated to their left.

The game continues until all players have had their turn. The cards are then revealed, with each player turning their hand over simultaneously on the word of the banker.

Counters can then be awarded on the following basis:

- Players with 16 exactly receive as many counters from the bank as there are players in the game.
- Players with 16 exactly in a hand that includes the eight of diamonds receive

two counters from the bank for each player in the game.

- Players with less than 16 pay the banker one counter.
- Players with more than 16 pay the banker one counter for every point above 16.
- Ten bonus counters are awarded to the player with the best hand. In the event of a tie, the counters are shared.

At the end of ten deals, the counters are totted up. The player with the most wins the prize.

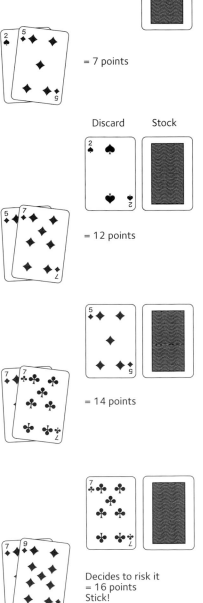

= 7 points

Discard   Stock

= 12 points

= 14 points

Decides to risk it
= 16 points
Stick!

Vingt et Un

With no complicated set-ups and no impenetrable rules, Vingt et Un is the undoubted king of prize-winning card games.

Number of players

This game is for two to ten players.

Cards

Shuffle a standard 52-card deck of cards and cut, the player with the highest card becomes banker. In this version of the game, the banker does not play but merely deals the cards and distributes the winnings. He or she starts by giving each player a set number of counters (25 is a good number to start with). The remainder goes to the bank.

How to play

The aim of the game is to assemble a hand that totlas 21, or as near to it as possible without going over ('busting'). The banker gives each player one card, which is dealt face down onto the table. Players look at their cards and place their stakes. A maximum and minimum starting stake should be set (say, a minimum of one counter and a maximum of three counters). Once all players have placed their stakes, the dealer hands round a second card to each player – again, face down.

The players look at their cards and assess their options; they each now have a chance to improve their hand if they want. The player to the left of the banker goes first, with the turn moving around the table clockwise thereafter.

Players can choose to buy, twist or stick.

'Buy': This is where players take an additional card and add to their stake. The additional stake must not exceed the maximum, but can be no less than the original amount they staked at the start of the game. Players can immediately buy a fourth and fifth card if they want, but on each occasion they must add to their stake again. Alternatively, they can stop buying cards and twist (see above right). For example, a player who has a ten and two may elect to buy a card first, but if the card dealt is another two, they may decide to be cautious and twist for their fourth card.

'Twist': If a player decides to twist, he or she does not add to their stake but simply takes another card from the dealer. Once a player has started twisting, they cannot subsequently 'buy', so their stake remains the same.

'Stick': If a player is happy with his or her two cards, either because they add

A winning hand, totalling 21

A 'royal pontoon'

up to 21 or because they are close to that total, they may decide to stick with them. He or she puts them on the table face down and takes no further cards. In our game we will make it a rule that players cannot stick with a total of 15 or under.

Players continue to twist and buy cards until either their total exceeds 21, at which point they are said to have 'bust', or they decide to stick.

When all players have finished their bidding, the banker asks them to turn over their cards.

The winning hand is that which totals closest to 21. A hand comprised of an Ace and a ten is called 'pontoon', but an Ace and a court card supersedes this and is called 'royal pontoon'. If no player holds such a hand, then any combination that adds up to 21 is victorious. Failing that, the total closest to 21 wins. In the event of two players holding a hand of equal value, the bank pays both. All losing players must pay their stakes to

the banker, while the victors receive payment equal to their stakes from the banker.

Card values

In Vingt et Un, the Aces are high or low (that is, they count as one or 11) and the court cards (King, Queen and Jack) count as 10.

Poker
Games

Poker Basics

The object of poker

The object of the game is to win money, or the chips representing money, from the other players. This is achieved in a succession of deals which last either until all the players remaining in the game agree to stop or until only one player remains, all the others having lost their stake money. Each deal is complete in itself and is not affected by previous or subsequent deals.

Each player in each deal is dealt a poker hand of five cards; in some games, e.g. Seven-card Stud Poker, each player selects his five-card hand from a larger number of cards. In successive rounds of betting, each player bets that he holds a better poker hand than any other player.

Players place their bets towards the centre of the table, the accumulated bets becoming the pot. A player may fold (pull out of a deal) at any time, but loses any stakes he has already bet in that deal.

A deal finishes when either all players but one fold, and he takes the pot, or a showdown is reached. The remaining players reveal their hands, and the player with the best hand takes the pot.

At the showdown, if two players or more have equally good winning hands the pot is divided between them.

Most poker games can be played in a 'High-Low' version, in which the player with the best hand, and the player with the 'worst', share the pot. In some versions, one player can win 'high' and 'low' with the same hand.

General rules of the game

This section relates to practices common to all forms of poker. How to play specific versions of the game follow in the parts on Draw Poker and Stud Poker, etc.

The cards

The standard pack of 52 cards is used, with the cards ranking:
A (high), K, Q, J, 10, 9, 8, 7, 6, 5, 4, 3, 2.

The Ace can also be used at the end of the sequence 5, 4, 3, 2, A, where it is ranked low. It can't be used in the middle of a sequence, e.g., 2, A, K, Q, J.

The suits are equal and not ranked.

Wild cards

By mutual agreement, any card or cards in the pack may be designated wild. The holder of a wild card may use it to represent any card he wishes, except that in some schools he cannot use it to duplicate a card he already holds, i.e. if he holds all four Aces, his wild card cannot represent a fifth Ace.

If a player has a pair of Kings and a pair of 4s, he can use a wild card to convert his two pairs to a full house, which ranks higher. Equally, if he has three of a kind, he can use a wild card to improve it to four of a kind.

Key to Poker illustrations
Chips
- Stakes and antes are represented by circles; the numbers in the circles represent the number of chips.
- White chips indicate those staked in previous betting rounds.

- Grey chips indicate those staked during the current betting round.
- Orange chips indicate those in a side-pot in Stud Poker.

Cards shown face up but shaded represent cards in the players' hands or face down on the table.

Players coloured orange represent those no longer in the hand.

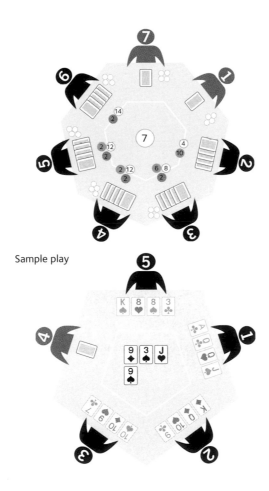

Sample play

POKER GAMES

Ranking of Poker Hands

The ranking of poker hands is shown below, from highest to lowest. 'Combinations' indicates the number of such hands possible in a 52-card pack without wild cards being used. Also shown is the probability of being dealt such a hand straight from the pack, and lastly, the probability of that happening, expressed as a percentage.

Table 1: The ranking of poker hands

		Combinations	Probability	Description
1st	Straight flush	40	1 in 64,974 0.0015%	Five cards of the same suit in sequence. Between two or more straight flushes, that with the highest-ranking top card wins. A tie is possible.
2nd	Four of a kind	624	1 in 4,165 0.00240%	Four cards of the same rank, with an odd fifth card. Between two similar hands, that with the higher-ranking four cards wins. There cannot be a tie, so the fifth card is of no consequence.
3rd	Full house	3,744	1 in 694 0.1441%	Three cards of one rank (i.e. a triple) with two of another (i.e. a pair). Between two full houses, the one with the higher-ranking set of three wins. A tie is impossible.
4th	Flush	5,108	1 in 509 0.1967%	Five cards of the same suit, but not in sequence. Between flushes, the one containing the highest card wins, if equal the second highest, and so on. Ties are possible.
5th	Straight	10,200	1 in 255 0.3925%	Five cards in sequence, but not of the same suit. Between straights, the one containing the highest card at the top of the sequence wins. Note that A, K, Q, J, 10 therefore beats 5, 4, 3, 2, A, where the Ace counts low. Ties are possible.

230

What happens if...?

• What happens if the cards in a flush are exactly the same value as each other, for instance, the hands are tied, as below?

♥10, 8, 7, 6, 3   ♣10, 8, 7, 6, 3

Answer: In this situation the pot is split between the two players.

• What happens if the cards of the two pairs are exactly the same? For instance:

♥K, ♦K, ♣7, ♠7   ♠K, ♣K, ♦7, ♥7

Answer: The fifth card determines the outcome. If this is also the same, the pot is split.

		Combinations	Probability	Description
6th	Three of a kind	54,912	1 in 47 2.1129%	Three cards of the same rank with two unmatching cards. Between similar hands, that with the highest-ranking three wins. Ties are impossible.
7th	Two pairs	123,552	1 in 21 4.7539%	Two cards of one rank, two of another and an odd card. Between similar hands, that with the highest-ranking pair wins, if equal the highest-ranking second pair, if equal the odd card. Ties are possible.
8th	One pair	1,098,240	1 in 2.3665 42.2569%	Two cards of one rank with three other unmatching cards. Between similar hands, the highest-ranking pair wins, if equal the highest-ranking odd card, if equal the next highest ranking, and so on. Ties are possible.
9th	Nothing	1,302,540	1 in 1.9953 50.1177%	This hand lacks an accepted name, and is sometimes called a 'no-pair' hand or a 'high-card' hand. Hands of this type are ranked by the highest-ranked card they contain, if equal by the second card and so on. Ties are possible.

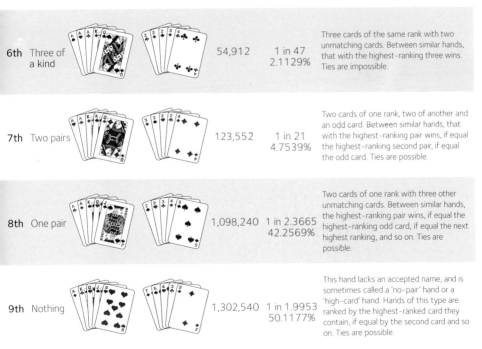

The Set Up

Here are a few useful things to know before beginning to learn the rules and regulations of poker. Because poker is a betting game, many players take the rules of the game very seriously so it's good to be prepared.

In a casino or club, where everything is supplied, from table to cards, the game will be played with chips. Usually there are four denominations, denoted by white chips, red chips, blue chips and yellow chips.

The value in cash of a unit is variable – some tables having higher stakes and being more 'valuable' than others. In private games cash may be used as stakes, but it is preferable to play with chips. The players determine in advance the value of each colour in units, and the value of the unit in cash, before anyone buys his chips. For example, a white chip worth one unit could represent anything between a penny and a pound in Britain, or anything from a cent to a dollar or a euro, etc. elsewhere.

In this book, in each example of specimen games, we will describe the betting in terms of chips only.

Common chip values

white	red	blue	yellow
1	2	5	10
1	5	10	25
1	5	25	100

Banker

If chips are being used, the players should select one player to act as banker, who has first choice of seat. He has charge of all the chips and issues them to the players, including himself, at their cash value, and redeems for the appropriate amount the chips of players who leave the game.

Time limit

Before play begins, players should agree on a time at which play will end. If other players join the game later they are bound by the time limit initially agreed upon. Players are free to leave the game earlier if they wish.

Seating

After the banker has chosen his seat, other players may choose seats if they wish. If there is a dispute, the cards are shuffled by any agreed player, and cut by another. The banker then deals a face-up card to all of the other players. The player dealt the highest card (Ace high) has first choice of seat, the next highest card the next choice, and so on. If two players draw equal cards, they are dealt a second card to break the tie.

Player 1	Player 2	Player 3	Player 4	Player 5
6♥	A♣	7♦	A♦	2♠

K♥   4♣

Choosing seats Players 2 and 4 were both given Aces in the first deal, and in the second deal, player 2's King beats player 4's four, so player 2 may choose where to sit first, followed by players 4, 3, 1 and 5 – in that order

Changing seats Players can change seats at any time after one hour of continuous play, and again at any time after another hour of play. If a player wants to change seats and someone else disagrees, repeat the seat-choosing process, as already described.

Jargon-buster

Burned card A discard from the top of the pack.

Chips Tokens used in poker instead of money.

Pair Two cards of the same rank.

Pot The total of the stakes which have been bet, and which the winner takes.

Triple, trey or trip Three cards of the same rank.

Wild card A card which by prior agreement its holder can use as any card he wishes.

The Sequence of Play

In poker, everything passes to the left. The dealer deals the cards, clockwise, one at a time to all the players, beginning with the players to his left, the turn to bet passes from player to player to the left and when each hand is over, the player to the left of the previous dealer deals.

First dealer

Once everybody is seated, the first dealer is chosen in the same way as seats are chosen (see page 232), except the banker this time deals a card to himself as well as the other players. If two players or more hold equal highest cards the banker deals a second card to each of them. The player with the highest card is first dealer.

In a casino, where the dealer is not one of the players, a button or disc is used to designate the player who would otherwise be the dealer, and this button passes round the table to determine who receives cards first, who bets first, etc. This is a simple way of avoiding arguments about whose turn it is.

Antes

To make the game more rewarding, financially, in most forms of poker a number of chips are put into the middle of the table to start the pot before each deal. These are called the *ante*. Most commonly, each player puts one chip

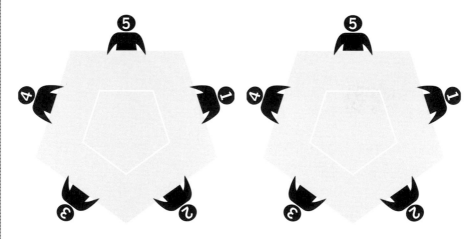

Progression of the deal and play The person to the left of the dealer is, in most circumstances, the first person to receive cards and to bet. When a hand is completed, the deal and turn to play first move to the left

into the pot before the deal. For convenience, sometimes the dealer puts in for all players, e.g. if there are eight players, the dealer puts in eight chips. After eight deals, each player's contribution in antes is equal. The ante is placed in the centre of the table and usually, for convenience, kept separate from the stakes each player bets during the deal, as the amount of each player's bet should be easy to see. The winner takes the ante and the stakes at the end of each deal.

Big and small blinds

Sometimes, instead of an ante, where all players put in, a blind bet is made by each of the first two players to the dealer's left. The first player puts in one chip called an ante, or small blind. The second player puts in a larger amount, agreed beforehand, say two chips, called a straddle, or big blind. The third player is the first to bet voluntarily. The small and big blinds are placed in front of the players making them, since they count as actual bets rather than antes.

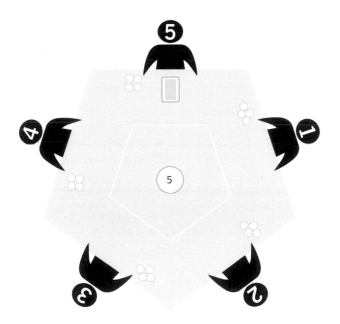

Antes and blind bets   In the ante, each player will contribute an equal amount, say one chip, to a pile in the middle of the table, as shown. Where only some players contribute, as in the system of big and small blinds, the chips count as part of the players' bets

Preparing the Deck

Shuffling

Before each deal, the cards must be shuffled at least three times. Any player may ask to shuffle, but the dealer shuffles last.

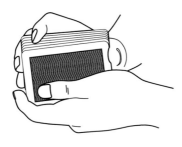

1. Hold the pack face down in the fingers of your left hand, with your left thumb holding the pack on top. With your right hand grasp the majority of the cards from the bottom of the pack.

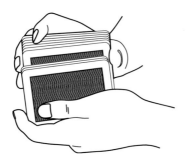

2. With your left thumb, pull off six to 12 cards from the top of the pack while your right hand takes the main part of the pack over them. The cards in your left hand drop into your palm.

3. Bring the pack over with your right hand, slip a few more cards off with your left thumb and repeat the process.

Cutting

After shuffling, the dealer then places the cards before the player to his right, who cuts by removing some cards from the top of the pack, placing them on the table and putting the remainder of the cards on top of them. Both parts of the pack during the cut should contain at least five cards.

If the player to dealer's right declines to cut, the obligation passes to the player to his right. The only reason to refuse to cut is superstition. If all the players refuse to cut, the dealer should do so himself.

1. Lift a proportion of the cards off the top of the deck, without looking at the bottom card or allowing anyone else to see it.

2. Place the removed cards next to the pack.

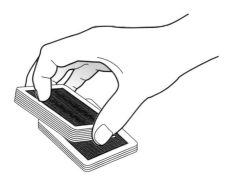

3. Put the main part of the pack on top of them.

Dealing

After the shuffle and cut, the dealer *burns* the top card of the pack by placing it face down on the table to begin what will become a pile of discarded cards as the game progresses. He then deals the cards one at a time to each player, including himself, beginning with the player to his left. The number of cards dealt, and whether they are face up or face down, depends upon the form of poker being played.

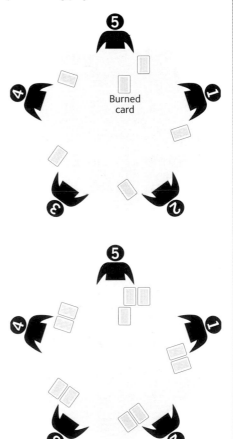

Burned card

Betting

In all forms of poker, betting takes place during what are known as 'betting intervals'. In each betting interval, one of the players has the right, or the obligation, to bet first. Each player thereafter in turn is required to do one of four things: bet, call, raise or fold.

There is, however, a fifth option open to players: to 'check'. This only applies in certain circumstances, and is discussed under 'Checking' below.

Bet

A player opens the betting by placing a certain number of chips into the pot, announcing the number of chips being bet. For example: 'I bet two'.

Call

The following player puts enough chips into the pot to make his contribution to it equal to the highest better so far, but no higher. By doing this he is retaining his interest in the pot. He announces he is calling, and the number of chips he is putting in. For example, he might say, 'I call for two.'

Raise

Another player puts enough chips into the pot to make his contribution equal to the highest better plus one or more chips. He announces the amount he is putting in, first to call and then to raise. He might say, 'I call two and raise another two'.

Fold

A player who feels he cannot win returns his cards face down to the dealer and announces that he is folding. This means that the player discards his hand. He relinquishes any interest in the pot for that deal and does not recover any chips he might already have contributed to the pot. Under no circumstances must other players see the cards he held as this would make the game unfair.

When placing chips into the pot, players do not mix their chips with those of the other players, since the value of each player's contribution to the pot must be seen. Players push their chips towards the centre of the table while keeping them separate from the rest.

Checking

In some forms of poker, there is a fifth option in addition to betting, calling, raising or folding, known as checking.

The first player whose turn it is to bet may check, which means he wishes to stay in the pot but not yet to bet, and he doesn't put any chips into the pot. Checking might be thought of as a 'bet of nothing'. Subsequent players may also

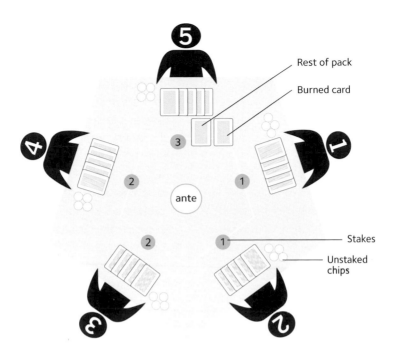

Rest of pack

Burned card

ante

Stakes

Unstaked chips

First betting round After a first round of betting, a table might look like the one shown above. After Player 1 bet one chip, Player 2 calls, Player 3 raises, Player 4 calls and Player 5 re-raises

check, but as soon as any player has made a bet it is no longer possible to check during that betting interval: players can stay in the pot only by calling or raising.

Betting after blind bets

After blind bets have been made in the form of small and big blinds (say of one and two chips, respectively), the third player (who is the first to bet voluntarily) must put in at least two chips to stay in the pot, i.e. what is needed to call, as the ante and straddle are regarded as normal bets. When the turn to bet has gone round the table and returned to the players who put in the ante and straddle, the chips they contributed count as normal bets: if the stakes are now six chips, player 1 has to contribute only five to call, and player 2 only four.

Betting etiquette

To avoid disputes, there are a few general guidelines about betting etiquette. Contravening them can result in penalties.

- A player should always state clearly whether he's betting, folding, raising, calling or checking, e.g. if he is raising,

he might say, 'Call two and raise two.'
- Players should always wait their turn.
- Players should only push their cards away or add them to the discard pile if they are folding.
- In most forms of poker, players should show their cards only during showdown.

Betting limits

It is usually considered desirable to limit the amount that the first better may bet, and the amount by which any player (or players) may raise. This prevents a player with a large bankroll dominating. It is sensible to have a lower limit for a bet or raise and that this limit should be one chip.

It might be, in the most sedate of games, that the upper limit on a bet or raise is also one chip. This is not so stifling or timid as it sounds, as continual raising by four or five players could raise a pot to 50 or more units in the first betting interval alone, as the table below shows.

Players				
1	2	3	4	5
First round				
1	2	3	4	5
Second round				
5(6)	5(7)	5(8)	5(9)	5(10)
Third round				
5(11)	fold	3(11)	2(11)	fold

On the other hand, if players feel daring or rich, they might decide on the upper limit on a bet or raise equivalent to the value of the highest chip, which might be 10, 25 or 100.

Some also think it desirable (and safer for all other players!) to limit the number of raises any one player can make during a betting interval, again as a means of preventing the richest players steamrollering the others. Three raises is a recommended number.

Other ways of establishing upper betting limits are by introducing a variable limit; by betting the raise; by having a pot limit; table stakes; or by freeze-out.

Variable limit

In Draw Poker the maximum limit might be higher after the draw than before; for example, one chip before the draw, two chips after the draw, or two chips before and five after. In Stud Poker the limit might be higher in the final betting interval than in previous betting intervals. For example; in Five-card Stud the limit might be one chip for the first three betting intervals and ten chips for the last.

Bet the raise

This means that a player may raise by the greatest number of chips that a previous player has put into the pot. For example, if the first bet was one chip, the limit for a raise is one chip: the first player to raise must put in two chips (one to call and one to raise) –

thereafter the limit is two chips, and so on, with the limit rising as the betting progresses. Players do not have to bet up to the limit, but if they were to do so, the stakes would rise rapidly. In the following example, each player either folds, calls or raises by the maximum. In three rounds, the pot reaches 144 chips.

Players				
1	2	3	4	5
First round				
1	2	3	4	5
Second round				
7(8)	14(16)	fold	28(32)	fold
Third round				
56(64)	fold		32(64)	

Pot limit

With this system, a player may bet or raise by as many chips as are in the pot, which would include the units the player himself needed to put in to call the previous bet. Beware, as when using this method, the limit can rise very fast. In the example shown below, each player folds, calls or raises by the maximum.

The result is, that in only two rounds, an initial pot of one chip has risen to a staggering 1,222 chips!

Players				
1	2	3	4	5
First round				
1	3	10	34	116
(total of pot)				
1	4	14	48	164

Second round				
394	fold	385	fold	279
(395)				
(total of pot)				
558	558	943	943	1,222

Table stakes

Each player buys an agreed equal amount of chips from the banker, let us say 100 chips. This is called the *take-out*. If a player wants more chips, he must buy them in the same amount of 100 chips, as often as he wishes. He cannot buy additional chips in the middle of a deal, and if he runs out he must wait until after that deal has been won, when he may buy another 100.

He can only buy fewer than 100 chips if he cannot afford the full amount. If he then loses these chips he must leave the game.

The only limit in this form of poker is the amount of chips a player has before him. If a player runs out of chips during a deal, he must 'tap out' (see page 243).

Freeze-out

A common form of poker, in which the overall amount of stakes that can be lost is limited, is called *freeze-out*.

In this version, all the players begin with an equal number of chips, which has been agreed in advance, and play until only one player is left, who of course wins the lot.

The game is called freeze-out because players are not allowed to prolong their play by buying more chips during the game. This form of poker is popular in casinos, and if you've ever played or witnessed a freeze-out game, you'll know that such a game can last an extremely long time.

Jargon buster

All-in To bet all one's chips, placing them in the pot.

Ante A compulsory stake placed into the pot before the deal.

Bet To place stakes into the pot.

Betting interval A period in the game when the players have been dealt some or all of their cards and in which they bet, call, raise, fold or check. The number of betting intervals varies with the form of poker being played.

Betting round During a betting interval, a betting round ends when all players have had an opportunity to bet once. The first player to bet then has the option to bet again, and a second betting round begins. Successive rounds take place until all bets are equal, when the betting interval ends.

Big blind Another name for the straddle.

Blind bet A compulsory bet made before the deal. It differs from an ante in being an active bet, i.e. it counts towards a better's total stake.

Call To place stakes into the pot to equalize your total stake with that of the previous better.

Check To stay in the game without adding to one's total stake. This is not

possible once a player has bet at that betting interval.

Equalize To make all players' stakes equal. A player who calls equalizes his stake with that of the previous better.

Flop The first three of the five community cards, dealt face up in Hold 'em and Omaha.

Fold To give up one's hand and drop out of the deal.

Freeze-out A game played to a finish, when only one player is left with all the stake money.

Nut hand or **nuts** The best hand possible, taking into account a player's hole cards.

Raise To place into the pot enough stakes to equal the previous better, and to add more.

Side-pot A separate pot begun when a player has tapped out.

Small blind The first blind bet, which precedes the big blind.

Straddle A second and final blind bet made in some poker games. It is larger than the first blind bet.

Suited If the two cards dealt face down to the player are of the same suit, they are said to be suited.

Take-out The agreed amount of chips that each player buys from the bank to begin a game at table stakes.

Tap out A procedure that is forced on a player during a betting interval when he is unable to continue betting because he has insufficient chips to call the bet (see page 243).

Fair Play

Tapping out

One principle of poker is that a player cannot be bulldozed out of a game by heavy betters who increase the stakes beyond his capital. If a player has insufficient chips to call, e.g. if he needs 12 chips to call but has only 10, he may put in all his remaining chips and call for that amount. This is called tapping out. He might say, 'I call for 10 and am tapping out'. Any excess that other players have already contributed is not withdrawn by them, but is moved into a side-pot, kept separate from the main pot, which is thus *equalized*. The player who has tapped out continues in that deal and competes for the main pot, although he takes no further part in the betting itself.

Players still active in the deal continue to bet in the side-pot until their bets are equalized. Should one of them have insufficient chips to call in the side-pot he can tap out of that and a second side-pot is formed. At the showdown, every player who has not folded, including the player who tapped out, competes for the main pot, while the final side-pot is contested only by those players who stayed in and contributed the full amount of chips.

If a player folds in a side-pot, he does not compete for the main pot, even though he folded after the main pot was closed.

1st betting round   Players 1 and 2 are not sure enough of their hands to bet so they check and the dealer folds

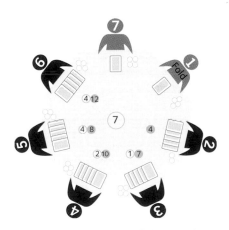

2nd betting round   Player 1 folds, while Player 2 calls Player 6's four chips. Player 3 raises the stake to eight chips, player 4 to 12, Player 5 calls and Player 6 raises to 16 chips

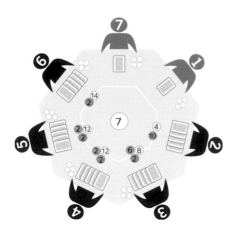

3rd betting round Player 2, with only 10 chips left, taps out with a total of 14 chips, two fewer than he needs to call. Players 3, 4 and 5 add sufficient chips to bring their contributions to the main pot to 14 chips and put two into a side-pot, while Player 6 takes two chips from his stake and puts those into a side-pot

The betting interval illustrated on page 243 and above has ended with players 3, 4, 5 and 6 as active players in the game, each having contributed 16 chips. Player 2 takes no further part in subsequent betting intervals, but retains his interest in the main pot, which is frozen at 77 chips (players 2, 3, 4, 5 and 6 each having put in 14 chips and the ante being seven chips). Players 3, 4, 5 and 6 withdraw two chips from the main pot each and keep these in a separate pile as the basis for the side-pot. They continue betting at subsequent betting intervals. At the showdown, if player 2's hand is the best remaining, he wins the main pot of 77 chips – if not, he leaves

the game. If player 2 takes the 77 chips, the player holding the best hand of those remaining in the side-pot at the showdown takes the side-pot. If his hand is better than player 2's, he takes the main pot and the side-pot.

A player can only tap out if all his chips are exhausted. If he wins the main pot, he can continue in the game, but if he loses he must leave the game, unless table stakes are being played (see page 241), when he can buy another set of chips.

Showdown

When the final betting interval has taken place, if more than one player is left, they show their hands by exposing them on the table, beginning with the last player to raise. Usually a player announces what he has, e.g. 'Full house, Kings', but it is not necessary to do so, and if he makes a mistake in what he says he is not bound by it – it is the cards that count. The player with the highest-ranking poker hand wins the pot. A player should not begin to take the pot before it is agreed by the others that he has won it.

All players, including those who have folded, are entitled to see the hands of those in the showdown. However, some players, if beaten in the showdown, are reluctant to show their hands in case it provides clues to their strategy, and will say 'You win' or 'Beats me' and fold their cards with the intention of discarding them. Many other players are fine with this, but they can insist on seeing the cards if they wish. To avoid ill-feeling it is best to agree before play starts whether or not all active hands will be exposed at the showdown.

Tied hands

If two or more players in the showdown have exactly tied hands (which is very unusual), then the pot is divided between them. If there is an odd chip that cannot be divided, it goes to the player who last raised.

Last man in

If there is only one player left in the game (e.g. one player bet or raised and nobody subsequently called) then there is no need for a showdown and that player takes the pot without having to expose his hand.

Exposing cards

A player who folds must not expose his cards. In fact cards should not be exposed unless the rules of the showdown require it. A player who accidentally exposes a card is not penalized, but if cards are exposed regularly, whether intentionally or not, a penalty should be payed on request of the dealer – say one chip to each player.

Going through the discards

No player may look at the cards remaining in the pack after the deal is completed, nor at cards discarded by players during the deal. A player who does so, if still in the game, must fold; if not in the game he must pay a penalty – say one chip to each player.

Dealer's responsibility

The dealer should watch for irregularities and draw the attention of the players to any that might occur. Any dispute in the action to be taken should be decided by the players.

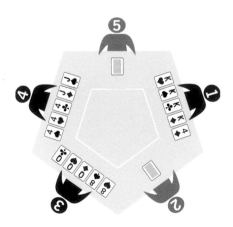

Showdown Usually all the remaining active hands are shown at the showdown. In this example, Players 3 and 4, each with a full house, would have felt confident of winning but are beaten by Player 1's four Kings

Draw Poker

In early poker games, players were dealt five cards upon which they bet. There was no provision for a player to change any of his cards – it was a game of deal, bet, showdown.

When the concept was introduced of allowing players, after what now became the first betting interval, to improve their hands by discarding some cards and drawing others to replace them, before a second round of betting took place, the game became called 'Draw Poker' to distinguish it from the earlier game, which is now not widely played at all.

Nowadays the name 'Draw Poker' is retained to distinguish it from forms of Stud Poker. It remains the most common form of poker played at home and beginners are advised to master it before attempting Stud, Hold 'em, etc.

The version described first is the basic game, which might be called 'Straight Draw Poker' but in the USA a slight variation called 'Jackpots' (see page 252) is so popular that some American books will describe that as the main game, and this version as a variation, called something like 'Anything Opens'.

'Draw' is a slight misnomer, since players do not 'draw' their replacement cards; these are dealt to them by the dealer. The game is best for between five and seven players.

Preliminaries

As described before in the general rules for poker games, players should agree a few things before they start playing:

- a time limit for the game, and agree that when that time is reached the game ends as soon as all the players have dealt an equal number of times
- which form of the game is being played (as will be seen, there are hundreds of variations, one of which is called Dealer's Choice, which allows the dealer to choose which variation will be played for that deal)
- the stake limits
- how any irregularities are dealt with.
- who is to be banker if chips are being used
- who is to be first dealer
- seating arrangements.

For this description of a six-handed game, we will assume the following have been agreed:

- chips of four colours, valued at one, two, five and 10 units, are being used.
- no bet or raise may be less than one chip.
- before the draw no raise may be larger than two chips, and after the draw five chips.
- the maximum number of raises one player can make is three per betting interval.

The play

1. The dealer places six chips in the centre of the table as an ante to start the pot. This represents one chip for each player, but for convenience's sake each dealer in turn may put in the ante for all players.

2. The cards are shuffled, cut and dealt as described in the general rules on page 236.

3. The dealer gives five cards to each player, including himself, one at a time, beginning with the player to his left (sometimes called the eldest hand). The dealer then places the remainder of the pack face down in front of him.

First betting interval

Between deals, players have the opportunity to bet in 'betting intervals', which may be divided into 'betting rounds'. The first opportunity to bet lies with the player to the dealer's left. He has three choices at this stage: to fold, to check or to bet. If he checks, the second player has the same option, and so on. But as soon as one player has bet, the option to check ends – from this point on players must either call, raise or fold.

If every player, including the dealer, checks on the first round, the deal comes to an end. The cards are collected, reshuffled and cut, and dealt by the next dealer, who puts in another ante of six chips, making the pot twelve chips for the next deal.

The draw

The betting interval ends when the bets of all the players who remain in the game are equalized. The draw then takes place.

1. The dealer takes up the undealt portion of the pack, and deals in turn with each player who remains in the game, i.e. those who haven't folded, beginning with the player nearest to his left.

2. This player announces how many cards he wishes to discard. If he does not wish to change his hand, he is said to 'stand pat'. This is usually done by announcing 'none' and tapping on the table. Otherwise he may discard between one and three cards. (If there were fewer than six players, he could discard up to four cards.)

3. The player passes the cards he has discarded face down to the dealer who lays them to one side to make a discard pile. He then gives the player an equal number of cards to restore his hand to five cards.

4. The dealer then deals in the same way with the next player. No player need announce how many cards he wishes to discard until the previous player has been dealt with.

5. The dealer draws his own cards last, taking care to announce how many cards he is discarding and replacing.

During the draw, before the first bet has been made, any player may enquire of another how many cards he drew.

Second betting interval

When the draw is completed, and all players have their final hands of five cards each, the second betting interval takes place. The first player to speak is the first player who bet on the first betting interval. If he has subsequently folded, then the first active player to his left has the same opportunity, and so on. The first options are to check, fold or bet, as before, but once a bet has been made, then subsequently the options are to fold, call or raise. Again the betting round continues until all active players have contributed the same amount to the pot, when the betting stops and the showdown takes place.

The showdown

Starting with the last player to raise, and continuing clockwise, each active player shows and announces his hand. The player who holds the best poker hand takes the pot.

Strategy before the draw

The first decision you have to make after the deal is whether to fold, check, call, bet or raise. In making this decision you will naturally be assessing your hand, at the same time deciding which cards you will discard in the draw if you remain in the deal that long. The cards to discard will almost always be obvious but it is essential that you do not set them aside or rearrange your hand by putting them to one end of the fan or in any other way

give other players a clue as to how many you intend to discard. There's no point in giving away any information before you have to.

Where are you sitting?

In some positions at the table you might not get the opportunity to check, and in fact wherever you sit your position relative to the dealer will affect how you act. The number of players also affects play. Suppose, for example, you are dealt a hand like ♠J, ♣J, ♦8, ♣5, ♥4 – a pair of Jacks. If you are one of six players, you have about a one in three chance of holding the best hand at the table.

General strategies

There are lots of sayings or beliefs of old poker players, and a couple are worth emphasizing here, since there is logic and truth behind them.

Don't throw good money after bad

It is hard for a player who has a good hand and has bet accordingly, contributing several chips to the pot, to come to terms with the knowledge that he is probably beaten and that to bet on would cost even more chips. It is no good thinking, 'I've put 20 chips into this pot – I'm not going to give up now. I must risk just a few more to protect my investment.' The point to realize here is that the chips you've put into the pot do not belong to you any more; they belong to the pot.

A bet is a good bet or a bad bet according to its prospects of being a winning bet and the amount it stands to win. A 3 to 1 chance that will win you six times your stake is a good bet, a 6 to 1 chance that will win you three times your stake is a bad bet – and neither fact is influenced at all by how much of the winnings (i.e. the pot) was originally yours to begin with.

Don't bet against a one-card draw

Assume you are holding three of a kind, and you are in a second betting interval with one other player who drew one card. It is your turn to speak first. The assumption is that your opponent's four cards were two pairs, in which case he might have drawn to a full house, or that he was drawing to fill a flush or a straight. In each case, the chances are that he will have failed, and that you hold the better hand. On the other hand, if, against the odds, he succeeded in improving his hand, he has got you beaten.

Whatever his fate in the draw, there is no point in you betting. You should check and wait to see what he does. If you bet, and he has failed to fill a straight or a flush, his hand is worthless and he will fold, so you will not win any extra chips from him. On the other hand you risk losing some, because if he has filled a straight or a flush, he will raise, and you will lose. So leave it to him. If he bets, call – you can be no worse off than if you'd bet in the first place. The only way you

can lose out against him is if he fails to improve two pairs, and checks rather than bets. You will win the pot, but could have won an extra chip or two had you bet and he had been silly enough to call.

Dealing with two pairs

In fact a hand of two pairs is a classic one in poker – one of the most awkward to deal with –and is likely to be the best hand at the table after the deal, even with as many as eight players in the deal. The trouble with two pairs is that the odds are more than 10 to 1 against improvement by drawing a single card, and while it may be the best hand before the draw, it seldom is afterwards.

In fact poker players have calculated that if, after the draw, you hold a hand of two pairs you have the following chances of winning:

Number of opponents still in:	Odds of winning if holding 2 pairs after the draw:
One	3 to 1 on
Two	slightly better than even
Three	6 to 4 against

With more than three opponents remaining your chances of winning get progressively worse.

Strategy for two pairs

Your strategy with two pairs at the deal will partly depend on where you are sitting. Suppose one player before you has bet, and there are three or four players yet to speak. On the assumption that your two pairs represent the best hand at the table, but might not remain so, your strategy should be to try to force out the remaining players, so you raise. If they all fold, you have a good chance of taking the pot, whereas if two or three of them stay in with middling pairs, say, the chances of you taking the pot have diminished. In fact many players fear holding two small pairs and if two players bet against them after the draw, will ditch them immediately.

Improving a hand in the draw

The better the hand you are dealt, the lower the odds of you improving it in the draw; the chances of improving your three of a kind in the draw are more than 8 to 1 against.

Usually the number of cards to exchange at the draw is obvious and straightforward. However, many poker players have differing views on the advisability of drawing two or three cards when holding a pair. Some players, with a hand like ♠A, ♥10, ♣3, ♦3, ♥2 would prefer to hold the pair and the ♠A (the odd card in this situation is called a kicker) rather than draw three cards to the pair.

By drawing three cards to a pair, the chance of improving the hand is about 14 per cent better than if only two cards are drawn. However, more than half the time,

the improvement will be to two pairs only (57 per cent with a draw of three and 66 per cent with a draw of two).

Bluffing

Much is said in poker literature about bluffing, and it is easy to come to the conclusion that bluffing is the most important element of the game. Certainly poker is a game of skill rather than luck, because a good player will win consistently, and he cannot always be lucky enough to be dealt the best cards. So where is the skill? Is it from mathematical superiority, psychological superiority, or a combination of both? The answer is that the best players need both these assets.

We have dealt already with the numerical aspects of poker, of hands in terms of their likelihood, and the probabilities of improving hands in the draw, etc. and clearly the best players need a knowledge of these things. It is not necessary to carry every fact in the tables in one's head, of course, but a general instinct of what they convey is essential.

The psychology of bluffing

The psychological aspect of poker lies in the ability to study and draw inferences from the behaviour and play of the other players. Is a particular opponent a good player or a bad player? Can you deduce the strength of his hand by the giveaway signs of excitement or by the way he has played previous hands? By the same token, can you prevent him discovering from your demeanour and style of play the same things about you? Or can you lead him to draw false conclusions about you or your hand by bluffing?

It is hard to say which of the two skills, numerical or psychological, is the more important to the complete poker player. It is true that, at the showdown, only the best hand wins. But this might not necessarily be the best hand that was held during the deal. The holder of the best hand may have been bluffed into folding before the showdown. Therefore, both skills are essential to being a well-rounded poker player.

Bluffing is used to mislead other players as to the value of your hand, and can be used in two ways.

1. You bet heavily to persuade opponents that you have a much better hand than you actually have, so that rather than contributing chips to the pot in order to call you, they fold. By this means you can sometimes win a pot despite having the poorest hand at the table.

2. Less spectacular but more subtle and more common, you attempt to persuade opponents that your hand is less good than it actually is, so that they stay in the deal longer and contribute more chips, which means a bigger jackpot when you eventually, as you hope, win the showdown.

The first type of bluff works best when the limits are high and to call

the bluff requires risking a large number of chips. If the limits are low, an opponent will be likely to call you and your bluff will fail.

Jargon-buster

Stand pat To decline to take cards at the draw. Since only hands of the value of a straight upwards cannot be improved by a draw, a player who stands pat either has picked up a straight or better at the deal, or is bluffing.

Draw Poker: Jackpots

There are hundreds of draw poker variations and while most can be dismissed as tinkering about to make the game more entertaining or less monotonous, and would be dismissed out of hand by serious players, a number have proved popular over a period of time. Descriptions of the more established variations follow.

THE MOST POPULAR

Jackpots must be mentioned first because it is the most popular form of Draw Poker, especially in the United States, and frequently textbooks will describe this version as poker itself, rather than a variation.

The difference from the game already described is merely that a player has to hold in the deal a hand of a pair of Jacks or better in order to open the betting. Once a player has opened, the other players can call, bet or raise as they wish.

A player who opens the betting must be able to show in due course that he held an opening hand, i.e. a hand of a pair of Jacks or better. If he folds before the showdown he must retain his hand in order to demonstrate that he had the necessary values. For this reason, he must also retain his discards at the draw because it is permissible for him to 'split his openers', i.e. to discard one or more of the cards that contributed to the combination that allowed him to open.

For example, if a player is dealt the hand shown below, his pair of Jacks entitles him to open the betting. When it comes to the draw, he might well decide to discard the ♣J, giving him the chance of a straight flush (with ♦10), a flush (with any other diamond) or a straight (with any other 10).

The player has roughly a 3 to 1 against chance of completing one of these hands, which might well take the pot. It is a better bet than drawing three cards to his Jacks, where the odds against him achieving a better hand than any of the above are about 75 to 1. However, if he discards the ♣J and the

discard is collected up, he will have no way of proving later, whether he folds or wins the pot with a straight flush, that he held a requisite hand to open. So he must keep the discarded ♣J, face down of course.

Example Jackpots hand

There are five players, with the dealer placing five chips in the pot as the ante and with a limit of two chips to bet or raise before the draw and five chips after the draw.

First betting interval
First betting round

1. Player 1 is dealer, so player 2 is first to speak. He holds a four-card straight, open at both ends, but hasn't the necessary hand to open.

2. Player 3 holds a four-card flush, but also cannot open.

3. Player 4 cannot open with a pair of 10s, and neither can player 5 with a pair of 6s. All of these players check.

4. The dealer, with his two pairs, opens with two chips, to the relief of players 2 and 3, with their chances of a good hand. He would have been able to open with two pairs, even if the higher pair had not been Jacks or above, since a hand of two pairs is clearly higher than the pair of Jacks required to open.

Second betting round

1. Players 2 and 3 call.

2. Players 4 and 5 fold. They know that

1st betting round Only Player 1 can open the betting, even though other players hold good hands

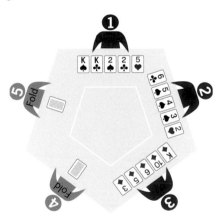

After the draw Players 2 and 3 have improved their hands in the draw, while Player 1 has not

player 1 has them beaten. Player 5 could have called, and drawn two cards to his pair, keeping the Ace as kicker, in the hope of drawing a third 6 or another Ace and winning the pot with three of a kind or two pairs Aces up, but he prudently decides to fold.

253

The draw

1. Player 2 discards ♥J, and receives ♣6, completing a straight.

2. Player 3 discards ♠10 and draws ♦10, completing a flush (there could be fireworks ahead).

3. The dealer discards ♥9 and draws ♥5.

Second betting interval
First betting round

1. It is dealer's turn to speak first, as the first to bet. He checks (if one or both of his opponents have filled to a straight or a flush, they will bet and eventually beat him, so there's no point in contributing any more to their winnings).

2. Player 2 is not interested in everybody checking as he holds a good hand and is confident. He therefore bets the maximum of five chips.

3. Player 3 realizes that player 2 could have filled to a straight, a flush or a full house, the last of which would beat him, but reckons that if he cannot raise with a King flush he never will, and calls five and raises five.

Second betting round

1. Player 1 now folds, his two pairs almost certainly beaten, but he keeps his hand because he must show his pair of Kings gave him the right to open.

2. Player 2 thinks his small run is probably beaten, but being a player who thinks it worth five chips to be absolutely sure (he hates the notion of being bluffed), he calls.

The showdown

Player 3 wins. His risk of continuing play, despite his suspicions of the hand player 2 may have held, has paid off and he takes the pot of 31 chips, making a profit of 18 chips.

Deal passed out: 1

If no-one has two Jacks or better, the deal is 'passed out'. The deal now passes to the next player, with the rules remaining the same. There is another ante (in this case the new dealer adds another five chips to the pot, making the ante ten) and the cards, after the shuffle and cut, are redealt. If the deal is passed out again, it continues round the table, with the ante increasing each time. It would be rare, of course, for more than two or three deals to be passed out consecutively. A pair of Jacks or better should appear approximately once in five hands, so with five players the odds against getting a run of three passed out hands are about 7 to 1 against and, with more than five they are over 60 to 1 against.

Deal passed out: 2

Rather than redealing the cards if nobody is able to open, an alternative is for all players to keep their hands and play then as Lowball (see page 258).

False openers

If, at the showdown, the opener cannot show that he possessed the required opening cards, the penalties are as follows:

- If the opener is involved in the showdown, he cannot win the pot and his hand is dead. If there is only one other player in the showdown, he takes the pot. If there is more than one, then the player with the best hand wins.
- If the opener bet and was not called, his bet is forfeited and remains in the pot for the next deal.
- If the opener bet and other players called and then folded, so that only the opener remained, all the money in the pot is returned to the players who made bets, the opener's bets remaining forfeit in the pot.
- If during the first betting interval, the opener announces that he lacked the cards to open before all bets are equalized, all other players withdraw their chips from the pot, with the exception of the ante. The opener's chips remain in the pot. Players in turn from the opener's left may open if they have the right cards.
- If one of the other players bets, the false opener may remain in by calling or raising but must put new chips into the pot – those he contributed earlier are forfeited.
- If no player after the false opener wishes to open, then the deal moves to the next player in turn, with the false opener's chips remaining in the pot for the following deal.

PROGRESSIVE JACKPOTS

Progressive Jackpots is played exactly like Jackpots until a deal is 'passed out'. While the deal still passes to the next player, and the ante is repeated, the next deal becomes Queenpots, wherein a pair of Queens or better is required to open the betting. Should the deal be passed out again, a pair of Kings is required, and if this is not achieved, the next deal requires a pair of Aces. After Aces, the requirement to open drops – it goes to Kings, then Queens, then Jacks, then back to Queens, Kings, Aces and so on back and forth.

Draw Poker: Spit in the Ocean

There are many variations of Spit in the Ocean. The distinguishing feature of the game is that the players are dealt four cards each face down, and a final card is then placed face up in the centre of the table. This card is the spit, and it is regarded as the fifth card in each players' hand.

However, this card, and the three others in the pack of the same rank, is regarded as a 'wild' card. This means that each player can regard the spit as whatever card he wishes. For example, a player who is dealt ♣A, ♣K, ♣J and ♣10, in effect holds a royal flush, the highest hand in most forms of poker, because whatever the spit, he can regard it as the ♣Q.

The hands of all players in Spit in the Ocean therefore consist of the four cards dealt them, plus one wild card. However, since all cards of the same rank as the spit are wild, a player might hold two wild cards in his hand, or even three.

It is vital in games of Spit for the players to agree beforehand how wild cards are to be evaluated. The general rule is that a wild card can't be used to duplicate a card already held in the hand, thus a hand of five of a kind would be impossible.

In the absence of official rules for the game, this is recommended procedure. However, there are players who prefer to allow a hand of five of a kind and other hands that are impossible without wild cards.

Players pay in their ante before the deal as usual. There is usually only one betting interval. First to speak is the player on the dealer's left, and he has the same options as in the standard form of Draw Poker, in other words, he must initially check or bet, and after betting commences he must call or raise or fold. When bets are equalized, the showdown takes place.

Example betting interval

The ♦5 in the centre of the table (see illustration, opposite) is the spit. Player 1 is dealer, there are five chips in the pot and it costs two chips to bet, with a maximum raise of five.

First betting round

1. Player 2 is in the lucky position of holding a second wild card as his ♣5 is the same rank as the spit. Nevertheless the best hand he can make is an A, K, Q, J, 10 straight, not a bad hand but one not guaranteed to win at Spit in the Ocean. He decides to bet the minimum of two chips and await events.

2. Player 3 has three of a kind (8s). It is not a bad hand, but he decides it is not unlikely that somebody will be able to do better than three 8s and folds.

3. Player 4 also has a second wild card, and has been dealt two Aces, so his hand is four Aces, almost an unbeatable hand in any form of poker, and a powerful one even in Spit in the Ocean, so he calls the two and raises by the maximum of five chips, hoping that somebody might call.

4. Player 5 also has an excellent hand, since with the wild card he can make a full house, beatable only by four of a kind or a straight flush. It costs him seven chips to stay in the game, but he calls.

Second betting round

1. Player 1, the last to speak as dealer, can use the wild card as an 8, and complete a straight, but in view of the level of betting so far decides to fold.

2. Player 2 now has the difficult choice of whether to fold, call or raise with the highest straight. There are 21 chips in the pot and he needs to put in five more in order to share a three-way showdown. The odds offered are just over 4 to 1. It is certainly not worth raising, he thinks. He can beat any other straight and three of a kind but anybody who has filled to a flush or better has him beaten. Reluctantly, but wisely, he folds.

3. In the showdown, player 4 wins with his four Aces, a profit of 13 chips.

As a matter of strategy it is interesting to consider what might have happened had he merely called on his first bet. Possibly no other players would have raised, in which case he would have five fewer chips. But suppose player 5, with

After the deal   The ◆5 wild-card spit strengthens the hands of Players 2 and 4 as they both hold 5s

his full house, had raised, as is probable, even by the minimum of two. Player 2 would probably have called for another 2, and then player 4 could have raised by five. If player 5 called, the pot would then be 27 chips, a profit of 17 to player 4.

Other Draw Poker Games

THE WILD WIDOW

This is an interesting variation of Spit in the Ocean. A widow is a community card dealt to the centre of the table, which can be played as part of any player's hand. Sometimes there may be more than one widow, and sometimes these cards can be wild. In this game, known as The Wild Widow, four cards are dealt face down to each player, followed by the spit face up in the centre of the table. However this time the spit is not part of any players' hand. It is a widow, and its purpose is to denote that the other three cards of its rank are wild.

During the first betting interval each player knows the identity of only four cards of his final hand, i.e. those four dealt face down to him. However, he knows if he has any wild cards, and can assess the possible values of his hand in respect of how it might be improved by his fifth card, which is dealt after the first betting interval. When all bets are equalized, this fifth card is then dealt face down to each player and the second betting interval takes place.

Of course it is quite possible that a player's fifth card could be a wild card, so the betting can be interesting and speculative, with the fifth card being a surprise to all and likely to change everybody's fortunes.

LOWBALL, OR LOW POKER

Lowball is played in the same way as Straight Draw Poker, with no minimum requirement needed to open, but with one great difference, the lowest hand wins. However, the ranking of the cards is simpler:

- flushes and straights are ignored.
- Ace counts low in all respects. Thus the lowest hand that can be held is 5, 4, 3, 2, A – the five lowest cards in the pack. It is known as a 'bicycle'. As straights are ignored, it doesn't count as a straight, and if all the cards were of the same suit, it wouldn't count as a flush either.

As between unmatched hands (i.e. those not containing a pair, triple or four), the highest-ranking card determines the order, and if equal the next highest.

- 10, 7, 6, 5, A beats 10, 8, 3, 2, A by virtue of the 7 being lower than the 8.

The same applies to pairs:

- 8, 8, K, 5, 2 loses to 7, 7, K, 5, 2 and loses to 8, 8, 10, 9, 6, but beats 8, 8, K, 6, A.

The procedure is as in Straight Draw Poker, with the first and second betting intervals, and a showdown.

HIGH-LOW POKER

This popular and interesting version of Draw Poker is played as a combination of standard poker, in which the highest-ranked hand at the showdown wins, and Lowball, in which the lowest-ranked hand wins. Each player has the option of playing for highest hand, lowest hand or high-low (it is possible, as we shall see, for a hand to be highest and lowest, although it is more likely in Seven-card Stud, High-low, as described in the Stud Poker section).

During the betting intervals, players do not know who is betting hoping to win the high hand and who is betting hoping to win the low. This is declared only at the showdown. At the showdown, the pot is divided equally between the player who wins high and the player who wins low. If there is an odd chip, it goes to the high player.

High hands are ranked as in standard poker, and low hands as in standard Lowball. This is where the possibility arises that a hand can be high and low. For example ♥A, ♥8, ♥5, ♥3, ♥2 could be the highest hand, ranking as an Ace-high flush, but it could also be the lowest, as in Lowball (see page 258) flushes are not recognized and Ace counts low, so the hand in Lowball is 8, 5 high, an excellent hand. Similarly a straight, 6, 5, 4, 3, 2 could be high and low – but this is very rare in five-card Draw Poker.

At the showdown, players must declare simultaneously whether they are competing for high, low or high-low. The commonest way to do this is for the players to secrete a chip in their hands under the table, say red for high, white for low, and one of each colour for high-low.

The following points are worth bearing in mind while playing:

- If in a showdown between two players one player is competing for high and one for low, they automatically share the pot.
- If two players are competing for high and one for low, the player competing for low automatically takes the pot for low – the other two players must show their hands, the higher taking the pot for high.
- If a player competes for high-low, he must beat both high and low players – if his hand isn't high and low, he loses, and the pot is divided among the other players as if he hadn't bet. This is to say that if a player declares high-low and holds the highest hand but not the lowest (or vice versa), he loses both. The lowest hand takes the low pot and the highest hand among those left takes the high.

Example hand

During the example hand shown on the following two pages, the ante is six chips and the limit, bet or raise, is two before the draw and five after.

After the deal Only Player 1 has an obviously poor hand – the others all have chances for improvement

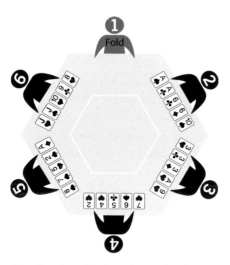

After the draw The four players who drew all improved their hands

First betting interval

1. Player 2 speaks first and bets two chips. He is thinking of drawing three to his Aces for high. He could go low by drawing two to A, 4, 2, but likes his Aces.
2. Player 3 calls. He is going high, too, drawing to a pair and an Ace kicker.
3. Player 4 calls. His idea is to ditch a 2, and hope for an Ace, 3 or 5 to give him a good low hand.
4. Player 5 calls. He is going low and will stand pat on 8, 7.
5. Player 6 calls. He will ditch his King and hope to complete a straight for high.
6. Player 1, the dealer, doesn't think much of his hand at all with all this activity, and cannot fold fast enough.

The draw

At the draw the pot is 16 chips, with five still in.
1. Player 2 discards his 10, 4 and 2 and picks up a pair of 6s and another 10.
2. Player 3 receives a 3 and 9 in return for his Queen and 8.
3. Player 4 discards one of his 2s, getting a 5 in return.
4. Player 5 stands pat.
5. Player 6 receives a second Jack for his King.

Second betting interval
First betting round

1. Player 2 has improved to two pairs, Aces up. He checks.
2. Player 3, who might well have folded on the first round, has improved to three

of a kind, and decides to bet two chips.

3. Player 4 has a very good hand for low and calls two and raises five (he is hoping that some of the high and low bidders will stay in and boost what he hopes will be his pot).

4. Player 5, who stood pat, decides to call seven and raise five more. Like player 4, he does not fear players 2 and 3, as their draws of two and three cards suggest they are going high.

5. Player 6, who improved to a pair of Jacks but failed to fill his straight, folds.

Second betting round

1. Player 2, requiring 12 chips to call, and holding two pairs, folds.

2. Player 3 fears that player 4 or player 5 might hold a straight or a flush to beat him for high, but in the hope they are going for low, he puts in ten chips to call.

3. Player 4 feels confident enough to raise again, putting in ten chips.

4. Player 5 now calls for five.

Third betting round

1. Player 3, with relief, also calls. Had player 5 raised again, he might well have folded.

The showdown

The showdown is reached with the pot standing at 67 chips. The three players select chips of each colour and under cover of the table put a chip of the required colour in one hand and place the fist containing that chip on the table.

Simultaneously they reveal its colour.

- Player 3 shows a red chip, and is delighted when the other two players show white. Player 3, with his triple of 3s, collects half the pot, 34 chips (he has the odd chip), for highest hand. The other two players expose theirs.

- Player 4 announces 7, 6 while player 5 states only 8, 7. Player 4 takes the other 33 chips for low. Each has put in 20 chips (including the ante), so player 3 won 14 and player 4 won 13.

- Player 5, dealt the pat hand, is the big loser, forfeiting 20 chips. Players 2 and 6 have lost three chips each, and player 1, who didn't bet, only his ante of one chip.

Although this might not be a typical hand, it shows why High-low is popular. There is plenty of action. If at the showdown all players still in go for high and none for low, then the highest hand takes all the pot. This presents the interesting situation whereby a player who all game has been going for high might find himself in the showdown with one other player who he feels has got a higher hand. He could therefore elect to go low, and share the pot. Of course if he is wrong, and his hand is higher, it would be a hard mistake to overcome as he could have had all the pot.

KNOCK POKER

Knock Poker is a good form of poker for those who like Rummy, since it combines elements of both games. The ante is one chip from each player.

The dealer deals five cards one at a time to each player, placing the remaining cards face down on the table as the stock. The top card is turned face up and laid by the pack to form a discard pile.

Each player, beginning with the player on dealer's left, must take either the face-up top card of the discard pile or the face-down top card from the stock into his hand and discard one card face up onto the discard pile. This can be any card from his hand, even the one he has just drawn. Play proceeds in this manner with each player trying to build up a good poker hand until any player, having drawn, knocks. He then makes his discard, and each of the other players in turn may draw and discard once.

In the showdown, the highest hand takes the pot. In many games the winner also collects bonuses from the other players for either:

1. knocking and winning without drawing a card (two chips each).

2. for special high hands: royal flush (four chips each), any other straight flush (two chips each), four of a kind (one chip each). Needless to say these are rare, but the bonuses encourage players to press on for special hands before knocking.

If the stock runs out, the discard pile is turned over to form a new stock.

RED AND BLACK

Red and Black is played exactly like standard Draw Poker, but hands aren't valued as poker hands. Instead, each red card in the hand counts as a plus value: face cards are 10 points each, Aces one point each and other cards by their index value. All black cards count as minus by the same calculation. After five cards have been dealt, there is the usual betting interval, then the draw, then a second betting interval, then the showdown, with the hand containing the highest number of points winning the pot. Players ante, check, bet, call and raise in the normal way.

The game is best played perhaps as High-low (see page 259). Of those left in at the showdown, the player with the highest score shares the pot with the player with the lowest score. It is impossible to win high and low. The players don't announce whether they are trying for high or low, although obviously at the draw each player will have one or other in mind.

PUT AND TAKE

Put and Take is sometimes called Up and Down the River. It is a simple banking game with little to suggest that it is a poker variant at all, but it is one of those games sometimes played in Dealer's Choice (see far right).

The dealer is in effect the banker. He deals five cards to each player face up. He then deals five cards to the centre, face up, one at a time. These are 'put' cards. As each card is dealt to the centre, players whose hands contain a card of matching rank put into the pot a specified number of chips (see 'settlement' below). When the five cards have been dealt, and players have put into the pot as required, the dealer collects up the five cards, puts them to one side, and deals, one by one, a second set of five cards, face up. These are the 'take' cards. Each player whose hand contains a card of matching rank, takes a specified number of chips. If all the chips previously put in are taken out, the dealer must replenish the pot.

Settlement

There are three main methods of settlement.

1. For the first card turned up in the 'put' and 'take' piles, each player with a matching card puts or takes one chip. For the second card the put and take is two chips, for the third three chips, for the fourth four chips and for the fifth five chips.

2. Instead of putting and taking 1, 2, 3, 4 and 5 chips as the cards are turned, players put and take 1, 2, 4, 8 and 16 chips.

3. The put and take does not depend upon the order of the five cards turned but upon their rank. Thus a player with a King in his hand puts and takes 13 chips, a Queen 12 chips, a Jack 11 chips, an Ace one chip and other cards according to their index numbers.

In each of the above methods of settlement, a player who holds two or three cards matching a put or take card in rank, must put in or take out two or three times the required amount of chips.

DEALER'S CHOICE

Dealer's Choice is one of the most popular forms of poker in 'social' games among friends. Each dealer can choose which form of poker will be played on his deal. It introduces variety and presents different mathematical problems from hand to hand. It is best, perhaps, when not played all evening, but intermittently.

Stud Poker: Five-card Stud

The main distinguishing features between Stud Poker and Draw Poker are that in Stud there is no draw and most of the cards are dealt face up.

The basic game is Five-card Stud Poker, in which there are four betting intervals. Because most of the cards are dealt face up, each player knows much more about the other players' hands than in Draw Poker, giving more scope for strategy.

Because there is no draw, it is possible to play with up to ten players, although should all ten players stay in to the showdown only two cards will not be used in the play, and 40 will be exposed. This is unlikely, of course, but nonetheless the more cards exposed, the longer players might take pondering the chances of improving their hands and the game could become clumsy. The game is best with six to eight players, although it is a better game than Draw Poker if there are fewer players, and can be played with plenty of action with only two players.

Preliminaries

As with Draw Poker, the seating, the first dealer, any special rules, the stake limits and the time limit should be agreed. The deal rotates to the left as usual.

The ante

It is not usual to have an ante in Stud Poker, but players may agree to have one if they wish.

The stakes and limits

A common way of limiting the stakes in Stud Poker is to set one chip as the low limit, and set differing upper limits, usually two chips for bets and raises during the first three betting intervals and five chips for the fourth betting interval.

It is also common practice for the higher limit of five chips to come into operation as soon as any player has an 'open pair', i.e. a pair showing among his face-up cards. This could be as early as the second betting interval.

An alternative way of limiting stakes is to set upper limits of one chip in the first betting interval, two in the second, three in the third and four in the fourth, again usually with the proviso that the limit of four comes into operation as soon as a pair is showing.

Pot limits (see page 241), in which a player can bet or raise the size of the pot, are also suitable for Stud Poker.

The play

1. After the shuffle and cut, the dealer deals one card face down to each player (known as the 'hole-card'), then one card face up. Each player examines his hole-card but does not reveal it. It is not shown until the showdown.

2. There is then a betting interval. The player with the highest card showing (i.e. the highest face-up card) must bet within the limits agreed. He has no option, i.e. he cannot check or fold. If two or more cards showing are of the same rank, the holder of the one nearest the dealer's left is the player who must open the betting. Thereafter, each player in turn must fold, call or raise. The betting continues round the table until all the bets of those players who haven't folded are equalized.

3. The dealer then deals a second face-up card to each player who remains in the game.

4. There is then a second betting interval. The first player to speak is the player with the highest poker combination in his face-up cards. Straights and flushes do not count for this purpose, so the highest possible combination at this stage is a pair. If more than one player holds a pair, the one with the highest pair speaks first. If there are no pairs, the person with the highest card speaks first (Ace, 2 beats King, Queen). If two or more players hold equal combinations, the player nearest the dealer's left speaks first.

On the second and subsequent betting intervals, the player to speak first may check rather than bet. Until a player has bet, subsequent players have the option to check, too. But as soon as a player bets, then subsequent players must call, raise or fold. When all bets are

equal the betting interval ends. If during any betting interval after the first all the players check, the deal continues.

5. After the second betting interval, players are dealt a third face-up card.

6. The third betting interval begins with the player holding the highest combination (highest triple, pair or high card).

7. After that, players are dealt their last face-up card.

8. Finally there is a fourth and last betting interval.

The showdown

If all the players except one fold at any of the betting intervals, then the remaining player wins the pot. Otherwise the two or more players left in after the bets are equalized in the fourth betting interval reveal their hole-cards and the one with the best poker hand wins the pot.

Dealer's obligations

The dealer has a more difficult task than in Draw Poker. He must point out who should bet first in each betting interval by pointing to the hand and saying 'King high' or 'Pair of 4s' or whatever. When dealing the third and fourth up-cards, he must also point out, as he deals the relevant card, whether it might be possible for the player to make a straight or flush. Thus, on the third up-card, if he deals ♥6 to ♣10 and ♦9 he should announce 'possible straight' and when dealing ♦J to ♦4 and ♦2 he should say 'possible flush'. He can also announce the pairs.

He should also ensure that players who fold don't reveal their hole-cards. The correct procedure when folding is to turn over the upcards and place them face down on the hole-card. One player's hole-card could be a vital card for another player and its premature display could affect the way the other player bets. It can be agreed that a player who folds without turning all his cards face down must pay a penalty to the pot.

If the dealer makes a mistake, other players are allowed to point out the error. If the dealer makes a mistake in indicating who should speak first at any betting interval, the mistake can be pointed out and corrected, but if two players have bet or checked out of turn because of the dealer's error then the situation stands and the betting continues as normal.

Strategy

Most players in Five-card Stud have a general rule that it is not worth betting if there is a better hand on the table than you hold, however pregnant with possibilities your hand might be.

It follows from this rule that if on the first betting interval a player has an Ace showing and is therefore obliged to bet, all other players should fold unless they happen to have an Ace in the hole. This is reasonable mathematically, but of course if everybody followed this method very few games would ever reach a showdown, and the whole session would be a bore. So everybody loosens up a little and very frequently the first better doesn't win the pot. If you bet only when you have the best cards, you will quickly get the reputation of being such a tight player that you won't get invited to games.

Jargon-buster

Hole-card The face-down card that is the first dealt to each player.

Open pair A pair showing among a player's face-up cards.

Five-card Stud, High-low

The procedure is as for regular Five-card Stud, with each player dealt a hole-card followed by four face-up cards, with a betting interval following each round of face-up cards. The ranks of hands are as in High-low Draw Poker (see page 259). At the showdown, players use coloured chips to declare whether they are contesting for the high or low pot.

Example hand

Even with four of the five cards in each hand showing, it is not always clear (see right) whether to call high or low.

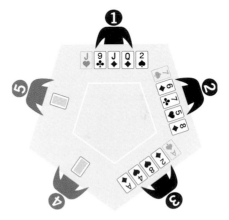

Player 1

Your hole-card is ♥J. You have a pair of Jacks. Should you call high or low? Player 2 is sure to be lower than you unless he has a straight, when he could be high and low. If he hasn't a straight, he might call low. Player 3 looks as if he might call low but could have a pair of Aces. Since player 2 is most likely low, you call high.

Showdown Judging whether your opponents are going high or low is vital for success at High-low Stud Poker.

Player 2

You too could be high or low. Has either player 1 or 3 completed a pair? If both, you are likely to be low; if neither, you are certainly high, with a pair of 7s. If only one has, you are unlikely to be either high or low. Because player 1 was unlikely to stay so far without a pair, you call low.

Player 3

You are sure you have player 1 beaten for high, but cannot beat him for low. But has player 2 a straight for high or a near-certainty for low? You doubt he has a straight, and go high. Player 2 wins half the pot for low (he doesn't need to show his cards, as he is the only low), player 3 wins the other half of the pot for high, after a showdown with player 1.

If a player holds a hand suitable for calling both high and low, he must win both hands to win the entire pot. If he fails to win both (a tie counts as a non-win) he loses both and the pot goes to the hands remaining in the showdown.

Stud Poker: Seven-card Stud

Seven-card Stud Poker has always been more popular than Five-card in the United Kingdom, and has also become so in the United States, making it possibly the most popular form of poker for home play at the moment. The object of each player is to achieve the best poker hand using any five of the seven cards available to him.

The extra cards, both of which are known only to their holders, make for better hands and more betting, and there is more scope for better players, too. In theory the game is limited to seven players, since if all stay in to the showdown 49 cards will be in action, but eight players can play as some players are likely to fold before the showdown.

Preliminaries

The preliminaries regarding the seating, the first dealer, special rules if any, the stake limits and the playing time should all be agreed. The deal rotates to the left and there are up to five betting intervals.

The ante

It is not usual to have an ante, as the betting is quite robust.

Stakes and limits

It is best to have limits to the bets and raises, but what they are is a question of taste:

1. Limit each bet and raise to one or two chips.

2. Limit all bets and raises to between one and five chips.

3. Compromise and limit the first three betting intervals (by which time each player still in will have five cards) to one or two chips, and then increase the upper limit to five chips for the last two betting intervals.

The usual convention in Five-card Stud, of increasing the limit as soon as a pair is showing, is not usually bothered with in Seven-card Stud as the two hole-cards reduce the significance of the cards showing.

The deal

After the usual shuffle and cut, the dealer deals one card to each player face down, then a second face down, then a third face up. Players carefully look at their face-down cards.

The play

As with Five-card Stud, at the first betting interval the player with the highest up-card must bet, and subsequent players fold, call or raise. When all active bets are equal, a second face-up card is dealt to all still in and a second betting interval takes place. As with Five-card Stud, the highest hand showing speaks first, but now, and on subsequent rounds, he may check. The dealer has the same obligations as in Five-card Stud, and must specify who is to speak first at each betting interval, and on the third and subsequent betting intervals should point out the possibility of flushes and straights as he deals the cards.

After the third betting interval (when each player has five cards), a sixth card is dealt, face up. There is a fourth betting interval, and then a seventh card is dealt to all players still in, but this time face down.

Players look at this last face-down card (but without revealing it to other players) and a fifth and final betting interval takes place. At this time all the players still in the deal have three face-down cards and four face up.

The showdown

If two or more players remain in the deal after the bets are equalized in the fifth betting interval, a showdown takes place. Each player exposes his three hole-cards and from the seven cards available to him forms his best poker hand. The player with the best hand takes the pot.

Strategy

The first decision you must make in Seven-card Stud is probably the most important. It comes when you have to decide whether to stay in or not at the first betting interval, when you have two hole-cards and an up-card. You should visualize the sort of hand you are looking for and look at the other players' up-cards to see if any of the cards you might need are already dealt. It is necessary, of course, to have chances of a good hand – two moderate pairs are unlikely to be good enough to take the pot at Seven-card Stud. Staying in with no clear possibilities in mind, hoping that you'll get a card that might suggest a hand developing, is a sure way to contribute to a pot you'll eventually drop from.

Betting strategy

When it comes to betting, if both your hole-cards are active in providing you with a winning hand, bet moderately at first – you want to keep the other players in and so shouldn't give away that your hole-cards are promising.

If your strength is showing (say a pair of up-card Aces) you could raise as if they completed three of a kind for you and scare off players who might if they stayed get a small triple themselves and beat you, or players who look as if they're developing a straight.

Always keep watch on opponents' up-cards and try to figure out their strengths. And however attractive your chances might look, if you are sure another player has a better hand, it's best to fold and cut your losses.

Stud Poker: Lowball

Both Five- and Seven-card Stud (or indeed Stud with any number of cards) can be played as Lowball. The rank of the hands is as for Lowball (see page 258), so flushes and straights are ignored, and the lowest possible hand is 5, 4, 3, 2, A.

The procedure in both cases is as in regular Stud Poker, with the lowest hand betting first on each round as opposed to the highest.

Because there are fewer ranks of hands, these games are less interesting than the regular or High-low versions.

The strategy in Lowball is to get out with a pair or with a high card. The illustration below shows a sample deal at Five-card Stud Lowball. The shaded cards are the hole-cards, known only to their holders, of course.

Example hand

First betting interval

1. Player 1 is dealer, so player 4 speaks first (two 4s are showing as lowest, and player 4 is the holder of the one nearest to the dealer's left). He bets.

2. Players 5, 2 and 3 call.

3. Player 1 is not a player to stay in with a King and folds.

Second betting interval

1. Player 3 speaks first (5, A is the lowest hand showing) and bets.

1st betting interval Player 1's King in the hole is a bad card for Lowball, so he will fold

2nd betting interval At this stage Player 3 has a good set of low cards, narrowly better than Player 2's

2. The others call. Player 3's possible flush and player 5's possible straight are immaterial, as these don't count in Lowball.

Third betting interval

1. Player 3 is still the first to speak, and he bets the maximum. He knows he beats all other hands going into the last round.

2. Player 4 has picked up a pair, and folds.

3. Player 5 knows his hand currently beats that of player 2, and calls.

4. Player 2 folds. He knows that to win he needs both players 3 and 5 (unless they're bluffing) either to get a pair with their last card or to get King or Queen.

Fourth betting interval

Player 3 unluckily draws a second Ace. Player 5 has the best hand showing, and is asked to speak first at the last betting interval. He knows that player 3 cannot beat him, and player 3 knows he has lost unless player 5's hole-card is a Queen. It isn't and player 5 takes the pot. A single card can ruin hands in Five-card Stud Lowball.

Of course a single card does not have such a big effect in Seven-card Stud Lowball because of the extra two cards.

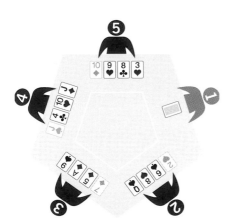

3rd betting interval Player 3 continues well with a 9, while Player 5's hand is helped by a 3

4th betting interval The second Ace gives Player 3 a pair, and ruins his hand

Texas Hold 'em

Texas Hold 'em, or just 'Hold 'em', has become possibly the best-known form of poker. This is because it is the game played in the World Series of Poker held annually in Las Vegas, which has been televised in the United States since the 1980s, and it is also the game played regularly on TV in Europe. In theory, up to 22 people can play but in practice it is rarely played with more than eight. Texas Hold 'em is a great beginner's game, as it is the easiest form of poker to play.

Outline of the game

Each player's object is to make the best poker hand from the two cards he holds and the five common cards in the centre of the table. A player can use both of his hole-cards or one, or none, using the five common cards as his hand. In this case he is said to be 'playing the board'. He cannot win with this, since the same option is open to all the other players.

In the televised game and in most casinos, a dealer is provided so that none of the players needs to deal. A disc or 'button' is moved round the table deal by deal to indicate who is the nominal dealer. In effect the professional dealer is merely acting for each player in turn. It is customary in casinos, after the cards have been shuffled and cut, for the top card to be 'burned', i.e. discarded unseen. This is to prevent possible cheating.

Betting

There is no conventional ante, but before any cards are dealt the first two players to the left of the dealer put in small bets known as 'blinds', which is short for blind bets. The first blind, known as the 'small blind', is a percentage of the minimum bet, usually a half or a third, and the second blind, the 'big blind', is usually the table minimum.

When the blinds have been posted (pushed towards the pot) the dealer deals two cards face down to each player. The players examine their cards. **1.** The first player to speak in the first betting interval is the one to the left of big blind. He cannot check because a blind bet has been made. He must call, raise or fold. Once the betting has gone all round the table, the two blinds may also call, raise or fold. Small blind must obviously increase his stake to the level of the betting in order to call. Big blind will have to increase his stake, too, if there has been a raise before the turn reached him.

2. When all bets are equalized, the dealer again burns the top card of the pack, and then deals three cards face up to the table. These three cards are known as the 'flop'. These (and the two more which follow after each betting interval) are common to all players, and are called 'community cards'.

3. A second betting interval now takes place, and in this and subsequent betting intervals, the first player to speak is the nearest active player to the dealer's left, not the first to bet on the previous round, as in Draw Poker.

4. After the second betting interval, and the top card again being burned, a further face-up card is turned up. This is called the 'turn' or the 'fourth street'. There is another betting interval, another burned card, and a fifth face-up card called 'the river' or 'fifth street'.

5. The final betting interval now takes place, and there is a showdown.

Minimum and maximum bets

In a casino, and advisedly in games played socially at home, there will be minimum and maximum bets. In a casino, for example, the small blind might be one chip, the big blind three chips and each bet and raise for that round would be in increments of three chips. Once face-up cards are dealt the bets and raises would be limited to increments of six chips up to the casino limit. The televised games are no-limit knock-out affairs in which all players start with an equal number of chips and continue to play until one player has won all the chips.

For games played at home the blinds of one chip and three chips are

recommended. Since the blinds are regarded as bets it will be necessary for all players to stake at least three chips to stay in for the first round. Three chips could therefore be the minimum bet or raise throughout, with say 10 as the maximum on the first round and 20 once cards are displayed on the table. That gives some scope for bluffing, although not as much as in the no-limit games. The game is also played as a pot-limit game, where the limit for bets and raises is the size of the pot.

Strategy

In Hold 'em the first two cards, the face-down ones, are the important ones. All the cards in the board are available to all the players; what separates one player's final hand from another's are the two hole-cards. So the first decision you need to make is the most important.

Hole-cards

Since the possible combinations of cards that can be held with two cards is very limited, experts have studied and ranked them, and in 1976 David Sklansky in his book, *Hold 'em Poker*, graded certain combinations. His ideas have been valued by poker players ever since.

Clearly the best combination to hold in the hole is Ace, Ace. The odds are 220 to 1 against getting this combination, so on average every 220 deals you will hold a hand on which you want to have all the money you can.

After a pair of Aces, the next best hands to hold are a high pair (e.g. K, K or Q, Q) or Ace with a high kicker (e.g. A, K or A, Q).

Pairs

Pairs are considered valuable, as there is always the possibility of improving to a triple on the flop, or even four of a kind. Pairs come round on average every 17 hands and if you stay in you can expect your pair to become a triple on the flop once in 8.8 times (odds of nearly 8 to 1 against).

When it comes to evaluating pairs, there are big gaps in value between Aces and Kings, and between Kings and Queens. After these, Jacks, 10s and 9s can be regarded as medium pairs, 8s and below small ones.

Ace with high kicker

More valuable than medium or small pairs is an Ace with a high kicker, i.e. Ace and King or Ace and Queen, particularly if they are suited. For example, if you have Ace, King, then an Ace or King appears in the flop, you hold the top pair, because if the pair is Aces, your King is the highest kicker, and if the pair is Kings, your Ace is the highest kicker. Only a triple, a flush or a straight can beat you. This is a good hand to bet on. Ace, Queen will be beaten if an Ace flops and an opponent holds Ace, King. Ace with a medium kicker of Jack, 10 or 9 can be useful and would be a good hand to bet on, but an Ace with a bigger kicker will beat you. Once you get down to Ace, Jack or Ace, 10, a pair of Jacks or 10s would be a better pair of hole-cards.

Ace with small kicker

An Ace with a small kicker, if they are not suited, is not a particularly good hand, and ranks below a combination with potential for flushes or straights. An Ace with a small kicker suited is, however, much more valuable, because of its potential for an Ace-high flush. For instance, if you hold Ace, 3 suited and three or more of the suit appear in the board you hold the top flush. If instead you held King, 3 you are in danger of losing to an opponent with the Ace of the suit among his hole-cards. And according to the other cards on the board, Ace-high flush could be the nuts (a hand that cannot be beaten).

Unpaired high cards

Hands such as King, Queen and King, 10 etc. are hands that might be the best-ranking hands before the flop but that can lead to problems, particularly if unsuited. For instance, suppose you hold King, Jack; you could flop a King and have the highest pair, but if you flopped a Jack, unless the other flopped cards are smaller, it is much less likely. Jack, 10, suited, with its potential for a flush and a straight is better to hold than, say, a small pair. If you hold a card below a 9 and it is not suited to an Ace, you are in the second class when it comes to rank of hands.

Flush and straight

Straights and flushes can win the pot, but when you hold two cards that are suited or consecutive, you have a long way to go to fill a five-card flush or straight. These combinations are sometimes called 'drawing hands' because you need to draw a series of cards to improve them. Obviously, if they are consecutive and suited it is a better bet than if they are one or the other. Combinations from 9, 8 suited down to 5, 4 suited are worth about the same as a small pair. Suited cards that cannot be part of a straight, such as 9, 4 or 10, 2, might be better folded sooner rather than later. When it comes to consecutive cards that are unsuited, then obviously the higher the better, with anything lower than Queen, Jack being valued less than a small pair.

Other combinations

If you hold two cards neither of which is high (so Jack and below), and if they are not suited and there are gaps between them (Jack, 4 or 9, 6), then they should not be bet upon. It doesn't follow that all other hands are worth betting on. For example 7, 6 unsuited or 3, 2 suited is not worth risking cash.

Bluffing

Anyone who has watched televised Hold 'em games will have seen bluffing come into its own. Some of the bigger pots have been won by the worst hand.

This is because of the no-limit format of the game.

Blinds are used and, as the game advances, the amounts required for them increase. The player with the fewest chips is likely to find that he has to force himself into the action, because if he goes more than a round or two without betting, his pile will get eaten up in blinds. Occasionally he is forced into a bluff. Equally, once a player's pile looks vulnerable, players with more chips try to bluff him out of hands, knowing that he will be reluctant to stake his diminishing stack of chips on inferior hands.

Jargon-buster

Back door A player who, usually inadvertently, completes a flush or a straight with the last two community cards in Hold 'em and Omaha, is said to have done so 'by the back door'

Bicycle or **wheel** The best low hand in Hold 'em and Omaha High-low games; any 5, 4, 3, 2, A, the suits being immaterial.

Case The fourth card of a rank in games like Stud and Hold 'em where there are face-up cards. If, for example, there are three 9s showing on the table, or two 9s are exposed and a player holds a third as a hole-card, the fourth 9 is referred to as the 'case 9'.

Omaha

Omaha is a game of increasing popularity, possibly approaching Seven-card Stud and Texas Hold 'em as being one of the most widely played versions of poker.

Omaha is a new phenomenon, and many authoritative textbooks published before the 1980s fail to mention it. The higher number of cards from which the final poker hand can be made, and therefore the chance of holding better hands, are the reasons for its success.

Outline of the game

Omaha is a very similar game to Texas Hold 'em – the difference lies in the number of hole-cards and so the number of cards available for making the final hand.

1. After the usual preliminaries of shuffle, cut and the top card being burned, four cards are dealt face down to each player. One of the anteing systems is used (i.e. either all put in, dealer puts in, or there's a small and big blind, etc.). Players examine their hole-cards and a betting interval takes place.

2. Three community cards (the flop) are then dealt face up to the table. There is then a second betting interval.

3. A fourth community card (the turn) is then dealt face up to the table and a third betting interval takes place.

4. A fifth and final community card (the river) is then dealt face up to the table

and a fourth and final betting interval takes place.

5. There is then a showdown, and the player with the best five-card poker hand wins.

So the game is identical to Texas Hold 'em except that each player has nine cards (four hole-cards and five community cards) instead of seven from which to make his best hand. However, there is a restriction: players must use two of their hole-cards and three of the community cards. This seemingly small difference from Texas Hold 'em does, in fact, make Omaha a more complex game.

Sample hand 1

The player with the hand on page 277 finds his hole-cards offer the promise of the top flush in hearts – he needs three hearts from the five community cards to come. After the flop, he still has this possibility, but also now has the chance of various straights, requiring a 9 or 6. The turn destroys his chance of a heart flush, but completes a straight. However, the river gives him a fifth spade, making his best hand a back-door Queen flush.

Flushes and straights are common in Omaha, since if three cards of a suit, for

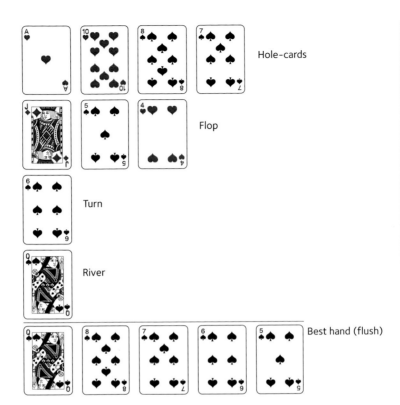

Hole-cards

Flop

Turn

River

Best hand (flush)

example, appear in the five communal cards, it only requires one player to hold two more of that suit among his four hole-cards to have a flush.

Sample hand 2

The hand on page 278 contains three 10s and an Ace, but the holder cannot think of the chance of four of a kind, or even a full house, because he cannot use all three 10s. Remember, he can use only two of his hole-cards. In effect he would be better off holding a pair of 10s rather than three. The flop comes up with another Ace, but, of course, this doesn't

give him a full house. Two pairs, even Aces up, would not win many deals of Omaha. Still available is an Ace flush in hearts. The turn is useless, but the river provides another Ace.

This unlucky player now holds three Aces and three 10s, but still cannot claim a full house. He must use exactly two hole-cards, so can claim the triple Aces but can use only one of the 10s. His best hand is as shown. Although the communal cards show that there is no chance of a player holding a flush (there aren't three cards suited), and no chance of a straight (there aren't three cards

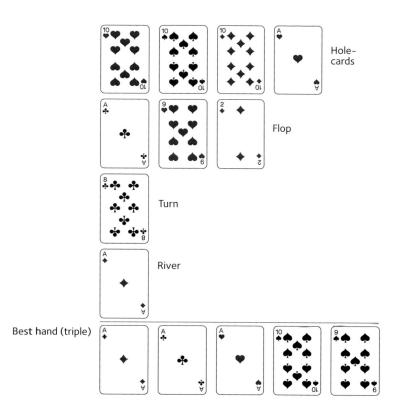

Hole-cards

Flop

Turn

River

Best hand (triple)

that could be used to form one), the triple Aces are not sure to win. Every player will have the two Aces at his disposal. A player who holds the fourth Ace and a card higher than 10 will beat the hand, as will a player who holds the fourth Ace with 9, 8, or 2, as well as one who holds a pair of 9s, 8s or 2s, because he will complete a full house.

Strategy

Much of the skill in Omaha comes in recognizing what constitutes a good hand. Unlike Texas Hold 'em, in which efforts have been made to grade the two-card hands held before the flop, the rules of Omaha make the four-card hands – of which two cards only, no more, no fewer, may be used – impossible to evaluate precisely. One can only know what a good hand, as opposed to a poor one, is.

A good hand consists of four cards that work with each other, giving opportunities to develop hands with the flop in many directions.

For example, see the hand at the top of page 279. With this, depending on the flop, you have a range of chances:
• triple or four Aces.

 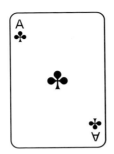  

POKER GAMES

- two cards to six straights from different flops: Q, 9, 8 – 9, 8, 7 – K, Q, J – A, K, Q – K, Q, 10 – K, Q, 9.
- two cards to Ace flushes – in fact these will be nut flushes (the best flushes possible) because there cannot be two flushes of different suits in Omaha, since a flush requires three suited cards among the community cards, and there cannot be two sets of three suited cards among five cards.

Obviously the best holding before the flop involves two cards of one suit and two of another, with all four cards connected or paired, with potentials for runs. The hand below is a good example of this. If you have one or two cards unconnected to the others by suit or rank, clearly the hand is not so good.

Because you can use only two of your hole-cards in making your hand, two Aces is actually better than three. With three Aces, one cannot be used, and there is only one left in the pack to achieve a triple with the remaining two.

After the flop you must look at your possible trips, full houses, flushes and straights in the same manner. Work out roughly, if not exactly, how many ways you can achieve these hands, without forgetting that communal cards are exactly that. If two Queens among the five common ones give you triple Queens, remember an opponent might well have triple Queens, too. If you have two Aces to go with them, fine. If your best to accompany them is, say, Jack on the board and 7 in hand, beware.

279

Card Handling for Tricks

Card tricks often demand particular kinds of shuffles and special card handling such as palming and performing a double lift. This section teaches you all the basics you'll need for doing great card tricks.

TYPES OF SHUFFLE

The following descriptions are for right-handed people. If you are left-handed, follow the steps using the opposite hands.

The overhand shuffle

.Although there are a number of ways to shuffle cards, the 'overhand' shuffle is the best one to use when performing card tricks, because it is the easiest one to adapt for false shuffling.

1. Start with the pack face down in your left hand, with all four fingers below the pack and your thumb resting on top (see illustration below).

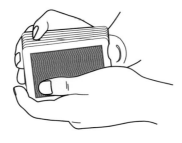

2. Using your right hand, grasp the majority of the pack with your fingers holding the top (short) edge of the cards and your thumb holding the bottom edge.

3. Raise the cards in your right hand up and over those that remain in your left hand, and use the left-hand thumb to drag down a number of cards – say ten or so – at a time (see above illustration).

4. These dragged-down cards should fall on top of those in your left hand, ready for the next lot to follow (above).

5. Repeat the steps until all the cards are shuffled and begin again, working through the pack two to three times before starting the trick.

FALSE SHUFFLES

False shuffles are essential skills to learn, as they are used in so many card tricks. If you practise enough your audience will never guess what you are doing and, in fact, a false shuffle can really add to the authenticity of a card trick in which you are trying to convince the audience that you couldn't possibly have positioned a card in a certain place.

'Top of the heap' shuffle

1. To keep a card in place at the top of the pack, hold the pack in your left hand, face down, with your thumb on top of the pack and your fingers holding it around the back.

2. Grasp the pack from underneath with your left hand, positioning the fingers of your right hand on the top edge of the pack and your right thumb on the bottom edge (as shown above). Now lift up the majority of the cards with your right hand and as you bring them over the top of the remaining cards in your left hand, subtly slide the top card towards you a little with your left thumb. This is now referred to as an 'injogged' card (above).

3. Now lower the main pack and use your left thumb to pull down a small pile of the cards from your right hand. Continue doing this until all the cards are used. Try not to make the pile too squared up otherwise the injogged card will become obvious to the audience.

4. When all the cards have been shuffled, use your right thumb to make a break above the injogged card and move this, and the pile of playing cards behind it, over the top of the pack and drop them down on the others (above). Your chosen card is now back on the top.

'Down under' shuffle

1. To keep a card in place at the bottom of the pack, perform the shuffle as above, but as you grasp the majority of cards in your right hand, use the fingers of your left hand to grip the bottom card and drag it down behind the pile in your left hand (right).

2. The bottom card remains in place and you can continue dropping small piles of cards over the top, safe in the knowledge that the card will remain where it is.

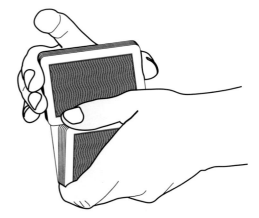

Shuffle up

1. To move a card from the bottom of the pack to the top, simply perform a normal shuffle – that is, grasp the majority of cards in your right hand and let them drop on top of the cards in your left hand.

2. As you approach the end of the pack you need to make sure that the last pile you drop contains just one card – the bottom card. Let it drop on to the rest so that it now becomes the card at the top of the pack (right).

Top to bottom shuffle

1. To move a card from the top of the pack to the bottom begin the shuffle as for Top of the Heap (see page 283). In grasping the majority of the pack with your right hand, make sure you take all but the top card.

2. Perform the rest of the shuffle as normal, knowing that the top card is now at the bottom of the pack.

FANNING OUT CARDS

Several tricks in this book involve you fanning out an entire pack of cards so that a member of the audience can pick a card. This can be quite difficult to achieve, especially for people with small hands. For these tricks, it is best to keep the fan tight if possible.

Square up the cards to start and then, holding them in your left hand, use your right hand to spread the cards in a circular motion, fanning them so that the top card moves towards the right and the bottom card is fanned out to the left, until you have a fan you can hold easily with your thumbs to the front of it and your fingers to the rear. Keeping the fan tight is particularly good advice, as a number of the tricks require you to keep the cards at the bottom out of sight, or use marked cards, which would be revealed if the fan was too loose.

Alternatives to fanning out the whole pack are spreading the cards out face down on a table or flat surface, or offering just a section of the pack for the volunteer to choose from as you shuffle through the pack of cards in your hands.

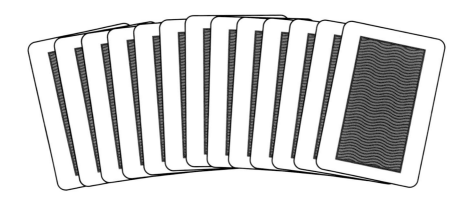

PALMING A CARD

This is another indispensable skill that will allow you to perform a greater number of card tricks. It requires some practice before incorporating it into your routine but is definitely worth the effort.

1. Hold the face-down pack of cards in your left hand and twist it at an angle towards you.

2. Perform the same movement as you would if going to square up the deck – indeed, this is what you want your audience to think you are doing. So, bring your right hand over the top of the pack and allow it to rest lightly on top of the cards, with the right side of your hand pressing down a little more firmly.

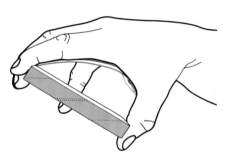

3. Use your left thumb to separate the top card from the rest of the pack and grip this with the little finger and right side of your right hand. Use your left thumb to push the card more firmly into your right palm and allow your hand to bend naturally, the card following the shape (see above).

4. You can now move your right hand away, in as natural a movement as possible, while keeping the audience focused on the main pack. Talk to the crowd and maintain eye contact while you carry out the manoeuvre.

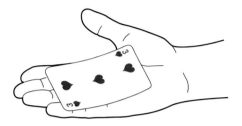

5. You can either put the palmed card in your pocket or keep it in your right hand (see above) depending on the trick requirements.

6. If you need to replace the palmed card, again pretend to be squaring up the pack and bring your right hand back over the top of the deck. Then simply release the card and square it up.

Colour Code Trick

The magician fans out a pack of cards face down and asks a spectator to choose a card, memorize it and return it to the pack. He then cuts the pack, squares it up and flips it over. He fans through once more to reveal that there is now one face-down card in the pack of a different colour. Turning it over, he reveals that this is the spectator's card.

Skill level 1

You will need
Two packs of cards, of different colours.

Preparation
Select one card from a pack of a different colour – say red, when your main pack is blue. Place the red card, face up, second from bottom in the main pack. Now find the blue equivalent of this card and place it face down at the top of the pack.

How to do it
1. In front of your audience, cut about one-third of the pack, flip the cards over and place them back on top of the pack. Now cut about half the pack and, again, flip the cards over and place them back on top of the pack.

2. Ask for a volunteer. Fan out the pack (the first cards should be face up) until you reach the first face-down card and ask the spectator to remove and memorize it. Discard the face-up cards and ask the spectator to replace her card back on the pack.

3. Cut the pack of cards, putting the top half underneath. Square up the pack and flip it over so that the cards are now face up. Fan out the cards (see page 285). There will be one face-down card among the others, which will be a different colour to the main pack. Flip it over to reveal that it is the spectator's card (below).

Cut and Locate

A member of the audience chooses a card from the pack. He memorizes the card and returns it to the top of the pack before cutting it. The magician then flips through the pack until she finds the chosen card. This is a good trick to perfect if you are a beginner, as it requires a peek at the pack but no special skills.

Skill level 1

How to do it

1. Shuffle the pack in front of your audience. While doing so, have a quick (and subtle) look at the card at the bottom of the pack.

2. Ask for a volunteer. Fan out the pack (see page 285) and ask a spectator to choose any card, memorize it and replace it on top of the pack.

3. Place the deck on the table and ask the spectator to cut the cards and complete the cut by placing the bottom pile on top (see below).

4. Square up the pack and slowly start dealing the cards on to the table, turning them face up as you go. When you reach the card that was the bottom card you peeked at, you know that the next one will be the spectator's chosen card. Hover over it to keep the audience in suspense, and then flip it over and reveal to all.

Top tip

By talking to your audience during the shuffle you will distract them from the pack of cards for long enough to take a quick look at the bottom card.

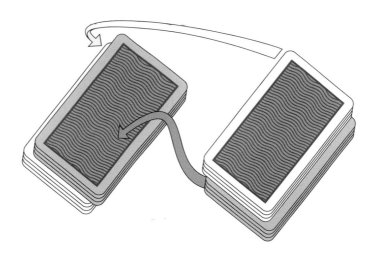

Shuffle Deduction

A spectator memorizes one of ten cards offered and its position in the pack. Following a swift process of elimination, the magician is left with a single card – the chosen card. This is a great trick that can be performed anywhere to any number of people.

Skill level 1

How to do it

1. Shuffle the pack and deal the top ten cards face down on to the table. Set aside the remaining cards. Ask for a volunteer from your audience.

2. Fan out the ten cards (see page 285) and ask the volunteer to choose one of them, memorize it and then return it to the fan. Tell her to remember the position of the card in the fan by counting cards from the left (see below).

3. Square up the cards, remove the top five cards keeping them in the same order and place them underneath the bottom five. Ask the spectator to tell you the position of her card and now count off that number of cards from the top of the pile and place them on the bottom of the pile. So, for example, if her card was the third one in, you count off three cards.

4. Square up the pile once more and eliminate the cards in the following manner: take the top card and move it to the bottom of the pile then take the next card and place it on the table. Repeat this process (one underneath, one on the table) until you're left holding one card. Turn it face up and the spectator will see that it is the card she chose.

4th card in

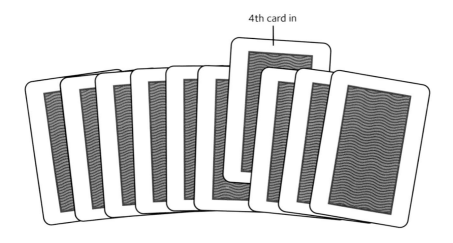

Leader of the Pack

The magician shuffles the pack in front of the audience and reveals the top card before returning it to the middle of the pack. The magician taps the pack on the table three times and turns over the top card to show that the revealed card has returned to its original position. This is one of those really simple tricks that will nevertheless leave your audience confused and impressed! It only takes a minute to perform so it is ideal for use in the middle of a routine, between two longer tricks.

Skill level 2

How to do it

1. Shuffle the pack in front of your audience. Next, instead of turning over the top card to show the audience, use a double lift so that the card you actually reveal is the second one down (see illustration below and page 287).

2. Slide the real top card away from the pack and, keeping it face down so the audience cannot see what it is, insert the card somewhere in the centre of the pack.

3. Wear a look of concentration as you tap the pack three times on the table. Slowly peel off the top card and reveal it – it will be the same one you showed the audience at the beginning of the trick.

Top tip

Make sure that you have perfected the double lift before you begin. The trick relies completely on this sleight and if it is not executed well, your audience will spot it immediately.

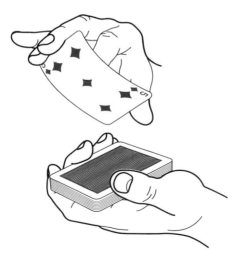

Facing Up to the Facts

Any five red and five black cards are removed from the pack. Half are reversed then the whole stack is shuffled well and placed behind the magician's back. When the stack is split and returned to the table in front of the audience, the same number of cards is face up in each pile and they are all the same colour, too.

Skill level 1

How to do it

1. Remove any five red and any five black cards from the pack and set aside the remaining cards.

2. Place the five black cards face down on top of the face-up red cards (see below) and shuffle the whole stack well in front of the audience.

3. Hold the cards behind your back and split them into two stacks of five. Turn one set over then set both stacks down

on the table. Spread out the two piles and there will be the same number of face-up cards in each pile – those in one pile being red and those in the other pile being black (below).

Top tip

This trick will not work if any of the cards get flipped over during the shuffle, so do not shuffle the cards too vigorously.

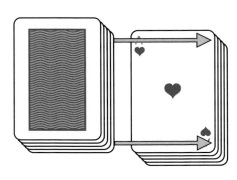

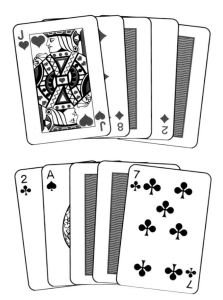

Empty Your Pockets

A member of the audience picks a card, looks at it and returns it to the pack, which is then shuffled well. The magician waves his hands over the pack, clicks his fingers or performs any other show-stopping turn while telling the waiting audience that the chosen card will be the only one facing up when the pack is fanned out. There will be murmurs of disappointment as this turns out to be a false claim but the magician redeems himself to gasps of astonishment as he pulls the spectator's card from his pocket!

Skill level 2

You will need

Any identical card from another pack.

Preparation

Before you start, place one of the identical cards in your pocket and make sure the other is at the top of the pack.

How to do it

1. In front of your audience, divide the pack into four stacks, remembering which stack contains the all-important rogue card.

2. Ask a willing spectator to choose two out of the four stacks of cards. If the two stacks she chooses contain the one with the trick card, hold on to them and discard the others. If not, put both the chosen stacks to one side and retain the stacks with the trick card (see illustration, opposite).

3. Ask the spectator to choose one stack and, again, if it is the one containing the trick card, hold on to it – if not, discard it. Either way, you should end up with the stack containing the trick card.

4. Give the top card (the trick card) to your spectator to look at, then reassemble the whole pack and ask the spectator to replace the card on top. Shuffle the pack well and tell the audience that the card will end up reversed in the pack. Of course, when you fan out the deck it is not reversed, so you pull it from your pocket instead.

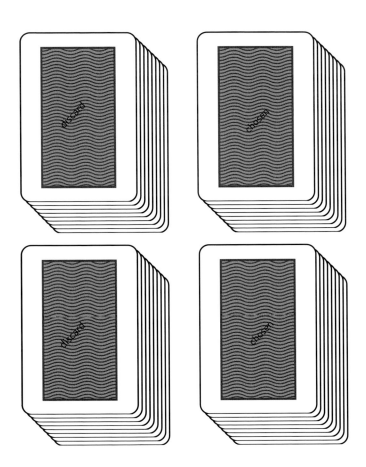

Top tips

Practise this trick a few times so that you can instinctively discard or retain the correct stacks – you need to do this quickly to keep your audience from working out how the trick works.

Being a good magician is also about being a good actor. So try to look genuinely surprised when your spectator's chosen card is not face up at the end. This will make the final stage of the trick look even more effective!

Counting Down

A spectator chooses a card from the pack. The card is replaced and the magician begins counting off cards from the bottom of the pack, stopping at the spectator's card.

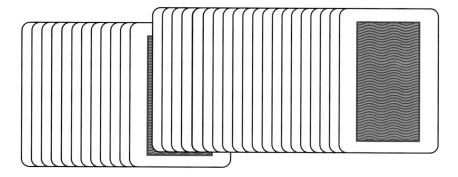

Skill level 1

How to do it

1. Shuffle the cards in front of your audience. Fan the cards out (see page 285) and, as you do so, discreetly count twelve cards from the bottom of the pack. Push the rest of the pack up and away from this group slightly, so it is easy to separate them (see illustration above).

2. Ask a spectator to choose a card and memorize it. While he is doing this, loosely gather together the two piles (the main pack and the twelve cards) and open them as if you've just randomly cut the pack here. Indicate for the spectator to replace his card in the cut and square up the pack.

3. Now you simply have to slide off twelve cards from the bottom of the pack, face down on to the table. When you reach the thirteenth card, turn it face up and it will be the card that was chosen by the spectator.

VARIATION

This trick can also be performed using a marker card. Before beginning the trick, make a tiny bend in the top left corner of any card. While you are fanning out the pack for the spectator, locate this card and make your cut just after it. Get the spectator to replace his card and then you can deal from the top of the pack, knowing that when you reach the marker card, the spectator's card will be the one that follows.

Suit Won't Shuffle

A complete suit is removed from the pack and the magician asks a member of the audience to give instructions to deal the cards. No matter how many times he does this, the suit still remains in consecutive order.

Skill level 1

How to do it

1. Remove all the cards of any suit from the pack and arrange them in their correct order, from Ace through to King. Place them spread out on the table to show the audience (as shown below).

2. Invite a member of the audience to help with the trick. Gather the pile and turn it over so the cards are face down then ask the spectator to give specific instructions for you to deal the pile of cards.

3. He must tell you either to 'single deal' or 'twist deal' each card until all the cards have been dealt. Single deal means simply placing the first card on the table. A twist deal is where you remove the first card, place it underneath the following card in the pile and then place them both on to the dealt pile.

4. Once all the cards have been dealt, pick them up and turn them face up to reveal the suit in the correct order! You can go through the pile twice before revealing the cards if you like and they will still remain in the correct order at the end.

Role Reversal

A spectator chooses and memorizes a card before returning it to the pack. The magician shuffles the pack and tells the audience that the spectator's card will return to the top. When it doesn't, the magician tries the bottom of the pack but the card is not there either. Looking confused, the magician fans out the pack and the spectator's card is the only face-down card in the middle of the pack. This trick employs all the basic skills that you need to have mastered before moving on to more complicated tricks., yet the trick itself is easy and effective.

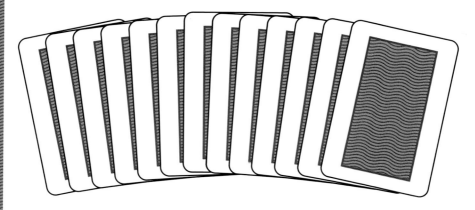

Skill level 2

How to do it

1. Shuffle the pack of cards in front of your audience and ask for a volunteer. Fan out the cards (see illustration above and refer to page 285) and ask the volunteer to pick one and memorize it. Square up the pack and ask him to replace the card on top.

2. Perform a false shuffle (see page 283) so that the spectator's card stays on top of the pack. Square up the pack.

3. Tell your audience that you have made the spectator's card return to the top of the pack. Perform a double lift (see page 287), revealing the second card down and look surprised when the volunteer tells you that this is not his card. Keep the top two cards face up and place them back on the pack.

4. Tell the audience that you suspect the spectator's card might have gone to the bottom of the pack by mistake and turn the pack over to show the bottom card. Obviously this will not

be his card either and now you must look doubly confused.

5. Keep your audience occupied by talking to them, as you need to distract their attention for the next part of the trick. With the pack still face up, you now need to turn the bottom card over. This will leave just the spectator's card facing a different direction (see right).

6. Cut the deck, being careful not to let the audience spot the face-down card. Tell them you're going to fan through the cards so that the spectator can pick out his card and you will try the trick again.

7. When you fan the cards out, there will be one face-down card. Tell the spectator to turn it over and he will see that it is his (as shown below).

The Flipping Trick

A spectator picks a card, memorizes it and returns it to the pack without showing it to anyone. With a flick of the wrist, the card miraculously reveals itself face up in a fan of cards that are all face down.

Skill level 2

Preparation

Before starting the trick, place the pack face up in front of you. Turn the top card over so that it is face down and turn the whole pack over so that the card is now on the bottom (below).

How to do it

1. For this trick you will need a volunteer. Begin by fanning the cards out face down in front of your volunteer (see page 285), being careful not to reveal the card facing up at the bottom of the pack. Ask her to remove a card and memorize it.

2. As you square up the cards, flip the pack over so that the odd card is now face down and the cards below are all face up. Split the pack, opening it just enough for a card to be inserted, moving the top half of the split slightly forwards as you do so to ensure the upturned cards are hidden, and ask your volunteer to replace her card face down within the pack so you cannot see it.

3. Put the pack behind your back, flip over the top card so that it now faces the same way as all the others and bring the pack back out in front of you.

4. Slowly fan the cards out in front of your volunteer and her card will be revealed as the only face-up card in the entire pack.

Top tip

Once you become more adept at this trick, you can try flipping the top card over without putting your hands behind your back. This will make the trick even more amazing.

Slip and Slide

The magician slides cards from a face-down deck until a member of the audience says 'Stop'. The magician then tells the audience the identity of the card that the spectator stopped at. On turning the card over, it is revealed to be correct!

Skill level 2

How to do it

1. Shuffle the pack well in front of your audience, peeking at the bottom card as you do so.

2. Square up the pack and place it flat, face down, in one hand. With your other hand, you need to put your thumb under the pack and your fingers on top, so that the pack is between your thumb and index finger.

3. Ask for a volunteer from the audience and tell her to say 'Stop' whenever she likes as you slowly slide cards back towards you from the top of the pack with your fingers, one at a time. Tell your audience that you will be able to predict the card that your volunteer has asked you to stop at.

4. As you slide the cards towards you from the top of the pack you must also slide the bottom card of the pack towards you with your thumb. Then, when the spectator tells you to stop, you slide the bottom card fully out to meet the rest of the pile, pulling them away together. Your memorized card will be at the bottom of the pile (see top right).

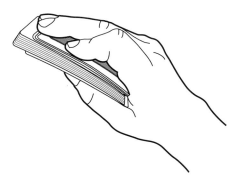

5. You are aware of the identity of this card so now you can tell your audience your prediction. Square up the pile and flip it over to reveal that you have guessed correctly.

Top tip

By explaining that you are going to predict the card as you perform this trick, you should distract the audience from the fact that you are moving the bottom card as well as those on top.

Making the Set

The magician picks three cards from the pack and places them face down on the table. A spectator is then invited to pick another card. When all the cards are turned over, they are revealed to be the four Tens.

Skill level 2

Preparation

Before you begin, place two Tens together a few cards in from the bottom of the pack (above).

How to do it

1. Shuffle the pack of cards in front of your audience, being careful not to move the two Tens together (see page 286).

2. Now fan out the cards (see page 285) and remove all four Tens, placing them face down in front of you on the table. It needs to look as if you are picking only three cards, so for the two that are together in the pack, you need to remove them as if they were one card (see top right) – it is probably best not to remove them first.

3. Turn the pack face down and fan it out on a table in front of a spectator.

Pick up the four cards and square them up. Ask the spectator to select any card from the fan and hand it to you. Place the chosen card face down on top of the other four cards.

4. Perform a double lift (see page 287) and show the audience that the

spectator chose a Ten. Carefully place these cards face up on the table so it is not obvious that there are two cards. Now fan out the remaining three cards and turn them over to reveal that you chose the other Tens in the pack.

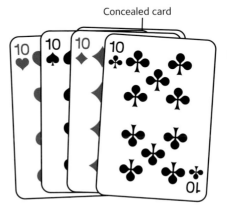

Concealed card

Top tip

You do not have to put the first Ten (with the other card) down on the table. You can simply turn it over and then return it to the other cards. Then you can fan them out in your hand to show them as the four Tens. Practise to see which method you are more comfortable with.

CARD TRICKS

Don't Bet On It

The magician deals out three piles of seven cards and asks a spectator to choose the top card of any pile, memorize it and return it. The magician then slaps the piles of cards and asks the spectator to point out the pile that contains his card. The spectator turns over the top card to discover that it is not his card after all – it has moved to a different pile. Practise palming a card before you perform this trick to others.

Skill level 2

How to do it

1. Shuffle the pack of cards in front of your audience and ask a volunteer if they would like to shuffle the pack as well.

2. Take the cards back and deal three piles on to the table, each containing seven cards. Ask the spectator to choose the top card of any pile, look at it and return it to the same pile.

3. Tell the audience that you are going to slam each of the three piles to wake the cards up and get them to move around.

4. Slam the pile containing the spectator's card first. As you do so, palm his card into your hand (see page 288). Keeping your hand low over the cards so the audience cannot see the palmed card, slam one of the other piles and drop the palmed card on top (see below). Slam the last pile for effect.

5. Ask the spectator to point out the pile that contains his card and turn over the top card. His card is no longer there. On turning over the top cards on the remaining piles he will find that his card has moved.

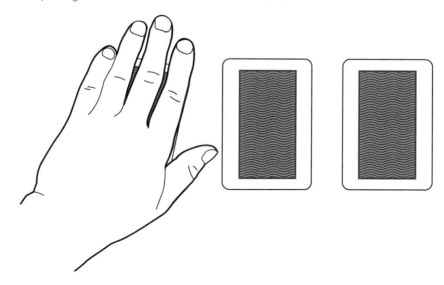

304

Top of the Heap

The magician places the four Kings at the bottom of a shuffled pack. With a flick of the wrist the Kings miraculously move to the top. This trick takes a good deal of practice, and the more you practise, the more convincing it will be.

Skill level 3

Preparation

Alternate the Kings with random cards at the top of the pack (random card, King, random card, King, random card, and so on). All cards should be face down.

How to do it

1. With the pack face down in your left hand, perform a double lift with your right hand, showing the first King (which in reality is the second card down) to the audience (see page 287). Put the cards face down on a table in front of you, placing them closer to you than to the audience, so they do not notice that there are two cards instead of one.

2. Repeat the double lift three more times so that the audience believes there are four Kings on the table. There should actually be eight cards with the Kings amongst them.

3. Place the pile of eight cards in your right hand and perform the double lift once more. Show the card(s) to the audience again, if you like, to confirm that it is just one King that you are holding. Now place the card(s) on top

of the main pack and slide the top card to the bottom. The audience will believe that you have moved the King to the bottom of the pack.

4. Repeat this three more times, until all the Kings are now together at the top of the pack (although the audience believes they are all at the bottom).

5. Taking the pack in your left hand, riffle through it with your right hand then square it up and deal the top four cards, face up, on to the table. The four Kings have managed to move back to the top of the pack.

Top tip

It is easier to conceal the fact that there are eight cards instead of four if you hold the pile in your right hand when putting them back on the pack. Obviously this looks a little clumsy, as you will have to break to slide each card with the remaining cards in your hand. However, with practice, you should be able to find your own way of doing this comfortably.

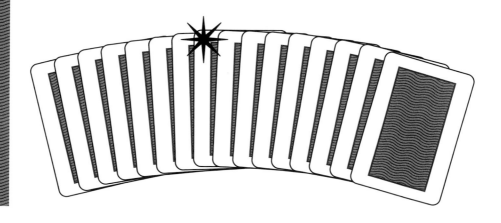

Feeling Vibes

A spectator deals two equal piles of as many cards as she likes, discarding the rest of the pack. She then cuts one of the piles, looks at the bottom card of the cut and places the cut cards on top of the untouched pile. The magician fans through all the cards and effortlessly picks out the spectator's card.

Skill level 1

How to do it

1. Ask a spectator to shuffle the pack and deal as many cards face down as she wants into two piles, with an equal number of cards in each. It is important that you count the number of cards in each pile. The spectator can set aside the remainder of the pack.

2. Now ask the spectator to choose one of the two piles and cut it wherever she likes, memorizing the bottom card of the cut (without showing you) before placing the cut cards on top of the untouched pile. The spectator should put the remaining cut cards on top of those.

3. The spectator has unwittingly placed her card at the centre of the pile. Assuming she dealt eight cards into each pile, you will know that her card is the eighth one from the top.

4. Fan the cards out in front of you, with the backs of the cards facing you (see page 285). Starting at your right, pretend to feel each card to determine whether or not it is the spectator's. Simply count along as you go.

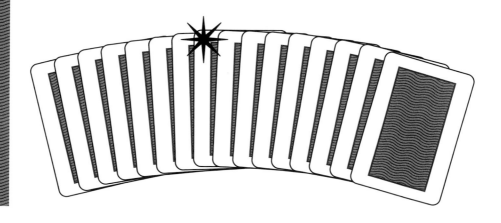

Psychic Powers

A spectator thinks of any card and keeps it in his mind. The magician flicks through the pack and extracts a card but it is not the card the spectator was thinking of. The spectator then locates his card and moves it to the top of the pack. The pack is cut and shuffled and the magician finds the card.

Skill level 2

How to do it

1. Ask for a volunteer and tell him to think of any card in the pack.

2. Shuffle the pack in front of the audience and begin counting cards face up on to the table, pretending to be looking for the spectator's card. When you reach the twenty-sixth card, hold it up and ask the spectator if this is his card – of course it won't be (unless you are incredibly lucky!). Remember the card and put it back on top of the pack. Place the other twenty-five cards that you counted out back on top of the pack too.

3. Now hand the pack to the spectator and ask him to fan through and remove his card without revealing it to you. Ask him to place the card on top of the pack and tell him to remove about one-third of the cards from the bottom of the pack and place them on top of his card.

4. Take the pack of cards back and fan it out with the cards facing you (see page 285). Ask the spectator to concentrate on his chosen card while you try to locate it. First you need to locate your card, which will be closer to the right end of the pack. Starting with the next card to the left, count up to 26. The 26th card will be the spectator's chosen card.

Fool's Gold

The pack is shuffled and the magician chooses a card. He then asks the spectator a series of simple questions and she is able to guess the card. This is not a trick but a mind game. Basically, you are telling the spectator what the chosen card is, while making it look as if she has guessed it completely at random.

Skill level 1

How to do it

1. Shuffle the pack and ask if the spectator wants to shuffle as well to make sure you are not hiding anything. Square up the pack, look at the top card and memorize it. Place the card face down on the table between you and the spectator and move the rest of the pack to the side.

2. Assuming that the card is the Four of Spades, ask the spectator to choose between red and black. If she chooses black, say she has made a good choice. If she says red, then say something like, 'Okay – so that leaves us with the black cards'. (Obviously you need to alter this according to which card the spectator is actually guessing.)

3. Now ask her which suit she prefers – in this case Spades or Clubs. Again, accept this suit or pick the other, depending on what her response is.

4. You now have the correct suit and need to get the spectator to guess the right number. Ask which she would choose – the cards running from Ace to

Seven or those running from Eight to King. Again keep the selection or eliminate it depending on her reply.

5. Now ask her to pick her favourite three cards from whichever set you have kept. If her selection doesn't contain the card, again eliminate these and you will be left with a possible four cards to choose from. If she has included it in her choice, you will be left with three. Whichever happens, you can now ask her to pick her favourite and repeat the process until you are left with just one card. Turn the card on the table over and it will be the same.

Top tip

Keep the banter quick and slick – if you keep the questions coming nice and quickly, she really will not realize that she is being steered towards picking the card on the table.

Upwardly Mobile

A member of the audience chooses a card from the pack and shows it to the magician who tells her that he has a psychic friend who will be able to verify the chosen card over the telephone. The magician calls his friend, passes him over to the doubting spectator and, sure enough, the friend reveals the chosen card.

Skill level 1

You will need

A mobile phone. An accomplice.

Preparation

Brief your friend in advance to make sure that he will be around at the appropriate time to take your call.

How to do it

1. Shuffle the pack well to prove that the cards are not in any particular order before the trick commences.
2. Fan out the pack face down in front of the spectator (see page 285) and ask her to pick a card. When she has chosen, set aside the remaining cards and ask the spectator to turn her card over and place it in the centre of the table.
3. Call your friend. As soon as he answers, he needs to begin slowly naming each of the four suits. When he names the correct one – say Hearts – you say 'Hello'. He must then start going through the numbers and, this time, when he reaches the correct one you say, 'I'll just pass you over', or something

similar. Your friend now knows the identity of the chosen card.
4. Pass the phone to the spectator and witness her amazement as your friend reveals the identity of the card.

Top tips

Use a mobile phone and not a landline so that your accomplice will be able to see that it is you calling and can start going through the suits immediately.

Practise the trick a couple of times before you try this on an audience. Your timing needs to be perfect and your accomplice should not go through the cards too slowly – the long gaps may give the game away.

Calling the Shots

With his back to the audience, the magician instructs a spectator to pick any card from the pack. The spectator is then instructed to deal out cards from the pack and the magician is able to stop her when she has reached her chosen card. This is an easy trick to master yet one that is quite impressive. You do not even touch the cards so your audience will be really baffled as to how it works.

Skill level 1

How to do it

1. Turn your back to the audience right from the beginning to add to the suspense. Ask for a volunteer and tell her to shuffle the pack to her satisfaction. Next, ask her to pick any non-picture card from the pack, memorize it and place it on top of the other cards.

2. Tell the spectator to take the value of her card and to count this many cards from the bottom of the pack, placing them back on top of the pack. So, for example, if her chosen card was a Nine, she must move nine cards.

3. Now tell the spectator to deal the cards, face up on the table, from the top of the pack. As each card is placed on the table, ask her to call out its value and suit.

4. In working out the chosen card, discount the first card that is dealt and called out. From the second card onwards begin to count, starting at one. When the spectator calls out a card that has the same number value as the number of cards you have counted, this will be her card. So, if she calls out a Nine of Hearts and you are on nine, that is the one.

Top tip

There is a possibility that there will be two or more cards that match the number you have counted to. This will not ruin the trick as there is still a good chance that the first one you guess will be correct. If it is not then just go with the other one and your audience will still be impressed.

It All Adds Up

A member of the audience chooses two cards from the pack at random. The magician asks her to do some simple maths and is then able to reveal the values of the cards she picked.

Skill level 1

Preparation

Before you begin this trick, you need to remove every picture card and every Ten from the pack.

How to do it

1. Ask a member of the audience to shuffle the pack and then take it back from her. Fan the cards out on the table in front of the spectator and ask her to choose any card and memorize the number before returning it to the pack.

2. Inform the spectator that some concentration is required, as she will need to do a little mental arithmetic. First, she must multiply the number of the card by two. Next she should add five and finally she must multiply the total by five.

3. Ask her to pick a second random card and add that number to the total she has reached already. She can then tell you the final number. In order to calculate her two cards, all you do is subtract 25 from the number she tells you. The resulting digits are the values of the two cards that were chosen. So, for example, if she says '64', you mentally subtract 25 which leaves you with 39. The two cards were therefore a Three and a Nine.

The Twins

The magician gives a spectator two black Queens. He then begins dealing cards face down on to the table until the spectator tells him to stop. At that point the spectator places one of her Queens on the pack. The process is repeated for the second Queen. At the end of the trick the magician fans through the pack to find that the two black Queens have located their red sisters.

Skill level 1

Preparation

Place one red Queen face down on top of the face-down pack and the other red Queen at the bottom of the pack. You also need to remove the two black Queens from the pack.

How to do it

1. Perform a false shuffle, keeping the top and bottom cards in place (see pages 283–4). Ask for a spectator and hand her the two black Queens, telling her that she is going to help you reunite them with their red twins.

2. Tell the spectator that you are going to begin dealing cards, face down, on to the table and she can tell you to stop whenever she likes. When she says 'Stop', instruct her to place one of the Queens face up on the dealt pile of cards. Place the remaining pack on top of this pile.

3. Repeat this process then square up the pack. Fan out the cards in front of the audience and ask the spectator to remove the face-up Queens and the cards directly to the right of them. On turning them over, she will discover that the black Queens have found their twins.

Top tip

This is a very easy trick to perform once the false shuffle has been mastered. However, it is important not to let the audience see that the bottom card is a red Queen or they will realize how the trick works.

Matching Pairs

The magician selects two random cards from the pack and places them face down on the table. A spectator cuts the pack and the magician picks the top cards from each pile – they match the cards chosen at the beginning of the trick.

Skill level 2

How to do it

1. Shuffle the pack of cards then fan through it, face up. Glimpse the top and bottom cards then pick out the two cards that match these. (So the Ten of Spades would be the match for the Ten of Clubs, and so on). It is important to remember which card is at the top and which is at the bottom.

2. Place the two chosen cards face down on the table. Perform a false shuffle with the rest of the pack so that the top and bottom cards stay in place (see pages 283–4).

3. Ask the spectator to cut the pack in two so that there are two piles of cards on the table. Turn over the top card of the top pile then turn over the matching card on the table (shown right).

4. Now flick over the other pile to reveal the bottom card. Turn over the remaining card on the table and you have two sets of pairs.

Top tip

Do not comment on why you turn the second pile over at the end – the audience will just assume that it is part of the trick and, once they see the matching card, it will not matter.

Glossary

All card games have a vocabulary of their own and this list is by no means complete and comprehensive; rather it includes only the words and expressions that are used in this book.

Above the line In games of the Bridge family, bonus scores and penalty scores are recorded above a horizontal line across the scoresheet. See *Below the line*.

Alone In Euchre, the right of the player who has named the trump suit to play without his partner.

Ante A compulsory bet made before the deal.

Assist In Euchre, a declaration made by the dealer's partner to accept the suit of the turn-up card as the trump suit.

Banco A bet equal to the amount staked by the banker.

Beg In games of the All Fours family, a rejection by the non-dealer of the suit of the turn-up card as the trump suit.

Bella In Klaberjass, an announcement made by the player who holds the King and Queen of the trump suit, after he has played the second one, allowing him to score 20 points.

Below the line In games of the Bridge family, scores for tricks bid and won are recorded below a horizontal line across the scoresheet. See *Above the line*.

Bete In Pinocle, failure to make the contract. See *Double bete* and *Single bete*.

Black Maria In games of the Black Maria family, the ♠Q.

Blitz In Gin Rummy, winning a game against an opponent who has failed to score.

Book In games of the Bridge and Whist families, the first six tricks won by a side, that do not count in the scoring.

Bottom layout In Monte Bank, the two cards from the bottom of the pack placed by the banker face upwards on the table. See *Top layout*.

Bower In Euchre, the Jack of a suit. See *Left bower* and *Right bower*.

Box In Gin Rummy, the score given for winning a hand.

Braggers In Brag, the ♦A, ♣J and ♦9, that serve as wild cards.

Build (1) In Casino, playing a card to a card in the layout to make up a total that may be taken with another card in the hand. (2) In games of Patience, the play of a card onto the next one above or below it in rank.

Buy Increasing a bet for the advantage of drawing a card face downwards.

Bury a card In Pinocle, discarding face downwards a card from the hand.

Calypso In Calypso, a complete suit, from Ace to 2, in a player's trump suit.

Canasta In games of the Canasta family, a meld of seven or more cards. See *Mixed Canasta* and *Natural Canasta*.

Carte blanche A hand that contains no court card.

Cash Leading and winning a trick with an established card.

Casino See *Great Casino* and *Little Casino*.

Centre In games of patience, that part of the table to which the foundation cards are played.

Check In Poker, a nominal bet that reserves the right to call or raise if another player bets.

Combine In Casino, picking up cards from the layout of the total pip value of a card in hand.

Comet In games of the Comet family, a wild card, usually a 9.

Conditions In Panguingue, certain melds by making which a player immediately collects chips from all other players.

Coup A winning play or bet.

Court card Any King, Queen or Jack.

Crib In Cribbage, an extra hand formed by the discards of the players.

Cut throat A version of what is usually a partnership game in which each player plays for himself.

Dis In Pinocle, the 9 of the trump suit.

Discard In a trick, the play of a card that is not of the suit led nor a trump.

Double bete In Pinocle, the penalty suffered by the bidder whose score for melds and cards taken in tricks fails to equal his contract. See *Single bete*.

Doubleton An original holding of two cards of a suit.

Dummy In games of the Bridge family, the partner of the declarer, and the hands he exposes on the table.

Elder hand In games for two players, the non-dealer.

Eldest hand The player who sits next to the dealer and whose privilege it is to play first. In most games, this is the player to the dealer's left, but in a few games, such as Panguingue, where play rotates anti-clockwise, it is the player to dealer's right.

Euchre In Euchre, failure to win at least three tricks.

Face card Same as *Court card*.

Fifteen In Cribbage, the play of a card which, with those already played, adds up to 15.

Finesse An attempt to win a trick with a card that is not the best held nor in sequence with it.

Flush A hand with all cards of the same suit.

Follow suit To play a card of the same suit as that of the led card.

Foot In Panguingue, the lower half of the stock set aside for use if the *Head* is exhausted.

Foundation In games of Patience, a card played to the centre on which a complete suit or sequence must be built.

Gate In Monte Bank, the bottom card of the pack.

Gift In games of the All Fours family, the point scored by the dealer if he begs and the dealer decides to play.

Gin In Gin Rummy, a hand in which all the cards are melded.

Go In Cribbage, the announcement that a player cannot play without exceeding 31.

Go down or **Go out** Same as *Knock* (1).

Grand slam In games of the Bridge and Whist families, the winning of all 13 tricks. See *Small slam*.

Great casino In Casino, the ♦ 10. See *Little casino*.

Head In Panguingue, the top half of the stock. See *Foot*.

Heel Same as *Talon*

High In games of the All Fours family, the score for being dealt the highest trump in play. See *Low*.

His heels In Cribbage, a Jack turned up as the start.

His nob In Cribbage, the Jack, either in hand or crib, of the same suit as the start.

Hole card In Stud Poker, the first card dealt, face downwards, to a player.

Honours (1) In games of the Bridge family, the Ace, King, Queen, Jack and 10 of a suit. (2) In Whist, the Ace, King, Queen and Jack of a suit.

Intrigue In Pope Joan, the Queen and Jack of the trump suit played by the same player.

Jack In games of the All Fours family, the score for winning the Jack of the trump suit.

Jackpot In Poker, a deal in which a player must hold at least a pair of Jacks to open.

Jasz In Klaberjass, the Jack of the trump suit.

Joker An extra card supplied with the standard

52-card pack used in some games as a wild card. See *Wild card*.

Kitty Same as *Pool*.

Knock (1) In games of the Rummy family, signification by a player that all his cards are melded. (2) In Poker, signification by a player that no further bet will be made by him.

Laying off (1) In Gin Rummy, the playing of cards to opponent's melds. (2) In Panguingue the playing of cards to one's own melds.

Layout Cards laid out on the table in a prescribed pattern either for the purpose of placing bets or to be moved in accordance with the rules of the game.

Left bower In Euchre, the Jack of the same colour as the Jack of the trump suit. See *Right bower*.

Left pedro In Cinch, the 5 of the same colour as the 5 of the trump suit. See *Right pedro*.

Little casino In Casino, the ♠2. See *Great casino*.

Loo In Loo, failure to win a trick.

Low In games of the All Fours family, the score made by the player who is dealt the lowest trump in play. See *High*.

Lurch In Cribbage, winning a game before the opponent is half-way round the scoring board.

Maker The player who names the trump suit.

March In Euchre, winning all five tricks by one side or one player.

Matrimony In Pope Joan, the King and Queen of the trump suit played by the same player.

Meld A matched set of three or more of a kind or a sequence of three or more of the same suit in consecutive order of rank.

Menel In Klaberjass, the 9 of trumps.

Miss In Loo, the widow-hand.

Mixed canasta In Canasta, a meld of seven or more cards of which one, two or three cards are wild. See *Natural canasta*.

Muggins In Cribbage, an announcement that enables a player to take points that his opponent has overlooked.

Nap A declaration in Nap(oleon) to win all five tricks.

Natural canasta In Canasta, a meld of seven or more cards of which none is a wild card. See *Mixed canasta*.

Non-comoquer In Panguingue, a group of Kings or Aces.

Order up In Euchre, the declaration of an opponent of the dealer accepting the suit of the turn-up card as the trump suit.

Pair (1) In Casino, the play of a card and taking up as a trick all the other cards of the same rank in the layout. (2) In Cribbage, playing a card of the same rank as the previous one played.

Pair-royal (1) In Brag, three cards of equal rank. (2) In Cribbage, playing a third card of the same rank as a pair.

Pam In Loo, the ♣J.

Pedro See *Left pedro* and *Right pedro*.

Peg In Cribbage, a marker used for scoring on a board.

Pinocle In Pinocle, the ♠Q and ♦J.

Pitch In Auction Pitch, the openin lead that determines the trump suit.

Plain suit A suit other than the trump suit.

Player In Calabrasella the player who elects to play on his own against the other two players.

Polignac In Polignac, the ♠J.

Pool The collective amount of players' stakes and fines.

Pope In Pope Joan, the ♦9.

Pot In Poker, a game in which all the players put up an ante.

Propose In Ecarté, a request by the non-dealer that cards may be exchanged for others from the stock.

Raise In Poker, increasing a bet by putting up more than needed to equal the previous player.

Refuse (1) In games of the All Fours family, the rejection by the dealer of a proposal by the non-dealer to make another suit trumps. (2) In

Ecarté, the rejection by the dealer of the non-dealer's proposal that cards may be exchanged for others from the stock.

Revoke Failure to follow suit when able to or to play a card in accordance with the game rules.

Right bower In Euchre, the Jack of the trump suit. See *Left bower*.

Right pedro In Cinch, the 5 of the trump suit. See *Left pedro*.

Rob the pack In Cinch, the privilege accorded to the dealer of selecting cards from the stock.

Round A division of dealing, betting or playing in which each player participates once.

Round the corner A sequence of cards in which the highest is considered adjacent to the lowest.

Rubber Three successive games between the same players: winning two of the three games.

Rubicon Failure of the loser of a game to reach a specified minimum total of points.

Ruff Playing a trump card on the lead of a card of a side suit.

Rummy In games of the Rummy family, the declaration by a player of all his cards in one turn.

Run Same as *Sequence*.

Run the cards In All Fours, to deal more cards and a new turn up after a beg is accepted.

Schmeiss In Klaberjass, an offer to play with the turn-up card as the trump suit or throw in the hand, as the opponent prefers.

Sequence Two or more cards of adjacent rank.

Side suit Same as *Plain suit*.

Single bete In Pinocle, the concession of defeat and payment of a forfeit, without playing. See *Double bete*.

Singleton An original holding of only one card of a suit.

Slam See *Grand slam* and *Small slam*.

Small slam In games of the Bridge and Whist families, winning 12 tricks. See *Grand slam*.

Smudge In Auction Pitch, a bid to win all four tricks.

Spread In Panguingue, a meld.

Stand (1) In All Fours, to accept the suit of the turn up card as the trump suit. (2) In Vingt-et-Un, to elect to take no further cards.

Start In Cribbage, the top card of the cut turned face upwards by the dealer.

Stock The undealt part of the pack which may be used later in the deal.

Straddle In Poker, a compulsory bet of twice the ante.

Stringer In Panguingue, a sequence.

Sweep In Casino, taking in all the cards in the layout.

Tablanette In Tablanette, what a player says when he is able to take all the cards on the table.

Take-it In Klaberjass, to accept as the trump suit the suit of the turn up card.

Talon In some games of Patience, cards laid aside in one or more packets for later use in the same deal.

Top layout In Monte Bank, the two top cards of the pack placed by the banker face upwards on the table. See *Bottom layout*.

Trail In Casino, the play of a card to the layout by a player who can neither pass, combine, build nor call.

Turn up A card faced after the deal to determine, or propose, the trump suit.

Twist In Vingt-et-Un, a request to be dealt a card face upwards.

Up cards (1) In Gin Rummy, the card turned up after each player has been dealt ten cards. (2) In Stud Poker, a card dealt face upwards.

Valle cards In Panguingue, the 7s, 5s and 3s, the melding of which wins chips.

Void Having no cards of a specified suit.

Vole In Ecarté, winning all five tricks.

Vulnerable In games of the Bridge family, being subject to bigger penalties and bonuses after winning a game.

Waive The privilege, in some games of patience, to lift a card and play the one under it.

Widow Extra cards dealt to the table at the same time as the hands are dealt to the players.

♣

Index

ACKNOWLEDGEMENTS

Acknowledgments

The illustrations used throughout were originally produced for Octopus Publishing Group Ltd by Publish on Demand Ltd, Brindeau Mexter, Line + Line, Peter Gerrish and 'ome Design, except for the following: **Fotolia**/pico *1*; R+R *4*; M. Schuppich *7*; james200035 *44, 184*; Leoco *226*; **Shutterstock**/makler 0008 *2, 206*; Laralova *8, 78*; Catalin D *152*; Elenapro *280*.